To the memory of my dear parents, Lillian and Jerry Lawrence, whose moral and emotional support instilled in me a life-long thirst for knowledge.

—Kenneth D. Lawrence

To my brother Jacob Moskovitz, who dedicated his life to public school education.

—Sheila M. Lawrence

To my wife, Helene, and to my sons, Bryan and Steven, for all their support and love.

—Ronald K. Klimberg

Contents

Chapter 7   **MULTIPLE LINEAR REGRESSION ANALYSIS IN FORECASTING** **133**

About the Authors

DR. KENNETH D. LAWRENCE is a Professor of Management and Marketing Science and Decision Support Systems in the School of Management at the New Jersey Institute of Technology. His professional employment includes over 20 years of technical management experience with AT&T as Director, Decision Support Systems and Marketing Demand Analysis, Hoffmann-La Roche, Inc., Prudential Insurance, and the U. S. Army in forecasting, marketing planning and research, statistical analysis and operations research. He is a full member of the Graduate Doctoral Faculty of Management at Rutgers, The State University of New Jersey in the Department of Management Science and Information Systems. He is a member of the graduate faculty at NJIT in management, transportation, statistics and industrial engineering. He is an active participant in professional associations as the Decision Sciences Institute, Institute of Management Science, Institute of Industrial Engineers, American Statistical Association, and the Institute of Forecasters. He has conducted significant funded research projects in health care and transportation.

Dr. Lawrence is the Associate Editor of the *Journal of Statistical Computation and Simulation*, and the *Review of Quantitative Finance and Accounting*, as well as serving on the editorial boards of *Computers and Operations Research*, and the *Journal of Operations Management*. His research work has been cited hundreds of times in 63 different journals, including: *Computers and Operations Research, International Journal of Forecasting, Journal of Marketing, Sloan Management Review, Management Science, Sloan Management Review, Technometrics, Applied Statistics, Interfaces, International Journal of Physical Distribution and Logistics,* and the *Journal of the Academy of Marketing Science.* He has 259 publications in the areas of multi-criteria decision analysis, management science, statistics, and forecasting, and his articles have appeared in over 25 journals including: *European Journal of Operational Research, Computers and Operations Research, Operational Research Quarterly, International Journal of Forecasting* and *Technometrics.*

Dr. Lawrence is the 1989 recipient of the *Institute of Industrial Engineers Award* for significant accomplishments in the theory and applications of operations research. He was recognized in the February 1993 issues of the *Journal of Marketing* for his *significant contribution in developing a method of guessing in the no data case, for diffusion of new products, for forecasting the timing and the magnitude of the peak in the adaption rate.* Dr. Lawrence is a member of the honorary societies *Alpha Iota Delta* (Decision Sciences Institute) and Beta Gamma Sigma (Schools of Management). He is the recipient of the *2002 Bright Ideas Award* in the New Jersey Policy Research Organization and the New Jersey Business and Industry Associates for his work in Auditing for his use of a Goal Programming Model to Improve the Efficiency of Audit Sampling.

In February 2004, Dean Howard Tuckman of Rutgers University appointed Dr. Lawrence as an *Academic Research Fellow to the Center for Supply Chain Management*, since "his reputation and strong body of research is quite impressive." The Center's corporate sponsors include Bayer HealthCare, Hoffmann-LaRoche, IBM,

Johnson & Johnson, Merck, Novartis, PeopleSoft, Pfizer, PSE&G, Schering-Plough and UPS.

The recognition of Professor Lawrence's research work is found in its broad level of citations, in various sources, in publishing in the finest research publication outlets, and the recognition of research abilities and skills by publications in companies and journal editors who continually seek Professor Lawrence as a referee and editor. Professor Lawrence's own editorial works are characterized by a thorough blend of refereed process, contributions by highly recognized scholars, including Nobel Prize winners, chaired professors from both domestic and international universities, who are considered world wide as experts in their fields. A majority of these publications are in blind refereed publications. The Institute of Industrial Engineers honored Professor Lawrence "significant accomplishments in the field of operations research, both in application and theory."

Many of Professor Lawrence's work have been cited multiple times. The citations for his works are found in 63 research outlets and include hundreds of citations. Some articles published decades ago are often cited.

Professor Lawrence's research has been listed as breakthrough research by the *Journal of the American Marketing Association* over a period of 35 years. His research in the Rutgers doctoral program has resulted in the awarding of multiple doctoral degrees under his direction. Furthermore, his research expertise and the skills have led to his frequent participation on other doctoral dissertation committees.

RONALD K. KLIMBERG, Ph.D. is a Professor in the Decision and System Sciences Department of the Haub School of Business at Saint Joseph's University, USA. Professor Klimberg received his B.S. in Information Systems from the University of Maryland, his M.S. in Operations Research from George Washington University, and his Ph.D. in Systems Analysis and Economics for Public Decision-Making from the Johns Hopkins University. Before joining the faculty of Saint Joseph's University in 1997, he was a professor at Boston University (10 years), an operations research analyst for the Food and Drug Administration (FDA) (10 years) and a consultant (7 years). Ron was the 2007 recipient of the Tengelmann Award for his excellence in scholarship, teaching, and research.

His research has been directed toward the development and application of quantitative methods, e.g., statistics, forecasting, data mining, and management science techniques, such that the results add value to the organization and the results are effectively communicated. Dr. Klimberg has published over 30 articles and made over 30 presentations at national and international conferences in the areas of management science, information systems, statistics, and operations management. His current major interests include multiple criteria decision making (MCDM), multiple objective linear programming (MOLP), data envelopment analysis (DEA), facility location, data visualization, risk analysis, workforce scheduling, and modeling in general. He is currently a member of INFORMS, DSI, and MCDM.

DR. SHEILA M. LAWRENCE has been a Lecturer in the Rutgers Business School (RBS) since 1993. For the academic year 2004-5, she had been an instructor in the MSIS Department in RBS. Professor Lawrence had been appointed to the Graduate Faculty at Rutgers as of May 2000. She has more then 30 years of technical management experience with AT&T, Hoffmann-LaRoche, PSE&G, and the State of New Jersey. Her teaching interests include supply chain, management science, survey research, quality and statistics. Her research interests include supply chain management, productivity analysis, quality management, forecasting, management information systems, and decision support systems. She has 96 publications in the areas of statistics, MIS, and supply chain. Dr. Lawrence is, also, an active member of professional associations such as the Decision Sciences Institute, American Society for Quality, INFORMS, POMS, and the American Statistical Association.

Chapter 1

Introduction to Forecasting

1.1 Introduction

During the past several decades the decision-making process and the manager's role in it have changed dramatically. A major cause of this change has been the advent of computer technology. The computing power of today's personal computers is greater than that of the large mainframes of the 1960s and 1970s. Computer technology has not only increased data storage capacity and made data easily accessible, but also has made tools to analyze the data more readily available to the manager. By far the most widely used management tool today is the spreadsheet. Spreadsheet software, and in recent years the dominance of Microsoft's Excel (included in the MS Office software), in particular, has radically changed the function and capacity of the manager. The accountant, the financial analyst, and the business manager in general, formerly spent a significant amount of time inputting or recording data and little time doing what they were trained and educated to do—analyzing data. Now, with the spreadsheet, managers can spend more time exploring the impact of different scenarios, asking "what if," and addressing more complex questions. Given today's managers' increased involvement in the decision-making process, an objective of this book is to provide the manager with the tools to analyze data and produce forecasts in Excel.

In the next section of this chapter, the importance of forecasting to the organization is first discussed. Subsequently, four forecasting factors to consider and a decision tree to determine which forecasting method(s) to contemplate utilizing, are discussed. The types of forecasting techniques are briefly examined in the last part of the next section. The last section demonstrates how to install Excel's data analysis ToolPak add-in.

1.2 Forecasting

1.2.1   Importance

Forecasting is the process of predicting the future. Whether it is predicting future demand, sales, or production, forecasting is an important yet unavoidable task that is an integral part of almost all business activities. Some of the top decision areas within the organization on which these forecasts have an impact, and which are considered important, are budgeting (54%), production planning (73%), and strategic planning (45%) (Mentzer and Cox). Although not exactly in the same categories in Rahmlow and Klimberg's 2001 study, the main areas of application were budgeting (85%), operations decisions (67%) and financial decisions (65%) as shown in Table 1.1. Additionally, in Table 1.1 we can see that forecasting is also notably used in staffing, investment, new product, and ordering decisions, as well as contingency planning. Forecasts not only have direct and indirect impact on almost every activity within the organization, but these forecasts can have an external effect, such as on stock values and perceived consumer confidence. Good forecasts can lead to lower costs, increased customer satisfaction, and so on. Good forecasts lead to an important competitive advantage.

Table 1.1   Areas within the Organization Used by Forecasting (Rahmlow and Klimberg)

Area	%
Budgeting	85
Operations Decisions	67
Financial Decisions	65
Staffing	50
Contingency Planning	47
Investment Decisions	41
New Product	39
Ordering	31

1.2.2   Four Forecasting Factors to Consider

Before starting a forecasting project, four factors must be considered to determine which forecasting technique(s) to apply. These four factors are:

- Time

- Data availability

- Money

- Who is the project for and how will the forecast be used?

Two dimensions of time must be addressed—the time of the project and the time horizon of the forecast. The time frame to produce a forecast, i.e., a few days, a couple of weeks or months or whatever, will affect the choice of the forecasting technique to use. The time horizon is how far into the future the model will predict. Short- to mid-range forecasts typically consider the immediate future up to two years ahead. Long-range forecasts usually encompass time periods of more than two years.

The questions to consider for the data required by the forecasting project are, is it available, does it need to be purchased or collected, or a combination of these. These data need consider not only the different explanatory variables and the amount of historical data desired, but also how difficult the data is to obtain and how accurate it is. A main source of data is internal, that is, from within the organization. Depending on the analytical competency of the organization (and the politics), retrieving and processing the required data may or may not be an easy task. Another primary source is published data, which can be found in printed material or electronically on disks or on the Internet. Data published by the organization that collected it, such as the Bureau of the Census, is called primary data. Data published by an organization other than the one that collected it, for example, by the business database services (in particular, the financial data published by Compustat), is called secondary data. The cost of gaining access to this data, whether it is primary or secondary, may range from zero all the way to quite expensive.

The amount of money assigned to the forecasting project will affect the type and amount of data that may need to be purchased. Additionally, costs would affect whether or not specialized forecasting software may be purchased. Another dimension to consider, along with the amount of money available, is whether or not the organization has the individual or individuals with the skills to produce the forecasting model. If there is currently no one capable of producing the forecasting model, the organization may hire someone, or obtain the expertise of a consultant.

The last factor to consider is who is going to use the forecast and for what purpose. Answering this question will define the level of detail required in the forecast (as well as the time horizon). In other words, if the forecast is to be used by a vice president, monthly or perhaps quarterly forecasts may be needed. On the other hand, if the forecasts are to be used by the plant floor operations manager, he (she) may desire daily or hourly updates. Answering the second question, of how it will be used, defines the level of importance and possibly the degree of accuracy required for the forecast to be useful.

1.2.3 Forecasting Method Decision Tree

After the above four forecasting factors have been evaluated, the forecasting method decision tree in Figure 1.1 is utilized to determine the type of forecasting method(s) to be used. The first step in using this forecasting technique decision tree is to decide whether the necessary historical data, or even more important, all the data deemed necessary, is available. In some situations, such as with a new product, no data may exist. Whether the data is available or not, the next question to answer is how important is the forecast. This question is directly related to the question of who is going to use the forecast, and how it is going to be used. Secondary factors to consider include how much money and time are available. If the forecast is believed to be unimportant, then knowledge of the organization and of the particular situation can be used to come up with a best estimate, or guesstimate. If the forecast is viewed as important and no data is available, and if at least one or two months is available, then there is enough time to use a qualitative method. Otherwise, there is not enough time, so a guesstimate must be used.

On the other side of the forecasting method decision tree, if the data is available and the forecast is important, then it is possible to determine the type of quantitative method to be used—time series or causal—depending on the importance of the forecast.

1.2.4   Forecasting Techniques

Forecasting techniques can be separated into two general categories—qualitative and quantitative—as shown in Table 1.2. Qualitative forecasting methods are commonly employed when there is little or no data available, such as with a new product. In general, these qualitative methods are less structured than quantitative methods. A judgment forecasting method elicits management's opinions to provide a forecast. The Delphi method is a formalized iterative forecasting technique that can be used to obtain executive opinions. The executives or managers use their industry knowledge, past industry experience, and intuition, to provide forecast estimates. Another qualitative method used, especially with a new product, is historical analogy.

Given data on a new product (or technology) information may be obtained or solicited from expert individuals who have faced similar situations.

Although market research can be considered to include product testing and surveys, market research today is often synonymous with focus groups. A focus group involves an objective moderator who introduces a topic, usually details of a new product, to a group of respondents, and directs their discussions in a nonstructured and natural fashion. The focus group is a source of rich information that cannot be provided by a survey. On the other hand, a major disadvantage of focus groups is that the results cannot be generalized, i.e., the information from a focus group is valid only for that homogeneous group. Two other techniques listed under qualitative methods in Table 1.2 are Markovian and diffusion models. Diffusion models are used to forecast the fate of new products, and Markovian models are employed to forecast consumer and buyer behavior. With both techniques, limited data is available.

A major possible problem with most of the qualitative methods is that the forecasts are subjective, that is, they are based on opinions that could be extremely biased. However, these qualitative forecasting techniques continue to be more popular than the quanti-

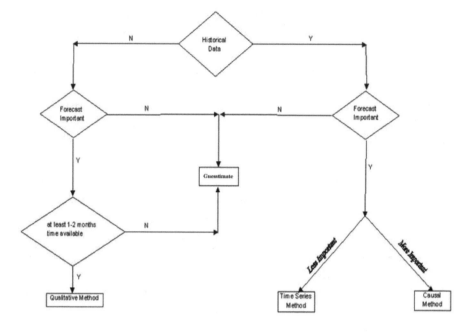

Figure 1.1   The forecasting method decision tree.

Table 1.2   List of Forecasting Techniques

Qualitative Methods	Quantitative Methods	
	Time Series Methods	Causal Methods
• Judgment	• Moving Average	• Regression
• Historical Analogy	• Exponential Smoothing	• Econometric
• Focus Group	• Trend Analysis	• Input-Output
• Market Research	• Decomposition	• Disaggregated
• Diffusion	• Advanced Time Series methods	• Neural nets
• Markovian	• Box-Jenkins (ARIMA)	

tative approaches, mainly because these techniques are easily understood and can be relatively inexpensive. This book will concentrate on the quantitative forecasting methods, although it will also examine the Markovian and diffusion models in Chapters 8 and 9 respectively.

Quantitative forecasting methods use historical data to predict the future, so a lot of data must be available. These quantitative forecasting techniques can be further categorized into either time series or causal methods. Time series forecasting methods only use the time series data itself, and not any other data, to build the forecasting models. These time series techniques isolate and measure the impact of the trend in seasonal and cyclical time series components. Table 1.2 lists several time series techniques ranging from basic moving average, exponential smoothing, and trend analysis, to the statistically sophisticated Box-Jenkins (ARIMA) models. Each of the time series techniques listed in Table 1.2 will be examined in Chapters 3 and 5.

Causal methods use a set of explanatory variables, possibly also including time series components, that are believed to influence the forecasted variable, e.g., sales. Regression techniques, discussed in Chapters 6 and 7, employ the statistical method of least squares to establish a statistical relationship between the forecasted variable and the set of predictor/causal variables. Other specialized causal methods, such as disaggregated, neural nets, and input-output models, are examined in Chapter 10.

Results from the 1984 Mentzer and Cox's survey, subsequently in Mentzer and Kahn's 1995 survey, and Rahmlow and Klimberg's 2001 survey, show that judgmental forecasting methods have been used somewhat more widely than quantitative methods. Although shown to be popular in Rahmlow and Klimberg's survey, the judgmental methods were low in satisfaction ratings. Among the quantitative methods, the moving average, exponential smoothing, and regression were most widely used. Overall, when a quantitative method was used, there was a corresponding high degree of satisfaction. The results also consistently showed that the Box-Jenkins (ARIMA) models were somewhat unknown (the relatively new data-mining methods were better known than the Box-Jenkins methods (Rahmlow and Klimberg)), and of those who did know of the Box-Jenkins methods, many were dissatisfied with them. Overall, users of quantitative methods have been more satisfied with the results than users of the qualitative forecasting techniques, (Rahmlow and Klimberg).

1.3 Excel

Excel is now the most popular spreadsheet program and most people have it on their computers. In Rahmlow and Klimberg's 2001 study of forecasting practices, the leading application software was overwhelmingly Excel (90%). For these reasons, and to avoid the need to purchase specialized forecasting software, the Excel software program was selected for use in this book.

It is assumed that readers of this text are somewhat familiar with Excel and its basic operation. If not, a visit to a local bookstore is strongly recommended, to examine the numerous Excel tutorial books to find one that speaks your language. If the reader is interested in a particular topic, for example, graphing, examine that section of the book, and if the author's discussion makes sense, buy the book! The purchase and study will be well worth the forty dollars, and the book will be used over many years and versions. The language of spreadsheets does not change significantly from version to version. The reader should use Excel (and this is true with the techniques discussed in this book as well!).

The book can be read often, but to learn how to use Excel it is necessary to sit in front of the computer and experiment. The authors guarantee that the first time it will not work (and will probably end up taking way too long), and you will wonder why you are doing this. The second time there will be a few less problems and less time needed. Come the third and fourth times, you will become expert, having learned by doing, and with some experiments you will most likely learn some shortcuts or new tricks.

A new version of Excel, 2007, was recently released, though the overall functionality of Excel did not change significantly. On the other hand, the graphical user interface of 2007 is significantly different and is called the Fluent User Interface. This new interface replaces the familiar menus and toolbars that were the cornerstone of prior Office products with a wide tabbed toolbar across the top of the workbook called the Ribbon, as shown in Figure 1.2. The Ribbon carries several major tabs including: Home, Insert, Page Layout, etc., running along the top. Below this list of major tabs is a row of related commands (related to the highlighted major tab). Some of the commands appear with just an icon, some with an icon and words, and some with drop arrows that lead to more commands. If you click on one of the major tabs at the top, a whole new row of related commands appears. The Ribbon and the list of related commands are the source of the new version's greatest achievement, making it easier for the user to get to all of Excel's powerful tools. The Ribbon is also the source of the greatest frustration, especially to experienced users, who have had to relearn and find where certain Excel functions, tools, or capabilities now reside.

1.3.1   Installing the Data Analysis ToolPak

Throughout this text, in addition to using numerous Excel functions, we will also be using Excel's Data Analysis ToolPak. Although the ToolPak comes with the standard Excel product, it usually is not installed during a regular installation, so instructions on how to install the Data Analysis ToolPak are included here.

In the upper left corner of the screen is a small circle containing the Office 2007 icon as shown in Figure 1.2. This icon is called the Office Button. Clicking on the Office Button brings up a list of options (similar to when you click on File in older versions of Excel). On the bottom toward the right, there is an option called Excel Options. Clicking on Options calls up a new dialog box, on the left side of which, several options are listed. If you click on Add-ins, the area of the dialog box toward the right will change. At the bottom of the dialog box, toward the left, as shown in Figure 1.3 these words will appear: Click Go.

Clicking on Go will cause a new dialog box to appear, similar to that in Figure 1.4. From the list of options listed, click on Analysis ToolPak and Analysis ToolPak—VBA. Then click OK. (In some installations, depending on the equipment, you may be prompted to insert your Microsoft Excel CD.)

Clicking on the Data tab on the Ribbon will bring up the screen shown in Figure 1.5. At the right, as shown in Figure 1.5, is the related command Analysis, and one of the options is Data Analysis.

Clicking on Data Analysis brings up the Data Analysis dialog box, as shown in Figure 1.6. Numerous statistical tools are listed here in alphabetical order. Several of these data analysis tools are covered in Chapters 2 and 3.

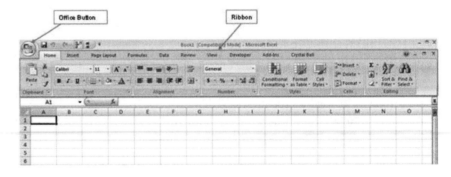

Figure 1.2   Excel 2007 Interface.

Figure 1.3   Add-ins box.

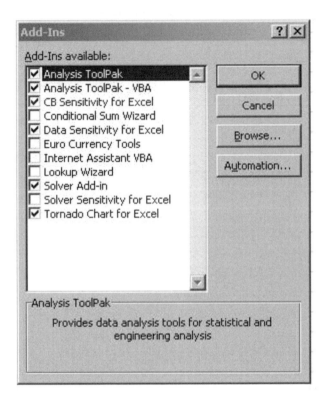

Figure 1.4   Add-ins dialog box.

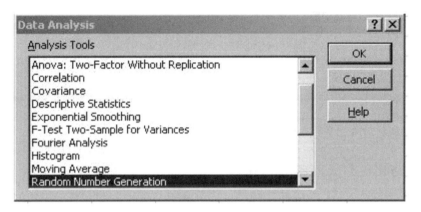

Figure 1.6   Data Analysis dialog box.

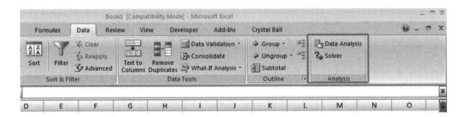

Figure 1.5   Data Analysis command tab.

References

Mentzer John T. and James E. Cox, Jr. "Familiarity, Application, and Performance of Sales Forecasting Techniques." *Journal of Forecasting* 3 (1984): 27–36.

Mentzer John T. and Kenneth B. Kahn. "Forecasting technique familiarity, satisfaction, usage, and application." *Journal of Forecasting* 14 (1995): 465–476.

Rahmlow, H. and R. Klimberg. "Forecasting Practices of MBAs." *Advances in Business and Management Forecasting* 3 (2002): 113–123.

Chapter 2

Summarizing and Displaying Data in Excel

2.1 Introduction

As discussed in Chapter 1, one of the first steps an individual takes in the forecasting process, once the data has been acquired, is to graph the data and to produce summary statistics. As a result, the analyst gets an immediate feel for the data, i.e., it is apparent if there is a trend or seasonality what the central value is, and how disperse the data is. The particular display tools and statistics to be applied depend upon whether the data is qualitative or quantitative. Qualitative data is data that is classified into categories such as gender, month, store, or on a Likert scale (e.g., 1 to 5) of answers to a survey question. Quantitative data is subdivided into whether the data is discrete or continuous. Discrete data is the result of a counting process, e.g., the number of males or females, the number of people in an age group, or the number of magazines purchased. Qualitative and discrete data cannot be fractional. On the other hand, continuous data is usually from a measuring process and can be fractional, e.g., sales, ROI, or P/E. In the following sections of this Chapter, tools to summarize and graph continuous, qualitative, and discrete data in Excel will be presented. Subsequently, because some forecasting techniques in later chapters will require the use of the statistical methodology called hypothesis testing, a general framework to hypothesis testing and the interpretation of the results using Excel will be presented. In the last section of this chapter some Excel procedures are presented; they are not so well known, but are ones that we have found to be extremely useful in the real world. We call these procedures simply, Excel nuggets.

2.2 Summarizing Continuous Data (Descriptive2.xls and Boxplot.xls)

2.2.1 Descriptive Statistics (Descriptive2.xls\Worksheet: Descriptive)

Measures of central tendency, such as mean, median, and mode, and measures of dispersion, such as standard deviation and variance, can be produced using the Descriptive Statistics tool from the Excel Data Analysis ToolPak.

For example, to generate descriptive statistics for the sales of a product over the past 8 months, as listed in Table 2.1, take the following steps:

1. Click on the **Data** tab from the Ribbon.

2. Click on the **Data Analysis** command (all the way to the right).

3. Choose **Descriptive Statistics** from the list of analysis tools.

4. A dialog box, as shown in Figure 2.1, will appear. As in Figure 2.1, fill in the appropriate boxes in the dialog box–

   Enter B1:B9 in the **Input Range** box

   Click on **Labels in the First Row**

   Click on **Summary Statistics**

   Enter D1 in the **Output Range** box (This identifies D1 as the upper left-hand corner of the output.)

5. Click **OK**.

Figure 2.2 displays the output from the Descriptive Statistics option under Data Analysis tools. This output provides measures of central tendency, measures of dispersion, and shape.

Another way of generating descriptive statistics is by using the functions provided by Excel. As shown in Figure 2.3, the Insert

Table 2.1   Sales Quantitative Data (Worksheet: Descriptive)

	A	B
1	Month	Sales ($M)
2	Jan	116
3	Feb	109
4	Mar	117
5	Apr	112
6	May	122
7	Jun	113
8	Jul	108
9	Aug	115

Function dialog box can be accessed either by clicking on the f_x button directly to the left of the formula box, or by clicking on the Formulas Ribbon tab and then the Insert Function command.

Exploring the numerous categories provided in the Insert Function dialog box, shown in Figure 2.4, and their long list of functions, you will find that an abundance of powerful Excel functions is provided. In particular, if you click on the statistical category, a long list of statistical function names will appear. A few of these statistical functions in common use are listed in Table 2.2, and their use is illustrated in Figure 2.5.

The syntax for the functions listed in Table 2.2 starts with an equals sign, then some function name, followed in parentheses by the range of values to which the function should be applied. For example, if we want to find the standard deviation of the eight values in Table 2.1 we would input: =STDEV(B2:B9), as shown in cell B15 in Figure 2.5.

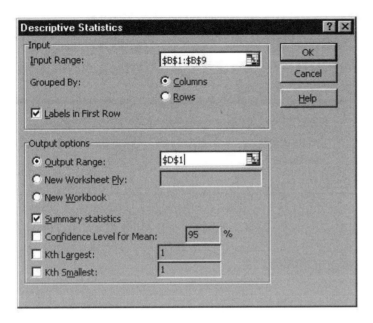

Figure 2.1 Descriptive Statistics dialog box.

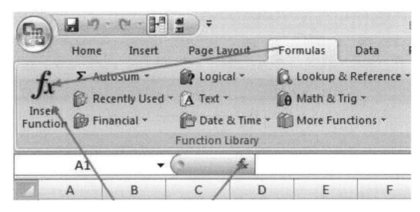

Figure 2.3 Two ways of getting to the Insert Function dialog box.

	A	B	C	D	E
1	**Month**	**Sales ($M)**		*Sales ($M)*	
2	Jan	116			
3	Feb	109		Mean	114
4	Mar	117		Standard Error	1.603567
5	Apr	112		Median	114
6	May	122		Mode	#N/A
7	Jun	113		Standard Deviation	4.535574
8	Jul	108		Sample Variance	20.57143
9	Aug	115		Kurtosis	0.068056
10				Skewness	0.404212
11				Range	14
12				Minimum	108
13				Maximum	122
14				Sum	912
15				Count	8

Figure 2.2 Output from the Descriptive Statistics option under the Data Analysis tools (Worksheet: Descriptive).

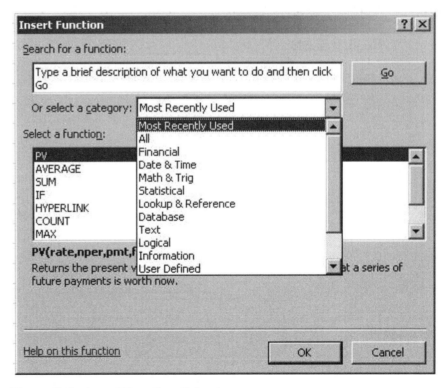

Figure 2.4 Insert Function dialog box.

Table 2.2   Partial List of Excel Summary Statistical Functions

Statistical Measure	Excel Function
Mean	=Average(B2:B9)
Median	=Median(B2:B9)
Minimum	=Min(B2:B9)
Maximum	=Max(B2:B9)
Standard Deviation	=Stdev(B2:B9)

Figure 2.5   Descriptive Statistics using the Excel functions (Worksheet: Descriptive).

Note	**All functions or formulas in Excel start with an equals sign.**

2.3   Graphing Continuous Data (Descriptive, Worksheets: Histogram1, Histogram2, and Time Series Plot)

2.3.1   Box plot (Descriptive2: Worksheet: Descriptive; Boxplot.xls: Worksheet: Simple)

One of the basic statistical summary displays is a box-and-whisker plot, a five-number display—or simply, a box plot. The box plot graphically displays five summary statistics of a data set:

- smallest number

- Q_1

- median

- Q_3

- highest number

The box plot enables the analyst to gain a sense of the central values, dispersion, and shape of data. In Figure 2.6, the three basic distributions of data shapes, symmetrical, left and right skewed, and their corresponding box plots are displayed. When the distribution of data is symmetrical, the median and mean are relatively close to each other. When the data is skewed, the mean is either significantly less than or greater than the median, i.e., if the distribution of data is left skewed, the mean will be significantly less than the median, and vice versa for right-skewed data distributions. The shape of data distribution affects the box plot. In particular, if the distribution of data is symmetrical, the box, from Q1 to Q3 (which is 50 percent of the observations) is not very wide, and in addition the width of each whisker (one whisker is from the smallest number to Q1, the other whisker is from Q3 to the largest number, and each whisker contains 25 percent of the values) is about equal. Whereas, for the skewed distributions of data, the boxes are wider and the whiskers are not equal in width.

Excel does not directly provide a graphical procedure to generate a box plot. However, the authors do provide an Excel file, called Boxplot and a Worksheet called Simple, that will generate a box plot. Using the sales data in Table 2.1 and in Worksheet: Descriptive, the following steps will produce the associated box plot:

1. Highlight the cells with the data (here, B2:B9 in Worksheet: Descriptive) and copy.

2. Open the Boxplot file and the Worksheet: Simple. Then paste these cells starting in A2. If necessary delete any old values in the column after the last observation. Further, take care not to relabel the column, i.e., do not change cell A1.

The corresponding box plot will appear as shown in Figure 2.7.

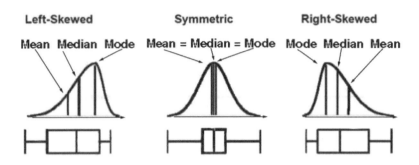

Figure 2.6 Shapes of distribution of data and their corresponding boxplots.

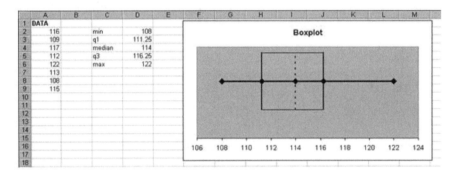

Figure 2.7 A boxplot of the data in Table 2.1.

2.3.2 Histogram

A histogram is a graph of the frequency distribution, and is one of the most common tools used in graphing continuous data. The histogram gives the analyst a sense of the shape of values. The Excel Data Analysis tools have a procedure to generate a histogram. To illustrate, review the data on the times (in seconds) that customers waited in line at a bank shown in Figure 2.8, and in Worksheet Histogram1, cells A2:E11. The summary statistics in Figure 2.8 are calculated in cells B13 to B17 using the statistical functions.

Prior to using the Data Analysis histogram procedure, it is necessary to define the bins (if you do not define them, Excel will create them). The bin numbers define the class intervals. A particular bin number is the last value or upper limit of a particular class inter-

val. In most instances, it will be found desirable to control the size and the number of the bins because, when Excel determines them they will most likely be some odd numbers and widths. A process useful in constructing the bins of a frequency distribution is:

Step 1. Determine the Range = Max value – Min value

Step 2. Iteratively compute the number of classes and width of classes until satisfied.

Number of classes = Range/(Width of classes).

Width of classes = Range/(Number of classes).

The width of the classes should be customary intervals, depending on the data. The number of classes should not be so large that many intervals have low numbers of frequencies, nor should the number of classes be so small that many intervals have too many observations (in general, use between 5 and 20 classes).

A rule of thumb to assist in initially determining the number of classes is the "2 to the k rule," which determines k, the number of recommended classes, as the minimum value such that $2^k > n$, where n is the sample size. For the example with customer waiting time, there are 50 observations. The minimum value of k is 6: $2^6 = 64 > 50$. So, the rule of thumb would suggest using 6 classes.

Step 3. Establish the lower boundary limit of the first class by determining the closest familiar value less than the minimum value. Subsequently define all the class boundaries.

In the example in Figure 2.8, the minimum and maximum values of the data are 51 and 351. These values are in seconds, so a customary interval would be 60 seconds. If this class width is found to be too large, it could be lowered to something like 30 seconds, or if it is too small, it could be increased to 90 or 120 seconds. Given that 51 is the lowest value, and must be included, and a 60 second class width is being used, the initial starting value will be 0, and the following are the lower and upper boundary limits for each class:

$0 \leq 60$	$180 \leq 240$
$60 \leq 120$	$240 \leq 300$
$120 \leq 180$	$300 \leq 360$

The bins are defined in Excel as the upper limit of each class. Therefore, as shown in cells G2:G7, in Figure 2.8, the upper limits of the classes (bins) are 60, 120, 180, 240, 300 and 360.

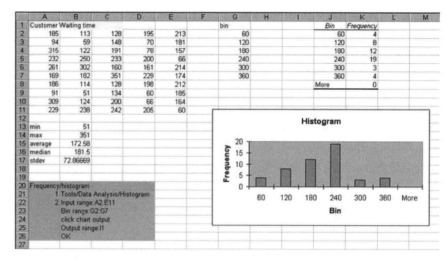

Figure 2.8   A histogram using the Data Analysis tools (Worksheet: Histogram1).

A frequency distribution and its corresponding histogram for this data can be generated using these steps:

1. Click on the **Data** tab from the Ribbon.

2. Click on the **Data Analysis** command.

3. Choose **Histogram** from the list of analysis tools.

4. A dialog box, as shown in Figure 2.9, will appear. As in Figure 2.9 fill in the appropriate boxes in the dialog box:

   Enter A2:E11 in the Input Range box

   Enter G2:G7 in the Bin Range box

   Click Chart Output

   Enter J1 in the Output Range box

   Click **OK**.

Figure 2.8 shows the output from the histogram procedure of the Data Analysis tools.

Another approach, which we call the two-step alternative approach, is found in Worksheet: Histogram2, and gives more control over the design of the histogram and the listing of frequency distribution. The procedure of this two-step alternative approach is:

Step 1. Produce Frequency Distribution

A. Highlight H2:H9

B. In cell H2 type the following: = frequency(A2:E11,G2:G9)

THEN BEFORE hitting the ENTER key, **simultaneously** hold down and hit the **CNTL**, **SHIFT** and **ENTER** keys.

The frequency function finds the frequency for each bin, G2:G9, and for the cells A2:E11. Also, by simultaneously holding down the keys an array is created.

Step 2. Produce Histogram

A. Highlight H2:H7.

B. Click on the **Insert** tab from the Ribbon.

C. Under the group of **Chart** commands, click **Columns**.

D. Under the 2-D Columns graphs, click the first (most left) graph.

E. Click the Select **Data** command (make sure the graph is hot (clicked on) and that the major Ribbon command **Design** is clicked). A new dialog box will appear. Toward the right, there is a column entitled **Horizontal (Category) Axis Labels**. Click on the **Edit box** as shown in Figure 2.10. The

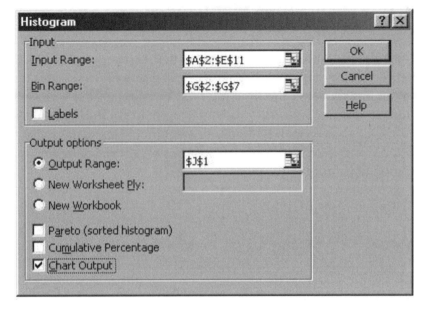

Figure 2.9   Dialog box for creating a histogram using the Data Analysis tools.

Axis Labels dialog box will appear. For the Axis label range: Highlight G2:G7. Click **OK**.

F. Add the title, and *x* and *y* axes labels. (Make sure the Ribbon tab highlighted is **Layout**.)

Using either of these approaches, you may desire to increase or decrease the distance between the bars. This distance between bars is called the gap width. You can change the gap width by:

1. Moving the mouse on top of one of the bars and right clicking the mouse. A new menu appears.

2. Click **Format Data Series**.

3. Decrease the value of the gap width (it is usually preset at 150) to zero.

2.3.3   Time Series Plot (Worksheet: Time Series Plot)

Frequently in forecasting, the data is time series data, that is, the data is collected sequentially over time. A graph of time series data, with the X-axis being the time interval, is called a time series plot. A time series plot is useful in identifying patterns in the data, such as trend and seasonal patterns. Using the sales data listed in Table 2.1 and in Worksheet: Time Series Plot, the following steps will produce a time series plot:

1. Highlight B2:B9.

2. Click on the **Insert** tab from the Ribbon.

3. Under the group of **Chart** commands, click **Line.**

4. Click the left-most graph in the first row.

5. Click the **Select Data** command (make sure the graph is hot (clicked on) and that the major Ribbon command **Design** is clicked). A new dialog box will appear. Toward the right, there is a column entitled **Horizontal (Category) Axis Labels**. Click on the **Edit box** as shown in Figure 2.10. The Axis Labels dialog box will appear. For the Axis label range: Highlight A2:A9. Click **OK**.

6. Add the title, and *x* and *y* axes labels.

Figure 2.11 shows the corresponding time series plot.

Looking carefully at the X axis it can be seen that the tick marks are not aligned with the points. To align the points and the tick marks:

1. Make sure the plot is hot and **Layout** highlighted; if not, left click anywhere inside the plot. Click the drop arrow, under **Axes.**

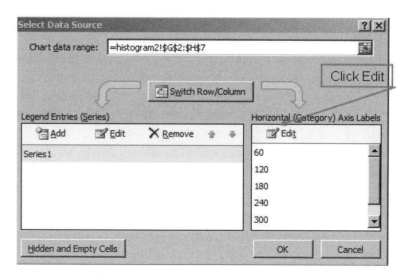

Figure 2.10   Adding bin names to histogram.

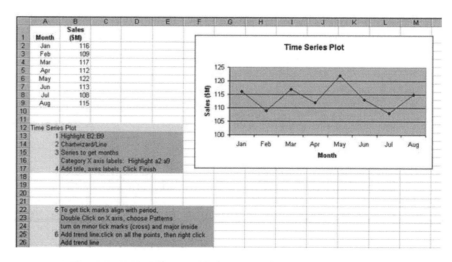

Figure 2.11   A time series plot (Worksheet: Time Series Plot).

2. Move the mouse over **Primary Horizontal Axis**. Then, move the mouse over and click on **More Primary Horizontal Axis Option** (toward the bottom).

3. A new dialog box appears. Around the middle of this dialog box there is an option called **Major tick mark type** with a drop box—choose **None**; Another option is called **Minor tick mark type** also with a drop box—choose **Cross**.

4. Click **Close**.

Additionally, two ways of adding a trend line to the time series plot are:

1. Make sure the plot is hot and **Layout** highlighted. Click **Trendline** command. Choose the type of trend wanted.

or

1. Move the mouse right over one of the points in the graph and right click the mouse.

2. All the points should be highlighted and a menu should appear. Choose **Add Trendline**.

3. Non-linear trend lines can be added, but for now let's just consider linear. So, just click **OK** and the trend line will appear.

Additional options that can be chosen include forecast time periods into the past and future, and the regression equation and R^2 can be displayed.

2.4 Summarizing Qualitative and Discrete Data; Graphs and Tables with Qualitative and Discrete Data (Descriptive2.xls)

2.4.1 Descriptive Statistics (Descriptive2; Worksheet: Countif)

The statistical measures commonly used for continuous data, such as mean, median, and standard deviation, are often not very useful when examining qualitative or discrete data. For example, in Figure 2.12, we have 22 survey responses from alumni of a university. There are qualitative variables of major, gender, and Likert-scaled responses to the question of how useful their statistics course was (1 – not very useful to 5 – very useful). In addition, there is one continuous variable, which is salary. In cells C25:D29 in Figure 2.12 there are some summary statistics for the usefulness question and salary. No summary statistics are provided for the other two qualitative variables, major and gender. The salary summary statistics provide some insight into the distribution of salary, i.e., the lowest salary is $31,235 and the highest is $65,437, with a mean of $49,017 and median of $51,430. The median is somewhat higher implying the data may be skewed to the left. Further supporting this left skewness is the fact that the minimum is further away from the mean (and median) than the maximum. In general, as discussed earlier in the chapter, the relationship of the mean to the median does give some indication of skewness:

Left-skewed data: Mean is significantly less than the median.

Symmetrical data: Mean and median are relatively close to each other.

Right-skewed data: Mean is significantly greater than the median.

2.4.2 Graphing Qualitative and Discrete Data

On the other hand, the summary statistics for the usefulness question do not provide any significant insights into the data. The information that would be useful for each qualitative variable is a frequency distribution, that is, how many times did someone answer 1, 2, and so on. The histogram procedure in the Data Analysis tools for quantitative data is not helpful with qualitative data. The bins in the histogram or bar chart are the different values, or the qualitative variables. If the histogram procedure under Data Analysis is used, the bins cannot be non-numeric. So, if a histogram of gender or major is required, it is necessary to either recode the data into numeric groups or use our two-step alternative approach.

Excel does provide two functions that facilitate the generation of the frequency distribution of qualitative data. These two functions are COUNTIF and COUNTBLANK. The COUNTIF function finds, for a specified range of cells, the number of occurrences of a specified value or phrase. For example, in Figure 2.13, to calculate the number of 1 responses to the usefulness question, enter into cell C32: =COUNTIF(C2:C23,1). Similar COUNTIF statements are used in corresponding cells for the other responses. (The function statement in cell C32 could be improved by changing it to =COUNTIF(C2:C23,A1). With this sequence entered, it is possible to just copy and paste the formula down until row 36.) In addition, the COUNTIF function can be employed to count alphanumeric data. For example, in order to count the number of business students, in cell C43, insert =COUNTIF(A2:A23,"Business").

Often when analyzing data, especially survey data, there are missing values or non-responses to a few questions, such as the individuals' missing answers in rows 10 and 16 in Figure 2.12. These non-responses or blank cells may be counted with the COUNTBLANK function. For the ongoing example, to count the blanks to the usefulness question insert in cell C37: =COUNTBLANK(C2:C23), as in Figure 2.13.

Last of all, a more often utilized type of graph of qualitative/discrete data is the pie chart and bar chart, which is one of the chart type options available in Excel; (in Excel, a bar chart is identified as either a column or a bar). For example, given the breakdown of how people responded to how useful their statistics class was in cells C32:C36, a pie/column/bar chart can be produced by:

	A	B	C	D
1	**Major**	**Gender**	**Usefullness**	**Salary**
2	Business	Male	3	52125
3	Business	Female	1	52325
4	Business	Male	4	63042
5	A&S	Male	3	54928
6	Business	Male	4	50599
7	A&S	Female	2	42036
8	A&S	Female	3	46427
9	A&S	Male	3	51865
10	A&S	Female		33263
11	Business	Female	5	58434
12	Business	Male	4	61551
13	A&S	Male	5	31235
14	Business	Male	2	58730
15	A&S	Female	4	35830
16	Business	Male		53267
17	Business	Male	5	65437
18	A&S	Female	4	47591
19	A&S	Female	4	42659
20	Business	Male	3	50996
21	A&S	Male	2	40185
22	A&S	Male	5	33155
23	Business	Female	1	52695
24				
25	min		1	31235
26	max		5	65437
27	average		3.35	49017.05
28	median		3.5	51430.5
29	stdev		1.268027893	9937.653

Figure 2.12   Qualitative and quantitative data (Worksheet: Countif).

1. Highlight C32:C36.

2. Click on the **Insert** tab from the Ribbon.

3. Under the group of **Chart** commands, click on **Column** (or/Pie or Bar).

4. Add your title, and x and y axes labels. (Make sure the Ribbon tab highlighted is **Layout**.)

PivotTables (Worksheet: Countif)

Contingency tables, crosstabs, or, using Excel's term, PivotTables are an OLAP tool that allows data to be sliced and diced, i.e., relationships can be examined and summarized between two or more variables/fields. The survey data in Figure 2.12 is used to illustrate how to construct and manipulate a PivotTable. Let's try looking at a table that counts the numbers of responses by major and by the response to the question on usefulness. The steps to generate such a PivotTable are:

1. Highlight A1:D23.

2. Click on the **Insert** tab from the Ribbon.

3. Under the group of **Tables** commands, click on **PivotTable**.

4. A new dialog box will appear. Just click **OK**. Then a new worksheet will appear similar to Figure 2.14.

5. Move the mouse to the right, on top of the word **Major** in the Pivot Table Field List box. Left click the mouse and hold it down while dragging **Major** all the way to Column A where it states in light blue "Drop Row Fields Here" and then release the mouse.

6. Similarly, move the mouse on top of **Usefullness**, left click and drag Usefullness on top of "Drop Column Fields Here."

7. There are two ways to obtain the count of the number of students by major and usefulness:

   A. Move the mouse on top of **Usefullness** (or choose any of the other fields (variables), left click, and drag it on top of "Drop Data Items Here" in the middle of the table, or;

   B. Move the mouse on top of **Usefullness** (or as above, any other field) and left click and drag it down to the lower right hand corner of the screen, in the white box under "Σ values."

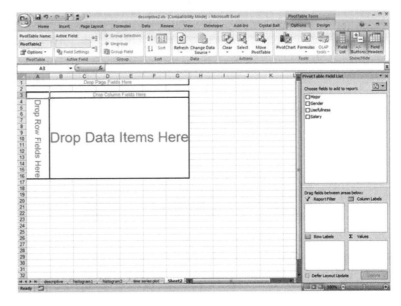

	C32		=	=COUNTIF(C2:C23,1)
	A	B	C	D
1	Major	Gender	Usefullness	Salary
2	Business	Male	3	52125
30				
31				
32	1		2	
33	2		3	
34	3		5	
35	4		6	
36	5		4	
37	blank		2	
38				
39	Male		13	
40	Female		9	
41				
42	A&S		11	
43	Business		11	

Figure 2.13 Use of the *countif* and *countblank* functions (Worksheet: Countif).

Figure 2.14 PivotTable worksheet.

Either way, the table should now look like the table in Figure 2.15. The number in a cell represents the number of people who had that major and gave a response of that particular number. For example, two business majors found their statistics course to be not very useful (response of 1).

> | **Note** | The Pivot Table Field List box will disappear if the worksheet is accidentally clicked on outside the table. To get the box back, click on the mouse anywhere inside the table. |

In that lower right-hand corner of Figure 2.15, in the white box, titled "Σ values," there is a row called "Count of Use" (its appearance would be slightly different if another field was selected in Step 7). Clicking on that row brings up a list of options, the last of which, as shown in Figure 2.15, will be Value Field Settings. Clicking that option will cause the Value Field Settings dialog box, Figure 2.16, to appear. In the Summarize value field by box, Count is highlighted. The setting can be changed so that various different summary statistics, such as averages, are displayed.

Different fields can then be clicked and dragged back and forth to create the desired PivotTable. Note that PivotTables become complex extremely quickly and it is advisable to try to keep them simple.

The data can be further sliced in a third dimension. For example, an analyst may be interested in examining the data in the table in Figure 2.15 by considering majors and usefulness by gender. In the Pivot Table Field List box, click on Gender and drag it down to the Report Filter box. The table will now look like Figure 2.17. If one now wants to analyze the data for males only, click on the drop arrow in cell B1, and a dialog box will appear as shown in Figure 2.17. Click on Male and click OK. Cell B1 will now be Male and the values inside the table will be correspondingly changed to

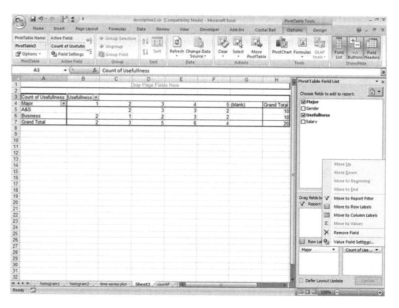

Figure 2.15   PivotTable of major by usefulness.

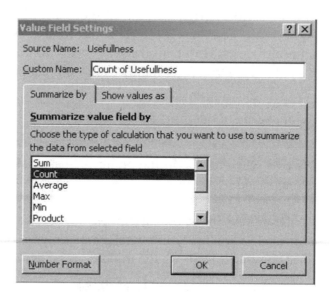

Figure 2.16   Value Field Settings dialog box.

represent only males. Repeating this process will allow only females to be displayed, or back will display everyone.

2.4.3 PivotTables with a Row or Column being a Continuous Variable

Thus far, qualitative/discrete variables/fields have been used as the row or column. If needed, a dimension of the PivotTable can be a continuous variable. However, a problem will most likely occur because the particular continuous variable in all likelihood will have numerous values and therefore will create large numbers of rows or columns. To illustrate this point, a new PivotTable of Salary versus Usefullness is generated, as shown in Figure 2.18. Such a table is not very useful. However, the continuous variable can easily be transformed into groups. In particular, salaries can be transformed into salary groups by following these instructions:

Move the mouse into any of the salary cells, A4 to A26. Right click. A dialog box will appear as in Figure 2.18. Click on **Group** and a Grouping dialog box will appear. Change the Starting at and Ending at values to 30000 and 70000 respectively. Click **OK**. The PivotTable in Figure 2.18 will change and should now look like the PivotTable in Figure 2.19.

2.5 A General Hypothesis Testing Framework

One of the basic underlying concepts of statistics is that it is improbable that the sample statistics, i.e., the sample mean, sample standard deviation, and sample variance, will exactly equal their corresponding population parameters. What is hoped is that they will be close, and statistics determines what is close. As a result,

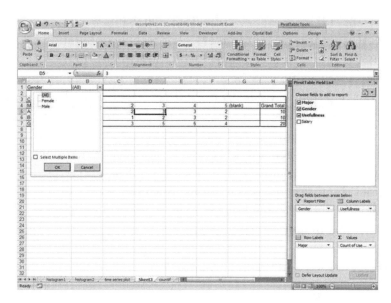

Figure 2.17 Adding a third dimension (Report filter) to the PivotTable.

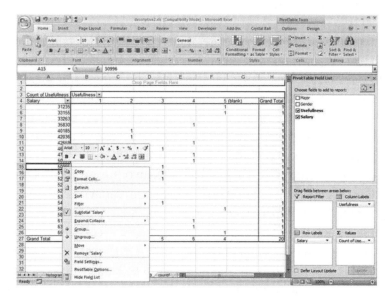

Figure 2.18 PivotTable output with one dimension using a continuous variable.

one of the objectives for collecting the sample may be to test whether a population parameter, such as the population mean or variance, is equal to, less than, or greater than a particular value. This particular value may be a constant or it may even be the corresponding population value from another population. The statistical process of testing whether a population parameter is equal to, less than, or greater than, a particular value is called hypothesis testing. In this section, a general framework is developed for hypothesis testing stressing the non-technical interpretation of the results. In no way does the following discussion substitute for the complete depth of understanding provided by standard statistical textbooks.

Statistical hypothesis testing consists of three major components:

- Hypotheses—null and alternative

- Statistical Requirements

- Decision and Conclusion

Two hypotheses are utilized here. One hypothesis is called the null hypothesis or H_0 and the other hypothesis is called the alternative hypothesis or H_1. The null and alternative hypotheses are statements about the population parameter(s) being tested. The null hypothesis is the historical/present value of the population parameter, or it is the hypothesized value. The alternative hypothesis is the opposite of the null hypothesis. Some of the more common applied hypothesis tests, as listed in Table 2.3, are performed on a population mean or means (comparing two population means), comparing two population variances, and a test of independence for comparing categorical data. To test whether a hypothesis is true or not, a random representative sample is collected, the appropriate sample statistic is determined, and the proper test statistic is calculated. Certain statistical requirements must be satisfied in order for particular statistical techniques to be considered valid, as listed in Table 2.3. Generally speaking, the statistical requirement is that a large enough random and representative sample must be collected.

Figure 2.19 PivotTable with the continuous variable converted into groups.

Table 2.3 Commonly Used Hypothesis Tests and Their Statistical Requirements

	Test	Statistical Requirement
Quantitative Data	One-Sample–Means	Central Limit Theorem (CLT)
	Two-Sample–Means (Independent)	CLT
	Two-Sample–Means (Dependent/Matched Pairs)	CLT
	Variances	Population distributions are normal or if used in conjunction with hypothesis testing of means, the CLT must hold
Qualitative/ Discrete Data	Π^2 Test of Independence	Expected frequencies are > 5

Depending on how close or far away the sample statistic is to or from the hypothesized value, a statistical decision and a non-technical conclusion can be made. The three major components of hypothesis testing are examined next in the context of one-sample hypothesis testing.

2.5.1 One-sample hypothesis testing of the mean (Continuous data)

One-sample hypothesis testing of the mean tests whether the population mean is equal to, less than, or greater than, a particular constant. For example, a dean at college A could claim the average SAT scores are 1200. A hypothesis test can be performed to see whether or not the population mean is:

(1) equal or not equal to 1200,

(2) significantly less than 1200, or

(3) significantly greater than 1200.

The corresponding null and alternative hypothesis for each situation are seen in Figure 2.20.

Situation (1) is known as a two-tailed test. In situation (1), a difference is sought, and this difference could be above or below the mean. Situations (2) and (3) are called one-tailed tests because in these situations some direction is implied, i.e., the sample statistic is expected to be significantly less than or greater than the population parameter.

The statistical requirement that allows performance of one-sample hypothesis testing of the mean is that the Central Limit Theorem (CLT) must be satisfied, as listed in Table 2.3. The CLT is satisfied if a random and representative sample greater than 30 is taken. (Otherwise, if the sample size is less than 30, the population distribution must be assumed to follow a normal or bell-shaped distribution for the CLT to hold (there are statistical tests to test for normality).) The one situation where the CLT does not hold is when the sample size is less than 30 and the population distribution is not normal. If it is assumed, in the ongoing example, that the dean collected a random sample greater than 30, the CLT is satisfied and the hypothesis test to determine whether or not the average SAT score

(1) Equal or not equal
$H_0: \mu = 1200$
$H_1: \mu \neq 1200$

(2) Significantly less than
$H_0: \mu \geq 1200$
$H_1: \mu < 1200$

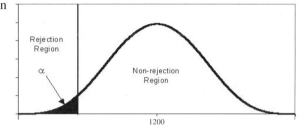

(3) Significantly greater than
$H_0: \mu \leq 1200$
$H_1: \mu > 1200$

Figure 2.20   Results of One-sample Hypothesis Testing of the Mean

is equal to 1200, or if it is significantly less than, or greater than 1200, can be performed.

The statistical decision from the hypothesis test is directed toward the null hypothesis. There are two possible statistical decisions:

- *Reject H_0*: The sample statistic, which we will call Z_{CALC} (depending on the test being performed it may not be a Z, but, could be a T or F or X^2 or something else), is far enough away to say that H_0 is not true, as in Figure 2.21.

- *Do Not Reject H_0*: The sample statistic, Z_{CALC}, is not sufficiently far away and it cannot be said that H_0 is not true as in Figure 2.21.

The ultimate burden of proof is on the alternative hypothesis, i.e., there must be overwhelming statistical evidence to say that the alternative hypothesis is true. To have statistically overwhelming evidence, in general, the hypothesis is regarded as having a small chance of occurring. This small chance of occurring is known as the level of significance, or α. Usually when performing hypothesis testing, we use an α of 0.01, 0.05, or 0.10. The level of significance, α, determines the location of the critical value, Z_C, and as a result determines what is to be considered far enough or not far enough away. When H_0 is not rejected, the sample statistic, Z_{CALC}, is still statistically close to the hypothesized value expressed in H_0 such that it is uncertain whether there is or is not a difference, i.e., $|Z_{CALC}| < Z_C$, as shown in Figure 2.21. Realize, it is not being concluded that H_0 is true, just that there is not enough evidence to say it is not true. On the other hand, when H_0 is rejected, the sample statistic, Z_{CALC}, is statistically far enough away, i.e., $|Z_{CALC}| > Z_C|$, as shown in Figure 2.21.

There is a direct analogy of hypothesis testing in the judicial system, in which the null hypothesis is that you are innocent; and the alternative hypothesis is that you are guilty. If you have overwhelming evidence, you reject H_0 and it is concluded that you are guilty. On the other hand, if the evidence is not overwhelming, then it is concluded that you are innocent. In reality, the system is really saying that there is not enough evidence to say you are guilty.

Not knowing what level of significance the analyst could be using, i.e., the level at which he(she) considers the evidence to be overwhelming, computer programmers of statistical software did not know how to present the results (which depended on the value

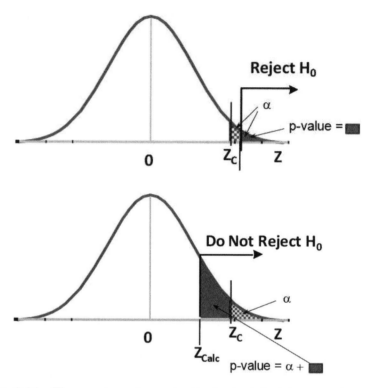

Figure 2.21   The p-value when reject/not reject decisions are to made.

of α). So, they ingeniously applied statistical hypothesis testing theory to develop a concept known as p-values. The p-value measures how close or far away the particular sample statistic is to the hypothesized parameter. The p-value is the probability of rejecting H_0. Thus, in Figure 2.21, the p-value is equal to the area under the curve to the right of Z_{CALC}. When Z_{CALC} is less than Z_C and we do not reject H_0, the p-value is equal to α plus the solid area at the right. Thus, when we do not reject H_0, the p-value is greater than α. When Z_{CALC} is greater than Z_C and we do Reject H_0, the p-value is equal to less area than α, i.e., the p-value $< \alpha$.

The smaller the p-value, the farther away the sample statistic is from the hypothesized value, stated in H_0. As shown in Table 2.4,

Table 2.4 Decisions and Conclusions to Hypothesis Tests in Relationship to the p-value

Critical value	p-value	Statistical Decision	Conclusion
$\lvert Z_{CALC} \rvert > Z_C$	p-value $< \alpha$	Reject H_0	There is enough evidence to say H_1 is true
$\lvert Z_{CALC} \rvert < Z_C$	p-value $> \alpha$	Do Not Reject H_0	There is not enough evidence to say H_1 is true

the meaning of the p-values in relationship to the two possible statistical decisions is:

- Reject H_0—the p-value is less than α.

- Do Not Reject H_0—the p-value is greater than or equal to α.

If the p-value is:

- less than 1 percent, there is overwhelming evidence that supports the alternative hypothesis.

- between 1 and 5 percent, there is strong evidence that supports the alternative hypothesis.

- between 5 and 10 percent, there is weak evidence that supports the alternative hypothesis.

- greater than 10 percent, there is little to no evidence that supports the alternative hypothesis.

The statement of the statistical decision, Reject H_0 or Do Not Reject H_0, is important, but it is almost meaningless to decision-makers (they do not understand it!). To be of any practical use, the statistical decision must be transformed and stated in a non-technical statement. This non-technical statement is called the conclusion. The conclusion statement, unlike the statistical decision, is directed toward the alternative hypothesis, H_1. As shown in Table 2.4, if the statistical decision is to:

- Reject H_0: The sample statistic is far enough away to conclude that the alternative hypothesis is true.

- Do Not Reject H_0: The sample statistic is "statistically close" and there is not enough evidence to say that the alternative hypothesis is true.

For example, continuing with our Dean example, let's say the Dean was testing whether or not the average SAT score is significantly greater than 1200, situation (3), and a 0.05 level of significance was applied. The corresponding null and alternative hypothesis would be:

$$H_0: \mu \leq 1200$$

$$H_1: \mu > 1200$$

If the resulting p-value is:

- 0.12, then the statistical decision is to not reject H_0, (0.12 > 0.05). The corresponding conclusion would be that there is not enough evidence to say that the average SAT score is greater than 1200.

- 0.02, then the statistical decision would be to reject H_0, (0.02 < 0.05). The conclusion would be that there is enough evidence to say that the average SAT score is greater than 1200.

2.6 Excel Nuggets (Datatable2.xls)

This section will demonstrate some rather unknown Excel procedures. Although not directly related to forecasting, these Excel procedures have been found to be extremely useful decision support tools for analyzing and presenting data.

2.6.1   Scroll bar and One and Two-way Data Tables (Worksheets: Mort1-4)

To facilitate presentation of the next three Excel procedures, the problem scenario of determining the monthly payments for a home mortgage given a certain cost, interest rate, time period, and down payment will be used. As shown in Figure 2.22, the hypothetical house costs $200,000 and a down payment of $10,000 is made, leaving a principal of $190,000 to be borrowed. Further, it is assumed that the interest rate is 6 percent and the loan is for 30 years. What would be the monthly mortgage payments? The Excel PMT function, in cell C11, shows that the monthly payment would be $1,139.15.

Decision makers often want to ask and perform "what if" analyses, asking what would happen to the results if a value changed or varied? In particular, with the ongoing mortgage example, how much would the monthly down payments change if the down payment or the interest rate changed? The scroll bar and one- and two-way data table are very powerful Excel tools that can be extremely useful in performing "what if" analyses.

The scroll bar allows incremental variations in the value of a cell, and the cell may be linked to other formulas or even to a graph so that, as the scroll bar is moved, the calculations and/or graph change. To illustrate this concept, examine what happens to the monthly payments as the down payment is varied from $10,000 to $30,000 in increments of $5000. The initial step is to create a scroll

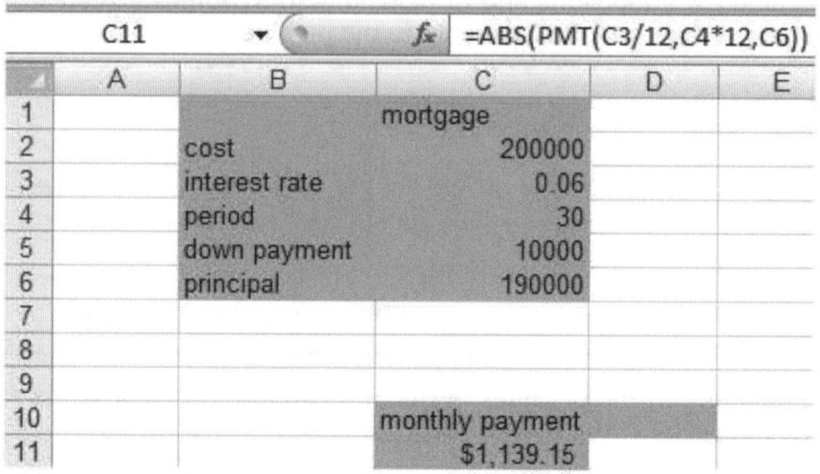

Figure 2.22   Mortgage payment example. (Worksheet: Mort1)

bar by first adding the Developer tab to the Ribbon, as follows: 1. Click the **Office Button**; 2. Click **Excel Options** (toward the bottom); 3. Click the check box next to **Show the Developer tab in the Ribbon**) then follow these steps:

1. Click on the **Developer** tab from the Ribbon.

2. Under the group of Control commands, click on **Insert**.

3. In the top Form Control, in the second row, click on the scroll bar icon.

4. A pair of crosshairs will appear. The crosshairs allow you to draw your scroll bar. Move the crosshairs to where you want the scroll bar to appear. Hold down the left mouse button, move the mouse to outline the scroll bar, and then release the button.

5. Move the mouse over the top of the scroll bar and right click.

6. A list of scroll bar options will appear. Choose the next to last option, which should be **Format Control**.

7. The **Format Control** dialog box will appear. As shown in Figure 2.23, enter:

   10000 in the Minimum value box

   30000 in the Maximum value box

   5000 in the Incremental change box

   Highlight cell **C5** in the Cell link box

8. Click **OK**.

Cell C5 is the down payment cell. When the scroll bar is moved, the down payment will change, and consequently the monthly payments in cell C11 also will change.

Like the scroll bar, the one-way data table allows changes or links to one cell. Instead of seeing the changes in the corresponding formulas however, the one-way data table generates a table with the changes. So, the advantage of the one-way data table over the scroll bar is that the changes in the results due to varying the value of one cell can all be seen at one time. In the ongoing mortgage example, this facility permits listing the different monthly payments for the different down payments. To produce a one-way data table for the different down payments follow the steps below (create this data table in Worksheet Mort2):

1. Put the numbers 10000 to 30000, in increments of 5000 in cells B12 to B16.

2. In cell C11, enter the Excel function <–ABS(PMT(C3/ 12,C4*12, C6))> to calculate the monthly payments

3. Highlight cells B11 to C16.

4. Click on the **Data** tab from the Ribbon.

5. Under the group of Data Tools commands, click on **What-If Analysis** and the Click **Data Table**.

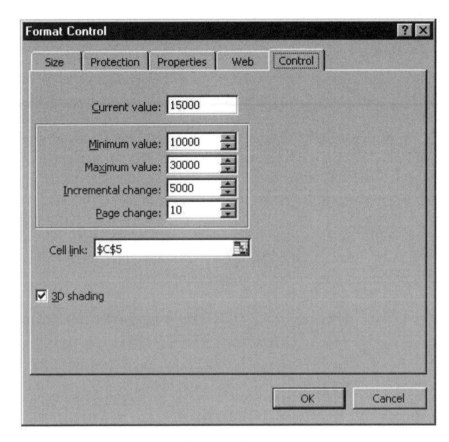

Figure 2.23 Format control for scroll bar.

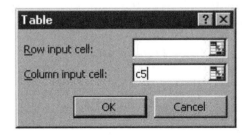

Figure 2.24 The Table dialog box of the one-way Data Table.

6. The **Table** dialog box will appear, as shown in Figure 2.24. Enter in the Column input cell box **C5**. Click **OK**.

Figure 2.25 shows the output from the one-way data table, which shows the different down payments for the corresponding monthly payments.

When the values in one cell are changed, the values in more than one cell may also change, e.g., when the down payment is changed, the total amount of the loan, i.e., the sum of all the monthly payments, also changes. The one-way data table can also list the changes of more than one cell. For example, in addition to the monthly payments, we may also want to see the different total amounts of the loan. To create such a data table, take the following steps (create this data table in Worksheet Mort2b):

1. Enter the numbers 10000 to 30000, in increments of 5000 in cells B12 to B16. In cell D10, enter “total loan.”
2. In cell C11, enter the Excel function <–ABS(PMT(C3/12,C4*12, C6))> to calculate the monthly payments.
3. In cell D11 enter = C11*C4*12
4. Highlight cells B11 to D16.
5. Click on the **Data** tab from the Ribbon.
6. Under the group of Data Tools commands, click on **What-If Analysis** and the Click **Data Table**.
7. The **Table** dialog box will appear. Enter in the Column input cell box **C5**. Click **OK**.

The data table in Figure 2.26 will appear, with the amount of the monthly payments and the total amount of the loan for the different down payments.

A15 fx

	A	B	C	D
1			mortgage	
2		cost	200000	
3		interest rate	0.06	
4		period	30	
5		down payment	10000	
6		principal	190000	
7				
8				
9				
10			monthly payment	
11		down payment	$1,139.15	
12		10,000	$1,139.15	
13		15,000	$1,109.17	
14		20,000	$1,079.19	
15		25,000	$1,049.21	
16		30,000	$1,019.24	

Figure 2.25 The output of the one-way data table.

	A	B	C	D
1			mortgage	
2		cost	100000	
3		interest rate	0.1	
4		period	25	
5		down payment	20000	
6		principal	80000	
7				
8				
9				
10			monthly payment	total loan
11		down payment	$726.96	$218,088.18
12		10,000	$817.83	$245,349.20
13		15,000	$772.40	$231,718.69
14		20,000	$726.96	$218,088.18
15		25,000	$681.53	$204,457.67
16		30,000	$636.09	$190,827.16

Figure 2.26 One-way data table output with two parameters. (Worksheet: Mort2c)

Excel additionally provides a two-way data table that allows changes to be made to two cells simultaneously. To illustrate how to produce a two-way data table, and continuing with the mortgage problem, besides varying the down payment, we could use different interest rates. Let's say the interest rates could vary from 7 to 10 percent. A two-way data table can be produced, displaying the monthly payments for the different down payments and interest rates by the following sequence (create this data table in Worksheet Mort3):

1. Enter the numbers 10000 to 30000, in increments of 5000 in cells C20 to C24. Enter the percentages 7% to 10% in increments of 0.25% in cells D19 to P19.

2. In cell C19 enter the Excel function <–ABS(PMT(C3/12,C4*12, C6))> to calculate the monthly payments.

3. Highlight cells C19 to P24.

4. Click on the **Data** tab from the Ribbon.

5. Under the group of Data Tools commands, click on **What-If Analysis** and then Click **Data Table**.

6. The **Table** dialog box will appear. Enter in the Row input cell box C3. Enter in the Column input cell box **C5**. Click **OK**.

This sequence produces a two-way data table with the different monthly payments for the varying down payments and interest rates, as shown in Figure 2.27.

2.6.2 Goal Seek (Worksheet: Goal)

Occasionally, a problem situation arises where the best value of a parameter that satisfies some specified goal is needed. The Excel procedure of Goal Seek will find this best value of one parameter while seeking a particular goal (if it is necessary to change more than two cells, perhaps it is advisable to try the management science technique of linear programming). For example, a common problem faced by sales managers is determining the selling price of a product, given the specified costs that will obtain a certain profit margin. As an example, take the numbers shown in Figure 2.28.

The projected demand for the product here considered is 10,000 units. The production cost per unit is \$12.63 and there is a fixed overhead cost of \$100,000. So, our total costs, B11, is equal to \$100,000 + \$12.63*10,000 = \$226,300 (or B10+B9*B4). The revenue per unit is equal to the discounted price per unit, i.e., B3*(1–B5). The total revenue, B6, is equal to the revenue per unit times the number of units sold, (B3*(1–B5)*B4). The total profit, B14, is equal to the revenue minus the costs (B6–B11). With the \$20.00 price per unit in Figure 2.28, the profit margin, that is, profit divided by revenue (B14/B6), would be –88.58 percent. It is necessary to find the price per unit at which the product must be sold to produce a profit margin of 30 percent. This result can be found by using the iterative Excel procedure called Goal Seek, as follows:

1. Click on the **Data** tab from the Ribbon.

2. Under the group of Data Tools commands, click on **What-If Analysis** and then click **Goal Seek**.

3. The **Goal Seek** dialog box will appear, as shown in Figure 2.29. In the Set cell enter **B15**. In the To value cell enter **.3**. In the By changing cell enter **B3**. Click **OK**.

Some values on the worksheet may vary, but the worksheet should be similar to that shown in Figure 2.30 where, with a price per unit of \$53.83, the corresponding profit margin is 29.94%.

Note	**The profit margin is not exactly 30%. If a more precise answer is needed, change the threshold used by Excel to converge on the solution.**

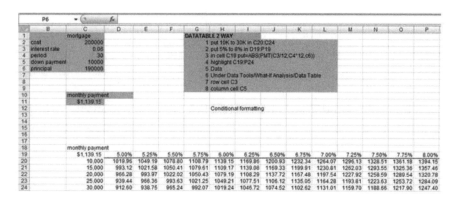

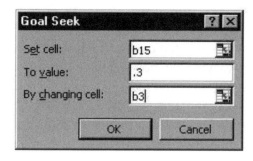

Figure 2.29   The Goal Seek dialog box.

Figure 2.27   Example of a two-way data table. (Worksheet: Mort4)

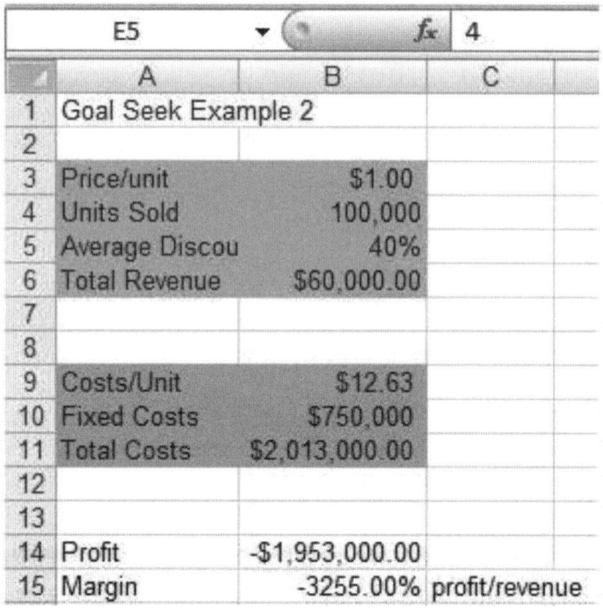

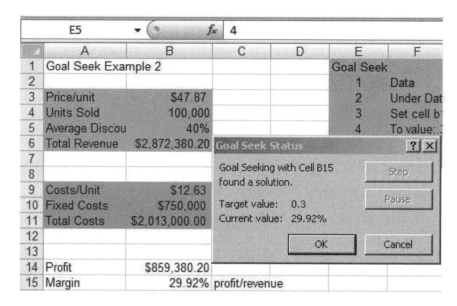

Figure 2.30   The results of using Goal Seek. (Worksheet: Goal)

Figure 2.28   A profit margin problem. (Worksheet: Goal)

References

1. Bradley, James V. *Distribution-Free Statistical Tests*. Englewood Cliffs, NJ: Prentice Hall, 1968.

2. Conover, W.J. *Practical Nonparametric Statistics*. 2nd ed. New York: John Wiley & Sons, 1980.

3. Daniel, W.W. *Applied Nonparametric Statistics*. Boston: Houghton Mifflin, 1990.

Chapter 3

Basic Time Series Analysis

3.1 Introduction

In this chapter the basic tools and techniques for analyzing time series data are presented. Time series data is data collected over time. The time period, i.e., the interval at which the data is collected, may be by year, month, week, day of the week, hour, and so on. Time series data consists of four components or patterns:

- *Trend—overall increasing/decreasing in values;*

- *Seasonal—short-term patterns in the data that repeat themselves;*

- *Cyclical—long-term patterns in the data that repeat themselves, and;*

- *Irregular—once the trend, seasonal, and cyclical components are removed, it is the remaining variability in the data.*

The first part of this chapter will focus on the process of teasing out and analyzing these components and in addition, understanding their impact on the data. This process is usually one of the major objectives of a time series forecasting project, as discussed in Chapter 1. Time series forecasting techniques are those that use only the time series data itself and not any other data to build the forecasting models. First, this chapter will discuss the time series forecasting technique of decomposition. The decomposition techniques isolate and estimate the effect of each time series component. In the latter part of this chapter, the two most common smoothing techniques of moving averages and exponential smoothing will be introduced. The objective of the smoothing methods is to even out or smooth out the variations. More complex smoothing methods are presented in Chapter 5.

3.2 Components of a Time Series (Files: Datats.xls and Randomness.xls)

3.2.1 Trend Component (Worksheet: Trend)

A trend is overall movements of the time series values, e.g., are sales increasing or decreasing. All the values will not necessarily appear along a smooth curve/line, i.e., there will most likely be some variations—a little higher or lower. One of the initial concerns is to discover the overall tendency of the data. In most instances only a linear trend is considered, but the trend may be non-linear (non-linear trends are discussed in Chapter 7). For example, in Figure 3.1, a linear trend and a non-linear (exponential) trend are displayed. In addition to the direction of the trend, the steepness (or rate of change) of the trend may also be of interest.

The slope of the trend line measures the rate of change of a linear trend such that the larger the absolute value of the slope the greater the rate of change. For example, in column C of Figure 3.2 the quarterly sales of a product are shown over the past five years. The quarterly sales are in hundreds of thousands of dollars. As the trend line in Figure 3.3 indicates, sales appear to be increasing over time. Additionally, the trend equation shows that sales are increasing at a rate of $1,772,200 per quarter (1.7722*100,000). (Steps in generating a times series plot and its corresponding trend line are discussed in Chapter 2.) The next section explains the statistical methods that can be used to determine the values of the y-intercept and the slope of the trend line, and whether or not there is a statistically-significant trend (slope).

3.2.2 Linear Trend Analysis

The trend line, the slope and the y-intercept shown in Figure 3.2, are developed using a statistical technique called regression (further discussed in Chapter 6). Regression finds the values of the slope

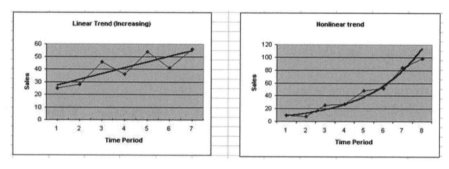

Figure 3.1   Example of linear and nonlinear trends.

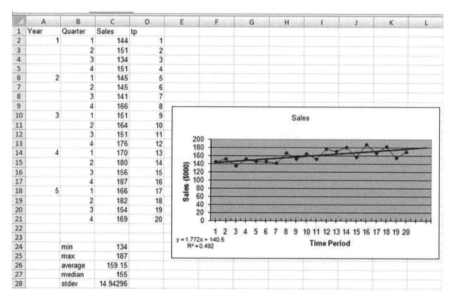

Figure 3.2   Linear trend of sales data.

and the y-intercept that minimize the sum of the squares of the differences between the regression line and the actual value. In other words, regression finds the line that minimizes the sum of the squares of the errors (where an error or residual is defined as the difference between actual and predicted values). This line is known as the best fitting line. The trend line is defined as:

$$T_t = b_0 + b_1 t$$

where:

T_t = the value of the trend line in period t

b_0 = the y-intercept

b_1 = the slope

t = the time period

The regression formulas to compute slope, b_1, and y-intercept, b_0, are:

$$b_1 = \frac{\sum\limits_{t=1}^{n} t Y_t - \dfrac{\sum\limits_{t=1}^{n} t \sum\limits_{t=1}^{n} Y_t}{n}}{\sum\limits_{t=1}^{n} t^2 - \dfrac{\left(\sum\limits_{t=1}^{n} t\right)^2}{n}}$$

$$b_0 = \overline{Y} - b_1 \overline{t}$$

where:

Y_t = time series value in period t

$\overline{Y}$ = average of times series values, i.e., $\overline{Y} = \dfrac{\sum\limits_{t=1}^{n} Y_t}{n}$

t = time period t

$\overline{t}$ = the average of time periods, i.e., $\overline{t} = \dfrac{\sum\limits_{t=1}^{n} t}{n}$

n = the number of time periods

In Figure 3.3, the time series data in Figure 3.2 has been manipulated to calculate some intermediary values used to calculate b_1 and b_0. These intermediary values are:

$\Sigma Y = 3183$
$\Sigma t = 210$
$\Sigma t Y_t = 34,600$

$\Sigma t^2 = 2870$
$\Sigma n = 20$ (as shown in Figure 3.3).

	A	B Sales (Y_t)	C Time Period t	D tY_t	E t^2
1					
2		144	1	144	1
3		151	2	302	4
4		134	3	402	9
5		151	4	604	16
6		145	5	725	25
7		145	6	870	36
8		141	7	987	49
9		166	8	1328	64
10		151	9	1359	81
11		164	10	1640	100
12		151	11	1661	121
13		176	12	2112	144
14		170	13	2210	169
15		180	14	2520	196
16		156	15	2340	225
17		187	16	2992	256
18		166	17	2822	289
19		182	18	3276	324
20		154	19	2926	361
21		169	20	3380	400
22	Sum	3183	210	34600	2870

Figure 3.3 Calculations for regression values.

We can then substitute into the b_1 and b_0 equations:

$$b_1 = \frac{34,600 - \dfrac{210(3183)}{20}}{2870 - \dfrac{210^2}{20}} = 1.772$$

$$\overline{Y} = \frac{3183}{20} = 159.15$$

$$\overline{t} = \frac{210}{20} = 10.5$$

$$b_0 = 159.15 - 1.772(10.5) = 140.54$$

As a result, the regression equation for the trend line is $T_t = 140.54 + 1.772t$. This equation is the same equation shown in Figure 3.2, which was the outcome of adding a trend line.

In addition to calculating the slope and y-intercept manually, as above, or by using the trend line option to the chart, the above trend line can also be generated in Excel using the Data Analysis Regression tool by following these steps:

1. Click on the **Data** tab from the Ribbon.

2. Click on the **Data Analysis** command (all the way to the right).

3. Choose **Regression** from the list of analysis tools.

4. A dialog box, as shown in Figure 3.4, will appear. Using the data shown in Figure 3.2, fill in the appropriate boxes in the dialog box, as shown in Figure 3.4:

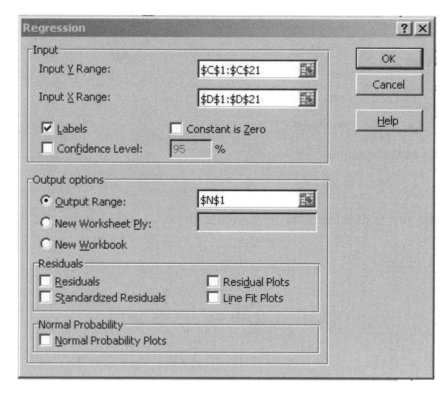

Figure 3.4   Regression dialog box for creating a trend line.

Enter C1:C21 in the **Input Y Range** box

Enter D1:D21 in the **Input X Range** box

Click on **Labels**

Enter N1 in the **Output Range** box (this identifies cell N1 as the upper left-hand corner of the output.)

Click **OK.**

Figure 3.5 shows the regression output. The b_0 and b_1 coefficients are 140.52 and 1.772 respectively, and are displayed in cells J17 and J18. Notice that these coefficients are the same values that were just generated using the regression equations. Using this trend line, the predicted value/forecast value for time period 1 is

$$T_1 = 140.54 + 1.772*1 = 142.312.$$

Additionally, the error or residual for the first time period is

$$Y_1 - T_1 = 144 - 142.312 = 1.688.$$

The predicted values and errors for each of the 20 periods are listed in Figure 3.6. Further, in Figure 3.6 forecasts for the next two periods, periods 21 and 22, are provided, i.e., the trend projection for the

21st period is: $T_{21} = 140.54 + 1.772*(21) = 177.752$

and

22nd period is: $T_{22} = 140.54 + 1.772*(22) = 179.524$

3.2.3 Test for Significant Trend

When a linear trend line using regression is produced, it is assumed that there is a theoretical regression line where: $T_t = \beta_0 + \beta_1 t + ,.$ β_0 is the y-intercept and β_1 is the slope. These model parameters, β_0 and β_1, are population parameters whose real values are unknown. The least squares regression procedure develops estimates, b_0 and b_1, of these population parameters, β_0 and β_1, respectively. The estimate b_1 is unlikely to equal β_1 exactly, but it is hoped that it is statistically close and the same is true for b_0 and β_0. A statistical hypothesis test can be conducted to test whether it can be assumed that β_1 is equal to zero or not. If there is a significant trend, and if the slope (trend) is positive, a significant positive trend exists, or if

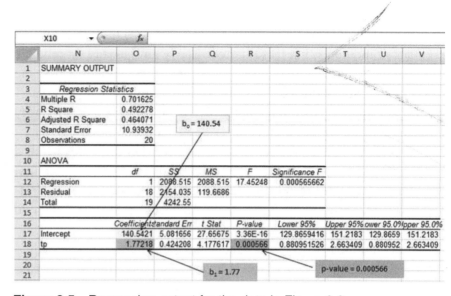

Figure 3.5 Regression output for the data in Figure 3.2.

Sales (Y_t)	Time Period t	Predicted	Error or Residual
144	1	142.312	1.688
151	2	144.084	6.916
134	3	145.856	-11.856
151	4	147.628	3.372
145	5	149.4	-4.4
145	6	151.172	-6.172
141	7	152.944	-11.944
166	8	154.716	11.284
151	9	156.488	-5.488
164	10	158.26	5.74
151	11	160.032	-9.032
176	12	161.804	14.196
170	13	163.576	6.424
180	14	165.348	14.652
156	15	167.12	-11.12
187	16	168.892	18.108
166	17	170.664	-4.664
182	18	172.436	9.564
154	19	174.208	-20.208
169	20	175.98	-6.98
	21	177.752	
	22	179.524	

Figure 3.6 Predicted and error values.

it is negative, a significant negative trend exists. Use of the word significant indicates that it is not necessarily a relatively large value but that there is a statistically significant trend showing that the trend is not equal to zero. Thus, the statistical hypothesis test determines whether the estimate of β_1, b_1, is statistically significantly close to zero, or is statistically significantly far enough away that it may be considered as not being equal to zero. On the other hand, it may be concluded that there is not enough evidence to say that there is a significant trend. In such a situation, subsequent forecasting modeling is unlikely to consider and find a significant trend component (although it is still possible).

This statistical hypothesis test, (statistical hypothesis testing is reviewed in Chapter 2), for trend has what is called null and alternative hypotheses, respectfully denoted as H_0 and H_1:

$$H_0: \beta_1 = 0$$

$$H_1: \beta_1 \neq 0$$

There are now two possible conclusions:

1. If H_0 is rejected, then there is a statistically significant trend, or

2. If H_0 is not rejected, then there is no statistically significant trend.

To determine whether or not to reject H_0, the p-value of the test is compared to a level of significance. The usual value of the level of significance, or α, is 0.01, 0.05 or 0.10 and is determined by the decision-maker/analyst. The p-value is based upon the data and is reported as part of the statistical computer results. Therefore, if:

- the p-value $< \alpha$ then reject H_0,

- the p-value $\geq \alpha$ then do not reject H_0.

In the example shown in Figure 3.5, b_1 is equal to 1.772 and the p-value is 0.000566 (cell R18), which is relatively small and definitely less than the commonly used values of α. So it can be concluded that, in this example, there is a statistically significant non-zero trend. More specifically, sales are increasing at a rate of about $1,772,200 per quarter.

3.2.4   Seasonal Component (Worksheet: Seasonal)

The seasonal component of a time series is a short-term pattern that repeats itself. What is considered to be short-term is relative to the time frame for which the time series data is collected. The time series data could be taken by the hour, day, week, month, year, or some other regular time interval. As a result, a seasonal influence could be time of day, day of the week, month of the year, quarter, or something similar. For some reason(s), the data tends to be higher or lower during a particular season, e.g., sales of skis are high in the winter and rather low during the summer, or restaurant sales are higher around meal times.

To demonstrate how to graphically observe a seasonal pattern, return to the data and graph in Figure 3.2. First it is necessary to remove the trend line and label the data points. To remove the trend line, simply:

- Move the mouse on top of the graph and click it on.

- Click on the **Design** tab from the Ribbon.

- Click on **Trendline** and a list of options appears. Click **None** and the trend line should disappear.

Next, because the data in Figure 3.2 is quarterly, each data point needs to be labeled according to its respective season by taking the following steps:

- To relabel Horizontal Axis values:

  Click the **Select Data** command (make sure the graph is hot (clicked on) and that the major Ribbon command **Design** is clicked). A new dialog box will appear. Toward the right, there is a column entitled **Horizontal (Category) Axis Labels**. Click on the **Edit box** as shown in Figure 3.7. The Axis Labels dialog box will appear. For the Axis label range: Highlight B2:B21. Click **OK**.

- To display Labels:

  Click the **Data Labels** command (make sure the graph is hot (click it on) and that the major Ribbon command **Layout** is clicked). A list of options will appear. At the bottom there should be More Data Label Option. Click it. The Format Data Labels dialog box should appear. At the top, under Label Contains click on Category Name (and if it is on, click off Value. Choose under Label Position—Right. Click Close.

As a result, the graph will now look like Figure 3.8. Examining Figure 3.8, it can be seen clearly that:

- sales are generally lower in the third quarter and

- sales tend to be higher in the fourth quarter, and most of the time in the second quarter as well.

If no seasonal pattern is uncovered, further forecasting model development may not need to consider any seasonal component. On the other hand, if a seasonal pattern is revealed, this pattern should definitely be considered in subsequent forecasting models.

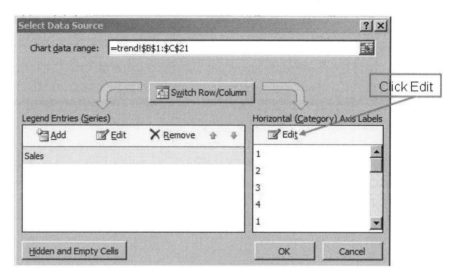

Figure 3.7   Adding quarter labels to graph.

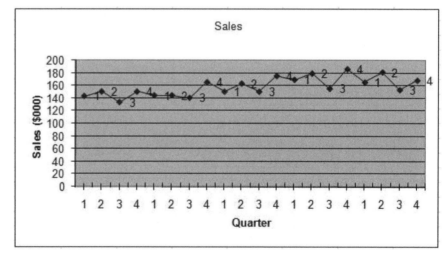

Figure 3.8   Illustration of the seasonal component of the sales data in Figure 3.2.

3.2.5 Cyclical Component

The cyclical component is a long-term pattern that repeats itself. The data then tends to stay above or below the trend line for long periods of time. Again, long-term is relative to how often the time series data is collected (e.g., monthly data as opposed to hourly data). Most of the time, cyclical patterns are assumed to be caused by economic factors such as the business cycle (hence, a cycle is usually at least 12 months). An example of a cyclical pattern would be the effect on prices caused by periods of rapid inflation, followed by modest inflation. The major difference between a seasonal and a cyclical component is that the seasonal component is of a constant length and occurs on a regular periodic basis, whereas a cyclical component varies in length and is usually longer than a seasonal component.

In many circumstances it is difficult to isolate the cycle effects. The question is whether the cyclical component should be addressed. To answer this question, three further questions should be considered:

1. Is the forecasting for the short term?

2. Does the data show a cyclical pattern?

3. Can this pattern be related to some economic/business indicator?

The cyclical component should be considered if all three of the above questions are answered in the affirmative. Further, there is a hierarchy to these questions such that they should be asked in sequence, i.e., there is no need to ask a subsequent question if a preceding question is not satisfied.

Usually the cyclical component should not be addressed if the exercise is for long-term forecasting. It is very difficult to estimate the cyclical effects in the long-term (one or two years into the

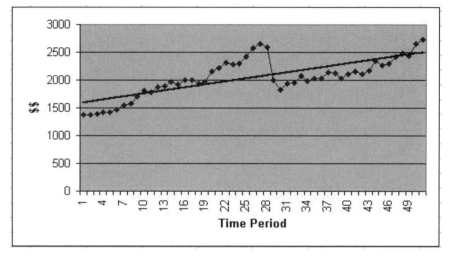

Figure 3.9   Example of cyclical graph.

future). For example, it is very difficult to forecast the economic conditions one year or two years from now. Thus, in most situations, simply using the trend component is adequate in estimating long-term increasing or decreasing effects. On the other hand, if the forecasting exercise is for the short-term, the cyclical component can be considered. To answer the next question, a significant cyclical pattern should be observed by examining a cyclical graph of the data. A cyclical graph is simply the time series plot of the data with its corresponding trend line.

For example, Figure 3.9 illustrates a cyclical graph with a definite cyclical pattern. For numerous periods the data values tend to be either above or below the trend line. Finally, where the first two criteria are satisfied, the forecasts are for the short-term, and a significant cyclical pattern in the data was found, a relationship between this pattern and some economic/business indicator must be established. The decision-maker/analyst needs to apply his (her) understanding of the particular industry, of the time series data, and his (her) knowledge of the relevant economic/business indicators collected by the federal government, to uncover this relationship. As Moore and Shisken[1] state:

> *Indicators provide a sensitive and revealing picture of the ebb and flow of economic tides that a skillful analyst of the economic, political, and international scene can use to improve his chances of making a valid forecast of short-run economic trends. If the analyst is aware of their limitations and alert to the world around him, he will find the indicators useful guideposts for taking stock of the economy and its needs.*

3.2.6   Irregular Component (Randomness.xls)

The irregular component is the variability remaining in the data when the effects of the other three components, (trend, seasonal, and cyclical), are taken out of the time series data. This irregular component is also called the residuals or errors. In most instances, this remaining component is nearly, if not completely, random. In such a situation, one of the smoothing techniques discussed later in this chapter could be used (as well as the Box-Jenkins approach discussed in Chapter 5). If the irregular component is random and normal (it follows a normal distribution) then no better time series models can be produced (unless another forecasting model uses additional explanatory variables). Why? Randomness implies that the data is unpredictable and has no pattern. No model can be developed from data that is unpredictable. On the other hand, if there is some pattern to the data then a model can be developed to predict this pattern. Thus, if the irregular component is not random, a model can be developed from the irregular component. The subject of detecting and testing for randomness is addressed in much detail in Chapter 4.

3.3 Decomposition (Datats.xls)

Decomposition techniques develop forecasting models in which the time series components—trend, seasonal, cyclical and irregular—are isolated and measured. These decomposition techniques assume either an additive or multiplicative model, i.e., the components are either multiplied by each other or they are added together. Originally developed during the 1920s, many variations of the additive and multiplicative models are still used today, e.g., the Census Bureau models of X-11 and Census II. In Chapter 7, the classical additive decomposition model: $Y_t = T_t + S_t + C_t + I_t$ will be discussed in the context of using the statistical technique of multiple regression.

The present chapter will focus on the classical multiplicative model $Y_t = T_t * S_t * C_t * I_t$. As discussed earlier in this chapter, the cyclical effects of this model are wavelike patterns due to economic factors such as the business cycle. In many situations it is difficult to isolate the cyclical effects, so a multiplicative decomposition model without the cyclical component is more commonly used. This multiplicative decomposition model, without the cyclical component is: $Y_t = T_t * S_t * I_t$ and it is assumed that whatever cyclical effect may or may not exist in the data is captured by the trend. The following section will demonstrate how the multiplicative decomposition model without the cyclical component is constructed, and the subsequent section will return to the more general multiplicative decomposition including the cyclical component, and show how this model is developed.

1.   Moore, G. H. and J. Shiskin (1976). "Early Warning Signals for the Economy," Statistics: A Guide to Business and Economics, eds. J. M. Tanur et al., Holden-Day, San Francisco, p. 81.

3.3.1 Multiplicative Decomposition (without cycle component) (Worksheet: Decomp1)

The multiplicative decomposition model that does not include the cyclical component uses a method called "ratio-to-moving averages" to calculate the seasonal variation, and trend analysis (using regression) to measure the trend component. Further, the effects of the trend component are measured directly from the data and on the other hand, the effects of the seasonal component are measured in the form of indices. To illustrate this multiplicative decomposition model, refer to the data in Figure 3.2. As mentioned earlier in the chapter, by examining the data in the graph in Figures 3.2 and 3.8, an obvious significant trend and a seasonal component are observable.

The first step in applying this decomposition technique is to remove the trend component, Y_t, from the data. Several methods can be used, including linear regression, differencing, or exponential smoothing. The most common method to remove the trend component uses moving averages and, subsequently, ratios, to develop the seasonal indexes, so this approach is called "ratio-to-moving averages." First, because the data in Figure 3.2 relates to quarters, a centered four-quarter moving average for the data is calculated. (Note: If the data were monthly, a centered twelve-month moving average would be calculated.) The following steps are taken to produce the centered four-quarter moving average shown in Figure 3.10:

1. Label columns D–G (i.e., in cells D1, . . . , G1), **Early MA**, **Late MA**, **Centered MA**, and **SI**, respectively.

2. In cell D4 enter the formula =AVERAGE(C2:C5). Copy and paste this formula into cells D5 to D19.

3. In cell E4 enter the formula =AVERAGE(C3:C6). Copy and paste this formula into cells E5 to E19.

4. In cell F4 enter the formula =AVERAGE(D4,E4). Copy and paste this formula into cells F5 to F19.

The 4-quarter moving averages calculated in columns D and E each include all the quarters in a year, so any seasonal effects are removed from the data. Further, notice that two quarters at the beginning of the series and two quarters at the end are not included (i.e., neither the Early nor Late MA in those periods is calculated).

There are two trend estimates for each time period. In particular, for the third quarter in Year 1:

Early MA = (144 + 151 + 134 + 151)/4 = 145

Late MA = (151 + 134 + 151 + 145)/4 = 145.25

However, because there is an even number of seasons (4), the middle (or center) of the Early MA is at 2.5 quarters and the middle of the Late MA is at 3.5 quarters for the first third quarter. In order to get a moving average exactly at the third quarter, the average of the Early MA and Late MA is taken (e.g., for the third quarter in Year 1: (145+145.25)/2 = 145.125). This average is called the centered moving average. Correspondingly, the centered moving averages for the remaining periods are calculated in similar fashion in Column F in Figure 3.10.

The centered moving average measures any effects from trend. The trend component, Y_t, is divided by its corresponding centered moving average (e.g., C4/F4). The resulting remaining component is a seasonal-irregular component, in column G, which is called the de-trended data, i.e.:

$$SI = \frac{Y_t}{T_t} = \frac{T_r * S_t * I_t}{T_t} = S_t * I_t$$

Each of the values in column G is an estimate of its corresponding seasonal index. One overall seasonal index for each season is calculated by taking the average of all the matching seasonal index estimates in column G. For example, using the seasonal indices in Figure 3.10, the quarter one seasonal index, in cell G24, equals:

$$\frac{G6+G10+G14+G18}{4} mp$$

$$= \frac{1.002593+0.963319+1.000736+0.9629319}{4}$$

$$= 0.982241$$

The base for these indices is 1.00. So the sum of the indices should be exactly equal to four. However, the actual sum of indexes, the value in cell G29, is slightly off at 4.004862. To make the sum of the seasonal indices add exactly to four, these indices are normalized by entering into cell H24 the formula =4*G24/$G$29 and then copying and pasting that formula into cells H25 to H27.

These seasonal indices, H24:H27, predict the seasonal influence of that part of the year in comparison to expected values for that segment of the year. A seasonal index greater than 1 implies higher values than expected for that season, and conversely, a seasonal index less than one implies lower than expected values for that season. For example, the seasonal index in Figure 3.11 for quarter 1 is 0.981049. So, sales are projected to be 1.8951 percent less than expected (−1.8951% = 100*(0.981049−1)). For the fourth quarter, sales are expected to be 6.5065 percent higher. Overall, sales for this example are above the norm in the second and fourth quarters and below the norm in the first and third quarters.

These four estimates of the seasonal indices are copied (use Paste Special and select values) and placed in their corresponding

	A	B	C	D	E	F	G
1		Quarter	Sales	Early MA	Late MA	Centered MA	SI
2	1	1	144				
3		2	151				
4		3	134	145	145.25	145.125	0.923342
5		4	151	145.25	143.75	144.5	1.044983
6	2	1	145	143.75	145.5	144.625	1.002593
7		2	145	145.5	149.25	147.375	0.983885
8		3	141	149.25	150.75	150	0.94
9		4	166	150.75	155.5	153.125	1.084082
10	3	1	151	155.5	158	156.75	0.963317
11		2	164	158	160.5	159.25	1.029827
12		3	151	160.5	165.25	162.875	0.927091
13		4	176	165.25	169.25	167.25	1.052317
14	4	1	170	169.25	170.5	169.875	1.000736
15		2	180	170.5	173.25	171.875	1.047273
16		3	156	173.25	172.25	172.75	0.903039
17		4	187	172.25	172.75	172.5	1.084058
18	5	1	166	172.75	172.25	172.5	0.962319
19		2	182	172.25	167.75	170	1.070588
20		3	154				
21		4	169				

Figure 3.10 Centered four-quarter moving average.

	E	F	G	H
23	Seasonal index			normalized
24		1	0.982241	0.981049
25		2	1.032893	1.031639
26		3	0.923368	0.922247
27		4	1.06636	1.065065
28				
29		sum	4.004862	4

Figure 3.11 Seasonal indices.

rows in column H, as shown in Figure 3.12. Given the seasonal indices, the actual sales, Y_t, are deseasonalized by dividing the value by its appropriate seasonal index. Thus, the data in column I, shown in Figure 3.12, are the deseasonalized data, i.e.:

$$TI = \frac{Y_t}{S_t} = \frac{T_t * S_t * I_t}{S_t} = T_t * I_t$$

In particular, for time period 1, the deseasonalized value is ((144/ 0.98194) = 146.7817).

The deseasonalized data in column I contains only the trend and irregular components. To estimate the trend from the deseasonalized data (column I), linear trend analysis is applied. (In the worksheet, cells I1:I21 are first copied into P1:P21 (again, using Paste Special and select values) and the label and sequential values for the time period are typed into column O as shown in Figure 3.13) As discussed earlier in this chapter, the Regression procedure under the Data Analysis tools is used to produce the trend line, as shown in Figure 3.13. As a result, the trend equation is: $T_t = 141.47 + 1.68t$.

The p-value for the hypothesis test, in cell V18 in Figure 3.13, to determine whether there is or is not a significant trend is 4E-06. This p-value is rather small, therefore, the data has a significant trend.

The projected/predicted trend for periods 1 and 20, respectively, using this regression equation is:

Period 1: 143.1497 = 141.47 + 1.68(1)

Period 20: 175.1468 = 141.47 + 1.68(20)

This trend equation, is used to generate trend projections or predicted trends for all the periods in column J of Figure 3.12 by: inserting into cell J2 =$S$17 + $S$18*O2 and copying and pasting this formula into cells J3 to J25.

Finally, the forecast for each time period, using this multiplicative decomposition approach, is found by multiplying the forecast trend by its corresponding seasonal index. So, in cell K2, enter the formula =J2*H2 and copy and paste this formula into

	A	B	C	D	E	F	G	H	I	J	K
1		Quarter	Sales	Early MA	Late MA	Centered MA	SI	Index	Trend	Forecast Trend	Forecast
2	1	1	144					0.981049	146.7817	143.1497	140.43687
3		2	151					1.031639	146.369	144.8338	149.41623
4		3	134	145	145.25	145.125	0.923342	0.922247	145.2973	146.5179	135.12566
5		4	151	145.25	143.75	144.5	1.044983	1.065065	141.7754	148.2019	157.84469
6	2	1	145	143.75	145.5	144.625	1.002593	0.981049	147.801	149.886	147.04544
7		2	145	145.5	149.25	147.375	0.983885	1.031639	140.553	151.57	156.36558
8		3	141	149.25	150.75	150	0.94	0.922247	152.8875	153.2541	141.33812
9		4	166	150.75	155.5	153.125	1.084082	1.065065	155.859	154.9381	165.01921
10	3	1	151	155.5	158	156.75	0.963317	0.981049	153.9169	156.6222	153.654
11		2	164	158	160.5	159.25	1.029827	1.031639	158.9703	158.3063	163.31494
12		3	151	160.5	165.25	162.875	0.927091	0.922247	163.7305	159.9903	147.55059
13		4	176	165.25	169.25	167.25	1.052317	1.065065	165.2481	161.6744	172.19373
14	4	1	170	169.25	170.5	169.875	1.000736	0.981049	173.284	163.3584	160.26257
15		2	180	170.5	173.25	171.875	1.047273	1.031639	174.4796	165.0425	170.26429
16		3	156	173.25	172.25	172.75	0.903039	0.922247	169.1521	166.7265	153.76305
17		4	187	172.25	172.75	172.5	1.084058	1.065065	175.5761	168.4106	179.36825
18	5	1	166	172.75	172.25	172.5	0.962319	0.981049	169.2067	170.0947	166.87114
19		2	182	172.25	167.75	170	1.070588	1.031639	176.4183	171.7787	177.21365
20		3	154					0.922247	166.9835	173.4628	159.97552
21		4	169					1.065065	158.6757	175.1468	186.54277
22										176.8309	173.4797
23					Seasonal index			normalized		178.5149	184.163
24						1	0.982241	0.981049		180.199	166.18798
25						2	1.032893	1.031639		181.8831	193.71729
26						3	0.923368	0.922247			
27						4	1.06636	1.065065			
28											
29						sum	4.004862	4			

Figure 3.12 Worksheet for trend, forecast trend, and forecast.

	O	P	Q	R	S	T	U	V	W	X	Y	Z
1	tp	trend		SUMMARY OUTPUT								
2	1	146.7817										
3	2	146.369		*Regression Statistics*								
4	3	145.2973		Multiple R	0.837954152							
5	4	141.7754		R Square	0.702167161							
6	5	147.801		Adjusted R Square	0.685620892							
7	6	140.553		Standard Error	6.666491299							
8	7	152.8875		Observations	20							
9	8	155.859										
10	9	153.9169		ANOVA								
11	10	158.9703			*df*	*SS*	*MS*	*F*	*Significance F*			
12	11	163.7305		Regression	1	1885.971263	1885.971	42.43659	3.99944E-06			
13	12	165.2481		Residual	18	799.9579124	44.44211					
14	13	173.284		Total	19	2685.929176						
15	14	174.4796										
16	15	169.1521			*Coefficients*	*Standard Error*	*t Stat*	*P-value*	*Lower 95%*	*Upper 95%*	*ower 95.0%*	*pper 95.0%*
17	16	175.5761		Intercept	141.46569	3.09679491	45.68132	4.56E-20	134.9595603	147.9718	134.9596	147.9718
18	17	169.2067		tp	1.684056713	0.258515444	6.514337	4E-06	1.140935498	2.227178	1.140935	2.227178
19	18	176.4183										
20	19	166.9835										
21	20	158.6757										
22	21	176.8309										
23	22	178.5149										
24	23	180.199										
25	24	181.8831										

Figure 3.13 Regression output for the trend component of multiplicative decomposition.

cells K3 to K21. To obtain the future forecasts, enter the formula = J22*H24 in cell K22 and then copy this formula into cells K23 to K25.

A graph of the actual and forecast values, from the data in Figure 3.14, can be produced by:

1. Select cells C1:C21.

2. Hold down the CTRL key and select cells K1:K25. (Cells C1:C21 and K1:K25 should be highlighted.)

3. Click on the **Insert** tab from the Ribbon.

4. Click on the **Line** command. A table of line charts appears. Click on the line chart in the first column and second row.

5. Add your title, and x and y axis labels. (Make sure that the Ribbon tab highlighted is **Layout**.)

Figure 3.14 shows the graph of the actual sales and forecast sales. Overall, the forecasts appear to be quite accurate except for small, yet consistent overestimation and underestimation in years 2 and 4 respectively.

The following section will examine the more general multiplicative decomposition method that does include the cyclical component.

3.3.2 Multiplicative Decomposition (with cycle component)

The multiplicative decomposition model that includes the cyclical component is: $Y_t = T_t * S_t * C_t * I_t$. To illustrate the procedure to develop this model, the same data just used for the multiplicative decomposition without the cycle component in Figure 3.2 and analyzed throughout this chapter will be used. In general, the process

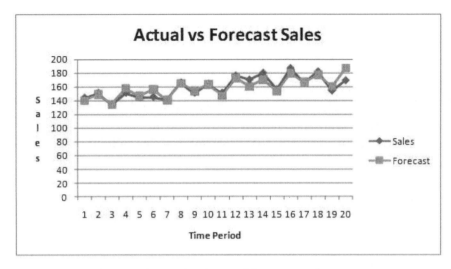

Figure 3.14 Graph of actual sales and forecast sales.

of developing forecasts using multiplicative decomposition with the cyclical component is quite similar to the process when the cycle component is not included.

The first step is to measure the trend component. Unlike the multiplicative decomposition without the cycle component approach, a "ratio-to-moving averages" approach is not employed here to estimate the trend. Instead, the trend line is produced using regression analysis with time period as the independent variable and the actual data as the dependent (similar to trend analysis discussed earlier in the chapter). Hence, as illustrated in Figure 3.15, the trend line for the example is: $T_t = 140.542 + 1.772t$. (The p-value for the slope is small, so there is a significant trend.) The trend value for the first time period is $140.542 + 1.772(1) = 142.314$. Using this trend line, the trend for each time period is calculated in column E of Figure 3.17.

The data is de-trended by dividing the actual sales by the trend, in column F in Figure 3.17, i.e.:

$$\frac{Y_t}{T_t} = \frac{T_t * S_t * C_t * I_t}{T_t} = S_t * C_t * I_t$$

For example, the first time period's de-trended value is 144/142.314 = 1.012. The values in column F are estimates of the seasonal indices. The average of all of a particular quarter's values in column F is averaged to calculate overall seasonal indices, in cells F23:F26. For example, the estimate of the first quarter seasonal index is equal to:

$$\frac{1.012 + 0.71 + 0.965 + 1.039 + 0.973}{5} = 0.992$$

Subsequently, these estimated seasonal indices are copied for time periods in their corresponding cells in column G of Figure 3.16.

The data is seasonally adjusted (or deseasonalized) in column H, by calculating the ratio of the actual sales divided by its seasonal index:

$$\frac{Y_t}{S_t} = \frac{T_t * S_t * C_t * I_t}{S_t} = T_t * C_t * I_t$$

For example, the first time period is equal to cells D2/G2:

$$\frac{144}{0.992} = 145.186.$$

These deseasonalized values in column H in Figure 3.17 are similar to the deseasonalized values for the multiplicative decomposition method without the cyclical component used on the same data and found in column I of Figure 3.12. The difference in these values is that in this example, a significant cyclical component is assumed, whereas the other deseasonalized values in Figure 3.12 assume that

	A	B	C	D	E	F	G	H	I
28									
29	SUMMARY OUTPUT								
30									
31	*Regression Statistics*								
32	Multiple R	0.70163							
33	R Square	0.49228							
34	Adjusted R Square	0.46407							
35	Standard Error	10.9393							
36	Observations	20							
37									
38	ANOVA								
39			*df*	*SS*	*MS*	*F*	*Significance F*		
40	Regression		1	2088.515	2088.515	17.45248	0.000565662		
41	Residual		18	2154.035	119.6686				
42	Total		19	4242.55					
43									
44			*Coefficient*	*Standard Err*	*t Stat*	*P-value*	*Lower 95%*	*Upper 95%*	*Lower 95.0%* *Upper 95.0%*
45	Intercept		140.542	5.081656	27.65675	3.36E-16	129.8659333	151.2183	129.8659 151.2183
46	Sales		1.77218	0.424208	4.177617	0.000566	0.880950835	2.66341	0.880951 2.66341

Figure 3.15   Trend regression of the actual data.

	A	B	C	D	E	F	G	H	I	J	K	L
1	tp	Year	Quarter	Sales	T	SCI	S	TCI	CI	C	I	forecast
2	1	1	1	144	142.314	1.012	0.992	145.186	1.020			
3	2		2	151	144.086	1.048	1.037	145.545	1.010	1.010	1.001	150.909
4	3		3	134	145.859	0.919	0.920	145.604	0.998	0.994	1.004	133.443
5	4		4	151	147.631	1.023	1.050	143.784	0.974	0.984	0.990	152.493
6	5	2	1	145	149.403	0.971	0.992	146.194	0.979	0.959	1.020	142.106
7	6		2	145	151.175	0.959	1.037	139.762	0.925	0.968	0.955	151.861
8	7		3	141	152.947	0.922	0.920	153.210	1.002	0.983	1.019	138.312
9	8		4	166	154.720	1.073	1.050	158.067	1.022	0.999	1.023	162.279
10	9	3	1	151	156.492	0.965	0.992	152.243	0.973	0.998	0.975	154.867
11	10		2	164	158.264	1.036	1.037	158.076	0.999	0.999	1.000	164.026
12	11		3	151	160.036	0.944	0.920	164.076	1.025	1.020	1.005	150.217
13	12		4	176	161.808	1.088	1.050	167.589	1.036	1.036	0.999	176.090
14	13	4	1	170	163.580	1.039	0.992	171.400	1.048	1.044	1.003	169.426
15	14		2	180	165.353	1.089	1.037	173.498	1.049	1.037	1.012	177.916
16	15		3	156	167.125	0.933	0.920	169.509	1.014	1.039	0.976	159.845
17	16		4	187	168.897	1.107	1.050	178.064	1.054	1.016	1.037	180.282
18	17	5	1	166	170.669	0.973	0.992	167.367	0.981	1.017	0.964	172.222
19	18		2	182	172.441	1.055	1.037	175.425	1.017	0.986	1.032	176.428
20	19		3	154	174.214	0.884	0.920	167.336	0.961	0.964	0.996	154.571
21	20		4	169	175.986	0.960	1.050	160.924	0.914			
22												
23							1	0.992				
24							2	1.037				
25							3	0.920				
26							4	1.050				
27								4.000				

Figure 3.16   Multiplicative decomposition with cyclical component.

Thus far, the trend and seasonal components in columns E and G respectively, in Figure 3.17 have been isolated and estimated. Next, the cyclical and irregular components are measured and isolated by dividing the actual sales by the trend and seasonal components in column I:

$$\frac{Y_t}{T_t * S_t} = \frac{T_t * S_t * C_t * I_t}{T_t * S_t} = C_t * I_t$$

In particular, for the first time period, divide cell D2 by cells (E2 * G2):

$$\frac{144}{142.314 * 0.992} = 1.020.$$

It was arbitrarily decided that a three-quarter cycle exists. An odd number was chosen to avoid the centering issue. Nevertheless, the choice of the number of periods for the cycle is left to the decision-maker/analyst to decide. To determine the cyclical component for a three-quarter cycle, a three-quarter moving average from the cyclical and irregular component in Column I must be calculated. In particular, for the second quarter of the first year, the cycle is equal to:

$$\frac{1.02 + 1.01 + 0.998}{3} = 1.01$$

I.e., it is the average of cells I2:I4, which is the value of cell J3.

Similarly, the cyclical component is calculated for the remaining periods in column J in Figure 3.17.

Figure 3.17 shows a graph of these cyclical indices. A definitely cyclical pattern appears with 8 straight periods below 1 (periods 3–10) and 7 straight periods above 1 (periods 11–18). Formal randomness tests (discussed in Chapter 4) to verify the existence of a pattern could be conducted, but it is not necessary here because the cyclical pattern displayed is obvious.

Column K contains the remaining irregular component (column I divided by column J or $C_t I_t / C_t$). Looking at the values in column

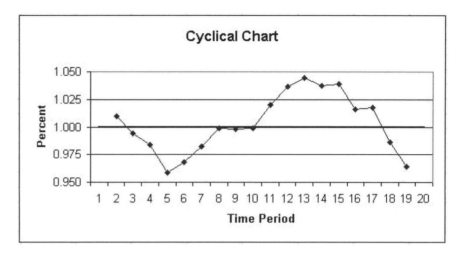

Figure 3.17 Cyclical chart of cyclical data in column J in Figure 3.16.

K, it can be seen that the numbers vary slightly but in general are close to 1.

The trend, seasonal, and cyclical components have been estimated and isolated in columns E, G, and J, respectively. Multiplying each of these components together generates a forecast for each time period. In particular, the forecast for the second quarter of year 1 is (=E3*G3*J3): 144.086 * 1.037 * 1.01 = 150.909.

Finally, a graph of the actual and forecast sales is shown in Figure 3.18. Except for the second quarter in the second year, the forecasts are extremely accurate.

In summary, regardless of which decomposition technique is utilized, additive or multiplicative (with or without the cycle component), one of the main objectives of a decomposition method is to estimate and isolate each of the time series components of trend, seasonal, cyclical, and irregular. This process in itself is very helpful to the decision-maker/analyst in understanding and providing insight to the underlying causes of the variations in the time series data.

3.4 Moving Averages (File: Datats.xls, Worksheet: MA)

The moving average smoothing method takes the average of the *k* most recent data values to predict the value of the series for the next period in the future. A moving average of order *k*, MA(k), is calculated as:

$$F_{t+1} = \frac{\sum\limits_{i=t-k+1}^{t} Y_i}{k} = \frac{Y_t + Y_{t-1} + Y_{t-2} + \cdots + Y_{t-k+1}}{k}$$

where:

F_{t+1} = is the forecast for period $t+1$

Y_t = is the actual value for period t

k = is the order of the moving average

After the *t*+1 data becomes available, the oldest value is removed from the equation and the most recent value is added to the equation to calculate the forecast for the next period.

    Taking the data that was used in Figure 3.2, which is also listed in Figure 3.19, arbitrary moving average of order three, denoted as MA(3) is chosen. The moving averages in column C are calculated using the AVERAGE function. The first moving average to be predicted is for the fourth time period, because the three previous period values are required for the MA(3) forecast. In particular, the formula in cell C5 is =AVERAGE(B2:B4). The remainder of the moving averages in column C are determined by simply copying and pasting the formula in cell C5 into cells C6:C22.

    Excel provides a moving average function as one of the Data Analysis tools. To produce a moving average of order 3, MA(3), as in Figure 3.19, take the following steps:

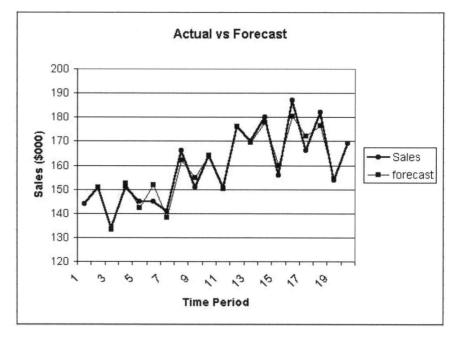

Figure 3.18   Graph of actual and forecast values.

1. Click on the **Data** tab from the Ribbon.

2. Click on the **Data Analysis** command.

3. Choose **Moving Average** from the list of analysis tools.

4. A dialog box, as shown in Figure 3.20, will appear. Using data as shown in Figure 3.19 for this exercise, fill in the appropriate boxes in the dialog box, as shown in Figure 3.20.

    Enter B1:B21 in the **Input Range** box

    Click on **Labels** in the **First Row**

    Enter 3 in the **Interval** box

    Enter D3 in the **Output Range** box

    Click **OK.**

As a result of using the Excel MA function, the data in column D in Figure 3.19 will appear. These values are the same as were calculated using the AVERAGE function. Here are a few warnings about using Excel and producing moving averages:

1. If the Moving Average function under the Data Analysis tools is used, no matter how many time periods are included in the moving average, the row in the **Output Range** box must always be entered one row below the first observation. In the example in Figure 3.20, this is row 3. Following this rule will line up the moving averages with the correct period.

2. Do not use the chart output option. The moving averages are one period early.

3. As discussed in Chapter 2, a trend line can be added to a graph. If one of the options is to add a moving average trend line and the number of periods can be chosen, do not use this option. As stated above, the moving averages are one period early.

The decision-maker/analyst must determine the order of the moving average, i.e., choose the number of periods to be used with the moving average method. The two extreme possible values of the order are 1 and n (where n is the total number of observations). A moving average of order 1, MA(1), simply uses the previous period's actual value to predict the value of the next period, i.e.: $F_{t+1} = Y_t$. This model implies that the best forecast for tomorrow is today's value, which is commonly called a naive forecasting approach. On the other hand, a moving average of order n, MA(n), simply uses the average of all historical values to predict the value of the next period.

The larger the number of periods used, the more smoothed out, or averaged out, are the forecasts. Conversely, a smaller order puts more emphasize on recent values. If the data suddenly shifts, a high order moving average would take longer to respond to the change

	A	B	C	D
1	tp	Sales	MA(3)	
2	1	144		
3	2	151		#N/A
4	3	134		#N/A
5	4	151	143.0	143.0
6	5	145	145.3	145.3
7	6	145	143.3	143.3
8	7	141	147.0	147.0
9	8	166	143.7	143.7
10	9	151	150.7	150.7
11	10	164	152.7	152.7
12	11	151	160.3	160.3
13	12	176	155.3	155.3
14	13	170	163.7	163.7
15	14	180	165.7	165.7
16	15	156	175.3	175.3
17	16	187	168.7	168.7
18	17	166	174.3	174.3
19	18	182	169.7	169.7
20	19	154	178.3	178.3
21	20	169	167.3	167.3
22			168.3	168.3

Figure 3.19 Sales time series data and moving average of 3 periods, MA.

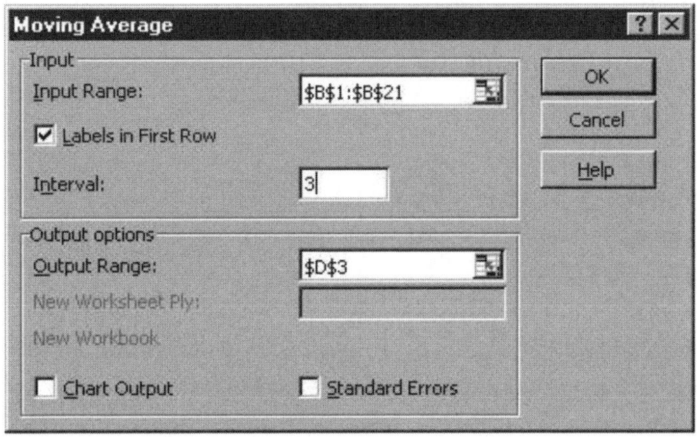

Figure 3.20 Moving average dialog box.

than a lower order moving average. Nevertheless, even a small order moving average will still lag behind the pattern by one or more periods. Decision-makers/analysts must use their understanding of the characteristics of the variable being predicted, and their judgment in choosing the order and the magnitude of various performance measurements. This subject will be discussed further in Chapter 4.

Lastly, the next period forecast for a moving average of order k can be calculated and is equal to:

$$F_{t+1} = \frac{\sum\limits_{i=t-k+1}^{t} Y_i}{k} = \frac{Y_t + Y_{t-1} + Y_{t-2} + \cdots + Y_{t-k+1}}{k}$$

The two-period ahead forecast for a moving average of order k is equal to:

$$F_{t+2} = \frac{\sum\limits_{i=t-k+2}^{t} Y_i}{k} = \frac{Y_{t+1} + Y_t + Y_{t-1} + Y_{t-2} + \cdots + Y_{t-k+2}}{k}$$

If the two-period ahead forecast is subtracted from the one-period ahead forecast, the result is:

$$F_{t+2} - F_{t+1} = \frac{\sum\limits_{i=t-k+2}^{t} Y_i}{k} - \frac{\sum\limits_{i=t-k+1}^{t} Y_i}{k}$$

$$= \frac{Y_{t+1} + Y_{t+1} + Y_{t-1} + Y_{t-2} + \cdots + Y_{t-k+2}}{k}$$

$$- \frac{Y_t + Y_{t-1} + Y_{t-2} + \cdots + Y_{t-k+1}}{k}$$

$$= \frac{Y_{t+1} - Y_{t+k+1}}{k}$$

The difference between Y_{t+1} and Y_{t-k+1} is assumed to be small, and if a high order of moving average is being used (that is a large k), this value will be even smaller. Therefore, in practice this difference is assumed to be equal to zero. Then, it can be seen that $F_{t+2} = F_{t+1}$. As a result, all future forecasts using the moving average method are equal to the one-period ahead forecast.

3.5 Exponential Smoothing (Worksheet: EA(.1))

The exponential smoothing method takes a weighted average of past values. The equation for the exponential smoothing model is:

$$F_{t+1} = \alpha Y_t + (1 - \alpha)F_t \tag{3.1}$$

where:

$F_{t+1}=$ forecast for period $t + 1$

$Y_t =$ actual value for period t

$\alpha =$ smoothing constant $(0 \leq \alpha \leq 1)$

This equation simply states that the forecast for the next period, $t+1$, is equal to a weighted factor of the period's actual value, plus a weighted factor of the same period's forecast value.

To demonstrate how the exponential smoothing model is the weighted average of past values, expand Equation 3.1 by substituting F_t in Equation 3.1 with:

$$F_t = \alpha Y_{t-1} + (1 - \alpha)F_{t-1} \tag{3.2}$$

The result is:

$$F_{t+1} = \alpha Y_t + (1 - \alpha)[\alpha \; Y_{t-1} + (1 - \alpha)F_{t-1}]$$

$$F_{t+1} = \alpha \ Y_t + (1 - \alpha)\alpha Y_{t-1} + (1 - \alpha)^2 F_{t-1} \qquad (3.3)$$

Next substitute F_{t-1} in 3.3, as with F_t, and then F_{t-2} and so on, and get:

$$F_{t+1} = \alpha Y_t + (1 - \alpha)\alpha Y_{t-1} + (1 - \alpha)^2 \alpha Y_{t-2} + (1 - \alpha)^3 \alpha Y_{t-3}$$

$$+ (1 - \alpha)^4 \alpha Y_{t-4} + (1 - \alpha)^5 \alpha Y_{t-5} + \ldots$$

$$+ (1 - \alpha)^{t-1} \alpha Y_1 + (1 - \alpha)^t F_1 \qquad (3.4)$$

Equation 3.4 clearly shows that the next period's forecast using the exponential smoothing method is a weighted average of all past actual observations. Further, the sum of all these weights is equal to 1, i.e.:

$$\alpha + (1 - \alpha)\alpha + (1 - \alpha)^2 \alpha + (1 - \alpha)^3 \alpha$$

$$+ (1 - \alpha)^4 \alpha + (1 - \alpha)^5 \alpha + \ldots$$

$$+ (1 - \alpha)^{t-1} \alpha + (1 - \alpha)^t = 1.0$$

The value of the smoothing factor, α, has a significant impact on how much or how little each past observation is weighted. Figure 3.1 lists and Figure 3.21 graphs the weights assigned to the current and the previous five observations for three different values of α: 0.1, 0.5 and 0.9. With $\alpha = 0.1$, the weighting of each period is approximately equal. Actually, there is a slight decrease in weights as data is taken from further back in time. In increasing α from 0.1 to 0.5 and from 0.5 to 0.9, more weight is given to recent observations with larger values of α. The weights assigned to past observations exponentially decrease as data is derived from further back in time (hence, the name exponential smoothing) and the rate of decreasing weights is greater, the larger the value of the smoothing factor, α.

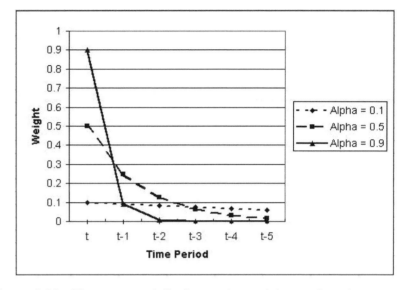

Figure 3.21 The exponentially decreasing weights assigned to past observations with the exponential smoothing method.

Table 3.1 Weights Assigned to Time Periods for α = 0.1, 0.5, and 0.9.

	Time Period					
α	t	$t{-}1$	$t{-}2$	$t{-}3$	$t{-}4$	$t{-}5$
0.1	0.1	0.09	0.081	0.0729	0.06561	0.059049
0.5	0.5	0.25	0.125	0.0625	0.03125	0.015625
0.9	0.9	0.09	0.009	0.0009	9E-06	9E-06

Another way of looking at the basic Equation 3.1 is to rearrange the right-hand side of the equation such that:

$$F_{t+1} = \alpha Y_t + (1 - \alpha)F_t$$

$$= \alpha Y_t + F_t - \alpha F_t$$

$$= F_t + \alpha(Y_t - F_t) \qquad (3.5)$$

The expression $Y_t - F_t$ is simply the error for the last period. Therefore, exponential smoothing using Equation 3.5 can be viewed as saying that the forecast for the next period is equal to the last period's forecast plus a weighted adjustment of the error in the previous forecast. The larger the value of α, the more weight is given to this error adjustment.

In Figure 3.22, forecasts are calculated for each period using exponential smoothing with $\alpha = 0.1$ in column C. Initially, to start the calculations, the first period forecast is assumed to be equal to the actual value of time period one, i.e., $F_1 = Y_1$. As a result, $F_2 = F_1 = Y_1$:

$$F_2 = \alpha Y_1 + (1 - \alpha)F_1$$

$$= \alpha Y_1 + F_1 - \alpha F_1$$

$$= \alpha Y_1 + Y_1 - \alpha Y_1$$

$$= Y_1$$

Thus, in the equivalent of Figure 3.22, cell C2, insert =B2. In cell C3, insert the formula =0.1*B2 + 0.9*C2. The formula in C3 is then copied and pasted into cells C4:C25.

As with the moving average, Excel provides an exponential smoothing function as one of the Data Analysis tools. To produce an exponential smoothing model with $\alpha = 0.1$, as in Figure 3.22, take the following steps:

1. Click on the **Data** tab from the Ribbon.

2. Click on the **Data Analysis** command.

3. Choose **Exponential Smoothing** from the list of analysis tools.

4. A dialog box, as shown in Figure 3.23, will appear. Using the data in Figure 3.22 (and Figure 3.2), fill in the appropriate boxes in the dialog box, as shown in Figure 3.23.

	C4		f_x	=0.1*B3+(1-0.1)*C3
	A	B	C	D	E
1	tp	Sales	EA(.1)		
2	1	144	144.0	#N/A	
3	2	151	144.0	144.0	
4	3	134	144.7	144.7	
5	4	151	143.6	143.6	
6	5	145	144.4	144.4	
7	6	145	144.4	144.4	
8	7	141	144.5	144.5	
9	8	166	144.1	144.1	
10	9	151	146.3	146.3	
11	10	164	146.8	146.8	
12	11	151	148.5	148.5	
13	12	176	148.8	148.8	
14	13	170	151.5	151.5	
15	14	180	153.3	153.3	
16	15	156	156.0	156.0	
17	16	187	156.0	156.0	
18	17	166	159.1	159.1	
19	18	182	159.8	159.8	
20	19	154	162.0	162.0	
21	20	169	161.2	161.2	
22			162.0	162.0	

Figure 3.22   Exponential smoothing with $\alpha = 0.1$.

Enter B1:B21 in the **Input Range** box

Click on **Labels** in the **First Row**

Enter 0.9 in the **Damping factor** box (the damping factor is equal to $1 - \alpha$)

Enter D2 in the **Output Range** box

Click on **Chart Output**

Click **OK** (to rescale the y axis move the mouse over the y axis and right click, then go to the Scale dialog box).

The data in column D in Figure 3.22 will appear. These values are the same as were calculated in column C except that in cell D2, Excel puts N/A. Further, if the mouse is moved on to one of the other cells in column D, those cells will be found to contain Equation 3.1 to calculate the forecasts. To forecast the next four time periods in columns C and D, copy the formulas in cells C25 and D25 and paste them into their respective next four rows.

As with the moving average, always put the row in the **Output Range** box one row below the first observation entry. On the other hand, unlike the problems Excel has with the moving average method with their Chart output, the data points are aligned correctly, as shown in the graph in Figure 3.21.

To start the exponential smoothing calculations, an assumption must be made as to what value to assign to F_1. It was earlier assumed that F_1 was simply equal to Y_1 and as was shown earlier, this assumption results in $F_2 = Y_1$. Excel's exponential smoothing function makes the same assumption about F_1, except that Excel's exponential smoothing function does not assign a value to F_1 but puts N/A in the cell as shown in Figure 3.22. Another initialization approach is to take the average of the first four, five, or six actual values. As Equation 3.4 demonstrates, F_1 does have an impact on all subsequent forecasts. The size of the impact depends on the smoothing factor chosen, because F_1 is weighted by $(1 - \alpha)^t$. As was illustrated by Equation 3.1, the effect of the initial forecast is more significant with a small α than a larger α.

Figure 3.21 further demonstrates that a large α would respond quicker to a change in the data than a small α (because significantly more weight is put on recent values). However, depending on the data, some or most of this changing in values may simply be due to random variations. Small αs are preferred, so as not to overreact to random variations, because small αs tend to smooth out the random fluctuations. Therefore, the choice of the α value plays a significant role in all the forecasts. Usually the decision-maker/analyst tries to find the best α by using an iterative process based on some speci-

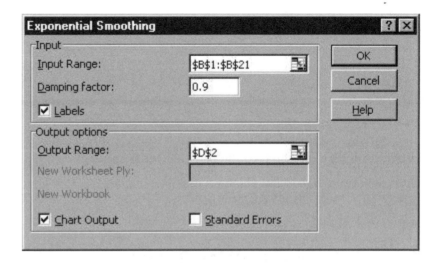

Figure 3.23   Exponential smoothing dialog box.

fied performance measurement criteria, which will be discussed in Chapter 4.

The first future forecast, i.e., for time period 21, for the example in Figure 3.22 is:

$$F_{21} = 0.1Y_{20} + 0.9F_{20}$$

$$= 0.1(169) + 0.9(161.2)$$

$$= 162$$

The two period ahead forecast, for time period 22, is equal to:

$$F_{22} = 0.1Y_{21} + 0.9F_{21}$$

It is established that F_{21} is equal to 162, however, it is not known what Y_{21} is, i.e., in real time we are in time period t so we do not know the actual value one period ahead. The best estimate of Y_{21} is the forecast F_{21}. Substituting in F_{21} for Y_{21} gives:

$$F_{22} = 0.1F_{21} + 0.9F_{21}$$

$$= F_{21}$$

$$= 162$$

In this outcome, and in general, this result implies that all forecasts $t+k$ periods ahead are equal to the forecast for period $t+1$:

$$F_{t+k} = F_{t+1} \quad k = 1, 2, \ldots, \infty$$

3.5.1   Optimal Smoothing Constant

An optimal smoothing constant, based on certain performance measurement criteria (several performance measurements are discussed in Chapter 4) can be obtained using Excel's Solver Add-in, but first, the Solver Add-in must be installed. Follow the same steps presented in Chapter 1 to install the Data Analysis ToolPak. When the Add-in dialog box, Figure 1.2, is reached, click on Solver Add-in.

Column B in worksheet Optimal EA, shown in Figure 3.24, contains the 20 time periods of sales from Figure 3.2. The Optimal EA worksheet can be used for any time series data set up to 1,000 time periods. In columns D–F, some intermediary calculations are made and in cells I2 to I5 are a few forecasting performance measures.

The following steps will find an optimal smoothing constant, α, using Solver:

1. Click on the **Data** tab from the Ribbon.

2. Click on the **Solver** command (all the way to the right).

3. A dialog box, as shown in Figure 3.25, will appear. In the Set Target Cell, click on the particular forecasting performance measurement to be minimized (cells I2 to I5) (in Figure 3.25, it

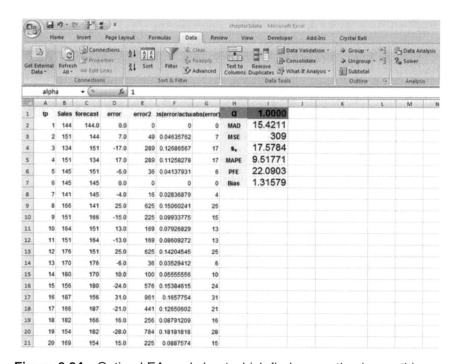

Figure 3.24   Optimal EA worksheet which finds an optimal smoothing constant.

Figure 3.25   Solver dialog box.

is set to minimize mean absolute deviation). In the By Changing Cells (DO NOT CHANGE), it is set to change alpha, cell I1.

4. Click **Solve**. The Solver results dialog box will appear. Click **OK**.

Alpha, α, cell I1, should change (as well as the intermediary calculations and performance measurements) to the optimal value that minimizes the forecasting performance measurement selected earlier.

3.5.2 Summary

The objective of the basic smoothing methods, that is moving average and exponential smoothing, is to even out or "smooth out" the variations caused by the irregular and possibly seasonal components in the data. If the data does have a significant trend or seasonal variation, techniques that estimate these components would most likely produce better forecasts. More complex smoothing methods that include these other components are presented in Chapter 5.

References

Moore, G.H. and J. Shiskin. "Early Warning Signals for the Economy." In *Statistics: A Guide to Business and Economics*, edited by J. M. Tanur et al. San Francisco: Holden-Day, 1976.

Chapter 4

Forecasting Performance Measurements, Tracking Signals, and Randomness Tests

4.1 Introduction

The forecasting model's forecasts are almost never exactly accurate, i.e., these forecast values may be slightly higher or slightly lower (depending on how good is the model) than the actual values. The difference between a forecast value and its corresponding actual value is the forecast error:

$$Forecast\ error = Y_t - F_t$$

The forecast error measures the accuracy of an individual forecast. This section will examine some of the more widely-used measures of overall performance: mean absolute deviation, mean square error, and mean absolute percentage error. In addition, a new measure developed by one of the authors to measure overall model performance will be introduced. After the forecasting model has been developed and implemented there will be a brief discussion of a tracking process to monitor the forecast to ensure it is under control. The second part of the chapter examines the meaning of randomness and discusses ways to test for it.

4.2 Forecast Performance Measures

One of the most popular measures of forecasting model overall performance is the mean absolute deviation, MAD. In summing them, the forecast errors tend to cancel each other out because some may be positive and some may be negative. To overcome this effect, MAD is the average of the absolute errors:

$$MAD = \frac{\sum |Y_t - F_t|}{n}$$

where

t = time period t

n = number of periods forecast

Y_t = actual value in time period t

F_t = forecast value in time period t

Figure 4.1 illustrates how MAD is calculated for the moving average model with a period of 3 and the data from Figure 3.19, shown in Figure 4.1. The forecast error for each time period is computed in column D, and the corresponding absolute values are calculated in column G. In cell J3, the MAD is calculated as an average of the absolute errors in column G.

The mean square error, MSE, historically, has been the primary measure used to compare the performance of forecasting methods, mostly due to its computational ease and its theoretical relevance to statistics. The MSE is calculated as the average of the square of forecast errors:

$$MSE = \frac{\sum (Y_t - F_t)^2}{n}$$

	J3		f_x	=AVERAGE(G6:G22)					
	A	B	C	D	E	F	G	H	I	J
1			Moving Average(3)							
2		tp	Sales	forecast	error	error2	abs(error/actual)	abs(error)		MA	3.0000
3		1	144							MAD	10.882
4		2	151							MSE	177.43
5		3	134							Se	13.32
6		4	151	143.0	8.0	64	0.052980132	8		MAPE	6.583
7		5	145	145.3	-0.3	0.111111	0.002298851	0.333333333		PFE	16.739
8		6	145	143.3	1.7	2.777778	0.011494253	1.666666667		Bias	2.9
9		7	141	147.0	-6.0	36	0.042553191	6			
10		8	166	143.7	22.3	498.7778	0.134538153	22.33333333			
11		9	151	150.7	0.3	0.111111	0.002207506	0.333333333			
12		10	164	152.7	11.3	128.4444	0.069105691	11.33333333			
13		11	151	160.3	-9.3	87.11111	0.061810155	9.333333333			
14		12	176	155.3	20.7	427.1111	0.117424242	20.66666667			
15		13	170	163.7	6.3	40.11111	0.037254902	6.333333333			
16		14	180	165.7	14.3	205.4444	0.07962963	14.33333333			
17		15	156	175.3	-19.3	373.7778	0.123931624	19.33333333			
18		16	187	168.7	18.3	336.1111	0.098039216	18.33333333			
19		17	166	174.3	-8.3	69.44444	0.050200803	8.333333333			
20		18	182	169.7	12.3	152.1111	0.067765568	12.33333333			
21		19	154	178.3	-24.3	592.1111	0.158008658	24.33333333			
22		20	169	167.3	1.7	2.777778	0.009861933	1.666666667			

Figure 4.1 Forecasting performance measures for the MA(3) model in Figure 3.19.

The process to compute MSE for the Chapter 3 data in Figure 3.22 using an exponential smoothing model with $\alpha = 0.1$ is demonstrated in Figure 4.2. In column E, the squares of the forecasting errors are calculated. MSE is calculated in cell J4 as the average of the squared forecast errors.

The smaller the MAD and MSE, the more accurate the forecasting results. Because MSE squares the forecast errors, large forecast errors are penalized. As a result, the forecasting method that minimizes MSE will not necessarily be the same forecasting method that minimizes MAD. Analysts who use the approach to minimize MSE do so because they prefer several small forecasting errors to one possibly large error.

The forecast errors typically follow a normal distribution with a mean of zero and a certain standard deviation (and they can be tested—see later in this chapter) . The standard deviation of error is usually simply called the standard error, s_e. MAD and MSE both estimate s_e:

$$1 \text{ MAD} \cong 0.8\sigma \cong 0.8\text{s}_\text{e}$$

$$\sqrt{\text{MSE}} = \text{s}_\text{e} \cong \sigma$$

A shortcoming of the MAD and MSE forecasting measures is that they do not take into consideration the magnitude of the actual values. To understand what this means, let's say that for a certain data set, the MAD and MSE both happen to result in an estimate of the standard error to be 10, i.e., $s_e = 10$. So, if the errors follow a normal distribution with a mean of zero, moving to ± 20 = 2*10 from the mean of zero would still cover approximately 95 percent of the values. Even after moving ± 20 from an estimated value of Y_{t+1}, $\hat{Y}_{t+1}$, an analyst would be still be highly confident (95 percent) that the forecast would be within ± 20 of $\hat{Y}_{t+1}$. Furthermore, if $\hat{Y}_{t+1} \cong 100$, the analyst could still be 95 percent confident that the forecast would be between 80 and 120. On the other hand, if the analyst said $\hat{Y}_{t+1} \cong 1000$, he (she) would claim with 95 percent surety that the forecast would be between 980 and 1,020. Even though the s_e is the same, the second example is a much more accurate model due to the magnitude of the actual values, Y_t.

A widely-used evaluation of forecasting methods, which does attempt to consider the effect of the magnitude of the actual values, is the mean absolute percentage error, or MAPE.

$$\text{MAPE} = \frac{\sum \frac{|Y_t - F_t|}{Y_t}}{n}$$

J4 =(AVERAGE(E4:E22))

	A	B	C	D	E	F	G	H	I	J
1			Exponential smoothing α = .1							
2	tp	Sales	forecast	error	error2	abs(error/actual)	abs(error)		α	0.1000
3	1	144	144.0	0.0	0	0	0		MAD	11.806
4	2	151	144	7.0	49	0.046357616	7		MSE	234.46
5	3	134	144.7	-10.7	114.49	0.079850746	10.7		Se	15.312
6	4	151	143.63	7.4	54.3169	0.048807947	7.37		MAPE	7.0072
7	5	145	144.367	0.6	0.400689	0.004365517	0.633		PFE	19.243
8	6	145	144.43	0.6	0.3245581	0.003928966	0.5697		Bias	9.5
9	7	141	144.487	-3.5	12.161052	0.024732411	3.48727			
10	8	166	144.139	21.9	477.9233	0.131695524	21.861457			
11	9	151	146.325	4.7	21.858536	0.030962326	4.6753113			
12	10	164	146.792	17.2	296.1077	0.104925489	17.20778017			
13	11	151	148.513	2.5	6.1851797	0.016470213	2.487002153			
14	12	176	148.762	27.2	741.92509	0.154763079	27.23830194			
15	13	170	151.486	18.5	342.78566	0.108908657	18.51447174			
16	14	180	153.337	26.7	710.91688	0.148127914	26.66302457			
17	15	156	156.003	0.0	1.074E-05	2.10121E-05	0.003277887			
18	16	187	156.003	31.0	960.8171	0.165759625	30.9970499			
19	17	166	159.103	6.9	47.573367	0.041550271	6.897344911			
20	18	182	159.792	22.2	493.17796	0.122019837	22.20761042			
21	19	154	162.013	-8.0	64.210583	0.052033446	8.013150622			
22	20	169	161.212	7.8	60.655505	0.046083813	7.78816444			

Figure 4.2 Forecasting performance measures for the exponential smoothing model (α = 0.1) in Figure 3.22.

Figure 4.3 demonstrates how MAPE is calculated for the multiplicative decomposition model using the data in Figure 3.12. The absolute value of the error is divided by each corresponding actual value in column F. In cell J6, MAPE is calculated as an average of the values computed in column F.

As with the other performance measures, the lower the MAPE the more accurate the forecast. Listed in Table 4.1 is a scale to judge the accuracy of a model based on the MAPE measure, developed by Lewis (1982).

The smaller the MAD, MSE, and MAPE values, the more accurate the forecasting model. A limitation of the MAD and MSE measures is that there is no context to indicate whether the model is good or not. Using the MAPE formula, and applying Lewis's scale, provides some framework to judge the model. However, depending on the data set, as to whether there is a significant trend or seasonal component, the MAPE may under- or overestimate the accuracy of the model. Additionally, all these overall forecasting performance measures have no real-world meaning.

This situation led one of the authors to develop a measure called the percentage forecast error, or PFE (Klimberg and Ratick):

$$\text{PFE} = \frac{2 * s_e}{\text{est } \hat{Y}_{t+1}}$$

The PFE is somewhat similar to the coefficient of variation that is used to measure the relative dispersion around the mean. In the numerator the standard error is multiplied by 2 so that it goes ± 2 standard deviates. The denominator is equal to the best estimate of Y_{t+1} so as to take into effect the magnitude of the forecast values. Depending on the data set, estimates of: (1) F_{t+1}; (2) $\overline{Y}$ or (3) Y_t have been used. As a result, the PFE allows analysts to say they are highly certain (actually 95 percent) that the forecast for the next time period will be within the PFE of the actual value, e.g., they are highly certain that the forecast will be within 20 percent of the actual value. Application of PFE has found highly accurate models to have a PFE of less than 20 percent, and good forecasting models having a PFE between 21 and 60 percent.

Each of the performance measures examined thus far, MAD, MSE, MAPE, and PFE, has assessed the size of the error. One measure, the bias, evaluates the direction of the error, that is, whether the forecast tends to over- or under-estimate the actual values. The bias is the average of the forecast errors:

$$\text{Bias} = \frac{\sum(Y_t - F_t)}{n}$$

J6 fx =100*AVERAGE(F3:F22)

	A	B	C	D	E	F	G	H	I	J
1			Multiplicative Decomposition							
2	tp	Sales	forecast	error	error2	abs(error/actual)	abs(error)			
3	1	144	140.4	3.6	12.695885	0.024743948	3.5631285		MAD	4.848
4	2	151	149.416	1.6	2.5083389	0.010488567	1.583773636		MSE	42.581
5	3	134	135.126	-1.1	1.2671078	0.008400439	1.125658814		Se	6.5254
6	4	151	157.845	-6.8	46.849805	0.045329084	6.844691723		MAPE	2.9833
7	5	145	147.045	-2.0	4.1838167	0.014106469	2.04543803		PFE	8.2004
8	6	145	156.366	-11.4	129.17645	0.078383324	11.36558192		Bias	0.0
9	7	141	141.338	-0.3	0.1143278	0.002398042	0.338123905			
10	8	166	165.019	1.0	0.9619452	0.005908362	0.980788044			
11	9	151	153.654	-2.7	7.0437402	0.017576189	2.65400456			
12	10	164	163.315	0.7	0.4693107	0.004177211	0.685062528			
13	11	151	147.551	3.4	11.898436	0.022843781	3.449411003			
14	12	176	172.194	3.8	14.487675	0.021626522	3.806267812			
15	13	170	160.263	9.7	94.817522	0.057278994	9.73742891			
16	14	180	170.264	9.7	94.78399	0.054087261	9.735706974			
17	15	156	153.763	2.2	5.003927	0.014339397	2.236945912			
18	16	187	179.368	7.6	58.243571	0.040811484	7.63174758			
19	17	166	166.871	-0.9	0.7588808	0.005247817	0.87113762			
20	18	182	177.214	4.8	22.90916	0.026298634	4.78635142			
21	19	154	159.976	-6.0	35.706829	0.038802073	5.975519179			
22	20	169	186.543	-17.5	307.74887	0.103803388	17.54277265			

Figure 4.3 Forecasting performance measures for the Multiplicative Decomposition model in Figure 3.12.

Table 4.1 A Scale of Judgment of Forecast Accuracy (Lewis)

MAPE	Judgment of Forecast Accuracy
Less than 10%	Highly accurate
11% to 20%	Good forecast
21% to 50%	Reasonable forecast
51% or more	Inaccurate forecast

The expected value of the bias is zero, and the closer to zero, the better the model. If the bias is positive, the actual values tend to be on average greater than the forecast value, so the model tends to underestimate the actual values. Conversely, if the bias is negative, the model tends to overestimate the actual values. The degree to which the model over- or under-estimates depends on the extent of the bias.

Table 4.2 summarizes the forecasting performance measures for the three forecasting techniques shown in Figures 4.1 to 4.3, with data from Chapter 3. The best is clearly the multiplicative decomposition model, in which all the performance measures are at their lowest.

Table 4.2   A Comparison of the Performance Measures for the Three Forecasting Techniques

MA	3	a	0.1	Multidecomposition	
MAD	10.88235	MAD	11.806	MAD	4.847977
MSE	177.4314	MSE	234.4647	MSE	42.58148
Se	13.32034	Se	15.31224	Se	6.5225449
MAPE	6.582968	MAPE	7.007181	MAPE	7.007181
PFE	16.73935	PFE	19.24253	PFE	8.200375
Bias	2.921569	Bias	9.468764	Bias	–0.02832

4.3 Tracking Signals

Once a forecasting model has been developed and implemented the forecasting errors should be monitored to ensure the forecast is under control. Several factors could cause the model to become inaccurate—changes in the trend or seasonal components, economical changes, or simply that it has been a long time since the model was updated. Several methods exist for tracking the forecasts. A straightforward approach is the control chart approach of tracking the errors. The errors are assumed to have a mean of 0 and a standard deviation α. The standard deviation, α, is estimated as:

$$\sigma \cong s_e \cong \sqrt{MSE} \cong 1.25 MAD$$

The forecast accuracy can be monitored by using the control limits of $\pm 3\alpha$'s. Any statistically significant deviations, as well as any significant non-random deviations, can be detected using some of the techniques discussed in the next section.

4.4 Randomness

Randomness implies that the data is unpredictable and has no pattern. If there is some pattern to the data, then a model can be developed to predict this pattern. Thus, if the forecast errors or irregular components are not random, a better model can be developed. To further understand randomness, it is necessary to first define stationarity. A series of data is stationary if it satisfies the following criteria:

C.1: has no trend and

C.2: has a constant dispersion (equal variance is known as homoscedasticity).

To test whether a data set has a significant trend or not, a linear trend analysis and its corresponding hypothesis test must be performed. If the null hypothesis, H_0, is not rejected, i.e., the result is a large p-value, then there is no significant statistical trend in the data and C.1 is satisfied. If the magnitude of the variance, the dispersion of the data, does not vary significantly in size over time, the data is considered to have constant dispersion and is said to be homoscedasticitic. On the other hand, if the spread of the data increases or decreases significantly in size over time, the data is considered not to have a constant dispersion and is said to be heteroscedasticitic. Although there are formal statistical tests, a simple visual inspection of the time series plot is usually sufficient to tell if there are significant changes in the dispersion of the data. If there are no significant fluctuations in the size of the variation in the data, then the data is homoscedasticitic and C.2 is satisfied. On the other hand, if significant variations in the magnitude of the data are discovered, i.e., the data appears to be heteroscedasticitic, whatever is causing the changes in variation should be removed (a model should be developed or a transformation of the data performed in such a way that the variation is removed). Formal statistical tests for stationarity are called unit root tests (the most prevalent is the Dickey-Fuller test).

A series of data is random if it is stationary, i.e., C.1 and C.2 are true, and, in addition, the following criteria are satisfied:

C.3: Data points do not stay either above or below the trend line for a large number of consecutive periods and

C.4: Data points do not seem to oscillate rapidly above or below the trend line.

An informal test to check whether the data satisfies C.3 and C.4, again, is just a visual inspection of the time series plot. A formal statistical test is the Runs test, which is a hypothesis test that tests both whether or not the data is meandering, C.3, and if the data is alternating back and forth too many times, C.4. In particular, the Runs test checks the number of values above or below a fixed value. This fixed value is usually the mean or median (when testing irregular components/residuals this value is equal to zero). If the

data is random, there should be approximately the same number of values above and below the fixed value. A run is the sequential occurrence of observations either above or below this fixed value. Further, if the data is random, the expected length of a run will be close to 2. Therefore, the expected number of total runs will be approximately equal to about one-half the number of observations.

For example, the mean of the 10 observations below is 4.4:

$$2\ 5\ 5\ 6\ 3\ 2\ 9\ 8\ 3\ 1$$

and there are 5 runs: (2) (5 5 6) (3 2) (9 8) (3 1).

Three of these runs are below the mean, (2), (3 2) and (3 1), and two runs are above the mean, (5 5 6) and (9 8).

There are, and always will be, two categories of runs, one above and one below the fixed value. To amplify, n_1 is arbitrarily assigned to the above category and n_2 to the below category, where n_1 and n_2 are the number of values in each category. So for the above example $n_1 = 5$ and $n_2 = 5$.

If the data is random it would be expected that:

- about the same number of values would appear above the mean as appear below the mean, i.e., $n_1 \cong n_2$, and

- there will not be too many nor too few runs.

The null and alternative hypotheses for the Runs test are:

H_0: The data is random.

H_1: The data is not random.

If n_1 and n_2 are greater than or equal to 10, the distribution of the number of runs is approximately normal and the following statistic can be used:

$$Z = \frac{R - \mu_R}{\sigma_R}$$

where:

n_1 = number of values above fixed value

n_2 = number of values below fixed value

R = total number of runs

$$\mu_R = \frac{2n_1 n_2}{n_1 + n_2} + 1$$

$$\sigma_R = \sqrt{\frac{2n_1 n_2 (2n_1 n_2 - n_1 - n_2)}{(n_1 + n_2)^2 (n_1 + n_2 - 1)}}$$

If the p-value is small, i.e., less than α, H_0 is rejected, and there is enough evidence to say the data is not random. Otherwise, H_0 is not rejected and the data is assumed to be random. (If n_1 or n_2 is less than 10, then the distribution of runs cannot be assumed to be normal and the Runs test therefore cannot be performed. In such a situation it is necessary to graph the irregular/residuals data and visually inspect the data for too many or too few runs, C.3 and C.4.)

For example, in Figure 4.4 the monthly short-term interest rate charged by a bank and collected for two years is listed in column B, B2:B25 (in Worksheet: Runs). The time series plot in Figure 4.4 obviously shows the data is not random. If the Runs test is performed anyway:

The sample mean is 8.73 (the value in cell H1). There are two runs:

(9.76 10.22 10.57 10 9.56 9.01 9.05 9.18 9.08 9.17 9.20 9.07 9.04 9.03)

(8.59 8.06 8.12 8.21 7.84 7.57 7.19 7.18 7.35 7.49)

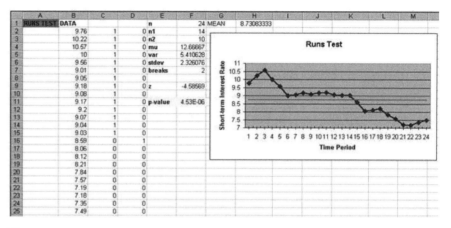

Figure 4.4 Runs test on short-term interest rate data.

The number of values above the sample mean is 14 and the number of values below the sample mean is 10. Thus, $n_1 = 14$ and $n_2 = 10$ and:

$$n_1 = 14 \quad n_2 = 10 \quad R = 2$$

$$\mu_R = \frac{2 * 14 * 10}{14 + 10} + 1 = 12.667$$

$$\sigma_R = \sqrt{\frac{2 * 14 * 10(2 * 14 * 10 - 14 - 10)}{(14 + 10)^2 * (14 + 10 - 1)}} = 2.326$$

$$Z = \frac{R - \mu_R}{\sigma_R} = \frac{2 - 12.667}{2.326} = -4.59 \qquad \text{(cell F9 in Figure 4-4)}$$

$$p - \text{value} = 4.53E - 06 \qquad \text{(cell F11 in Figure 4-4)}$$

The p-value is very small, therefore as conjectured, H_0 is rejected and the conclusion is that the data is not random.

In addition to randomness, if the data is approximately normal, two important results appear:

1. Control charts can be used to evaluate the data.

2. No other significant variation can be uncovered.

There are formal statistical tests for normality, but simply visualizing the distribution of observations would usually be sufficient. If the data roughly conforms to a bell-shaped curve with most of the observations within three standard deviations of the mean, then it can be assumed that the data is normal. If the data is normal, the empirical rule states that a little more than two-thirds of the observations (68 percent) will be within one standard deviation of the mean; about 95 percent will be within two standard deviations; and almost 100 percent will be within three standard deviations. More precisely, only 2.8 out 1,000 observations would be expected to be more than three standard deviations away from the mean. Generally, significant departures from normality are expected, which can most likely be detected visually. Figure 4.5 shows the distribution of observations of the data in column B in Figure 4.4. Below the graph in Figure 4.5, the average and the plus/minus two and three standard deviate limits are listed. Even though the data set is rather small, all the observations are within two standard deviations. So it would be reasonable to assume that the distribution is normal.

If the data is random and normal, the first important result allows the use of a control chart called an Individuals Chart (also called an I-chart) to examine the variation in the data. To construct an I-chart the center line (CL) and the upper and lower control limits (UCL and LCL, respectively) must be calculated. These values are calculated using the following formulas:

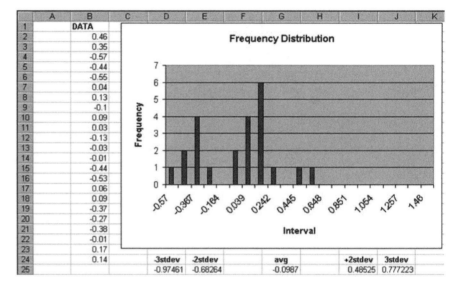

Figure 4.5   The graph of the distribution of data in column B to visually determine normality.

$$CL = \bar{x}$$

$$UCL = \bar{x} + 3\,\frac{\bar{R}}{d_2}$$

$$LCL = \bar{x} - 3\,\frac{\bar{R}}{d_2}$$

where:

$d_2 = 1.128$ for I-charts (from ASTM Table for sample size of 2)
$\bar{R}$ = average of the moving ranges and is used as an unbiased estimate of σ.

Figure 4.6 shows an example of an I-chart of the data in column B in Figure 4.4. CL, the value in cell H2, is calculated as the average of the observations (in cells B2:B24) and is equal to –0.0987. The moving ranges are calculated in column F. In particular, the value in cell F3, 0.11, is simply the absolute value of the difference of the values in B3 and B2, i.e., it is equal to |B3−B2|. Subsequent moving ranges in column F are calculated in similar fashion. As a result, $\overline{R}$, the average of the moving ranges in column F, is the value in cell I2, $\overline{R} = 0.231818$. The values of UCL and LCL are calculated as follows:

$$UCL = \overline{x} + 3\frac{\overline{R}}{d_2} = -0.0987 + 3\frac{0.231818}{1.128}$$

$$= 0.517842 \text{ (the value in cell H7)}$$

$$LCL = \overline{x} - 3\frac{\overline{R}}{d_2} = -0.0987 - 3\frac{0.231818}{1.128}$$

$$= -0.71523 \text{ (the value in cell H6)}$$

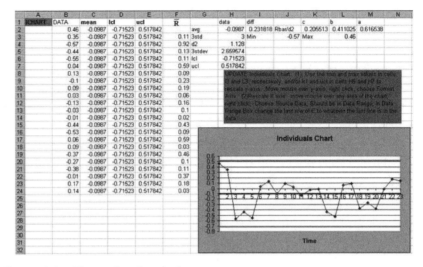

Figure 4.6 Example of an I-chart.

first subdivide the control chart into zones A, B, and C, as shown in Figure 4.7. Nelson's eight tests are:

Test 1: One point outside Zone A, i.e., a point outside the control limits.

Test 2: Nine points in a row in Zone C or beyond, and on one side of the CL (center line).

Test 3: Six points in a row, all increasing or all decreasing.

Test 4: Fourteen points in a row alternating up and down.

Test 5: Two out of three points in a row in Zone A or beyond, all on one side of the CL.

Test 6: Four out of five points in a row in Zone B or beyond, all on one side of the CL.

Test 7: Fifteen points in a row within 1F of the CL, on either side.

Test 8: Eight points in a row beyond 1F of the CL, on either side.

> **Note**
>
> **If the data is entered into the Runs worksheet of the file called Randomness, the data appears automatically in the worksheet called I-chart. Once the data is entered into the RUNS worksheet, the I-chart is generated (as well as what will now be discussed, which is Nelson's eight tests and normality (in the worksheet called normal)).**

Nelson[1] developed eight tests to identify special causes of possible non-random behavior in an I-chart. Nelson's approach is to

1. Nelson, L. S., (1984). "The Shewhart Control Chart–Test for Special Causes," *Journal of Quality Technology*, 16, pp.237–239.

A summary of the eight test results for the data in Figure 4.6 is shown in Figure 4.8. The data only violated Test 5 twice. To find which data points caused these particular violations, look at columns S through AH in Figure 4.9. As shown in Figure 4.9, points 3 and 5 caused the two Test 5 violations. Further, examining the I-chart in Figure 4.6, the causes of these two violations can be observed.

For a set of data to be considered random, does there need to be no violations for all eight of Nelson's tests? No, not necessarily. These tests simply provide insight into some of the patterns of the data. The degree of randomness depends on which test is violated and the number of violations, and furthermore, the decision is left to the decision-maker/analyst to determine the magnitude of each violation. In particular, with this example, the two Test 5 violations may not be significant enough to cause concern. Also, the degree of concern about the violation will not only depend on the type of violation, but also will depend on when it occurred, i.e., did it occur during one of the early time periods or toward the more recent values. In most situations, the decision-maker/analyst would be more concerned with recent violations because of their possible impact on forecasts.

Finally, it should be realized that randomness does not imply normality. Data is considered to be random if, by examining its time series plot, no pattern is observed (using the Runs test and I-chart). Testing for normality is carried out by either performing a formal statistical test or simply by looking at the distribution of observations, the histogram, and finding that the data appear to be normal. Hence, data can be:

- random and normal

- random and non-normal

- non-random and normal

- non-random and non-normal

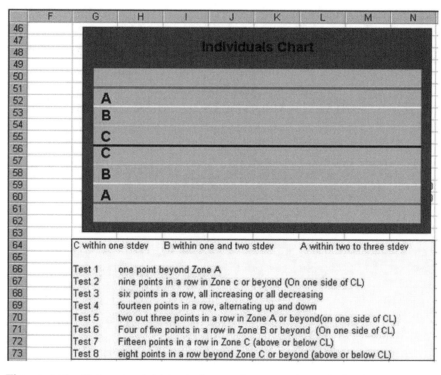

Figure 4.7   Nelson's eight tests for randomness in an I-chart.

	TEST RESULTS	
	Test 1	0
	Test 2	0
	Test 3	0
	Test 4	0
	Test 5	2
	Test 6	0
	Test 7	0
	Test 8	0

Figure 4.8   Nelson's eight tests results.

This observation leads to the second important result. If the data (error, irregular, or original data) can be considered to be random and approximately normal, then any other statistically significant variation in the data cannot be extracted. Thus, if the irregular component/residuals are being examined, all the significant time series components have been removed from the original data and no other statistically significant variation in the data can be extracted from the data—we cannot do any better with what we've got! (If the original data are being examined, and are found to be random and normal, then it can be concluded that there are no significant time series components in the data.) The only way to improve the model is to bring in one or more variables to help predict the variable—this is called causal modeling. On the other hand, if the data is random and not normal, the sources of variation are not acting independently and some time series forecasting technique may be used to remove the abnormality.

In many instances, after extracting from the data the trend, cyclical, and seasonal components by applying a forecasting time series method, the remaining irregular component is random. Data that is random shows no pattern and must satisfy all four criteria (C.1–C.4). If the data violates C.1, a significant trend exists and should be removed. If the data displays a non-constant variance, i.e., violates C.2, this suggests possibly that transforming the data using logarithms (usually the natural logarithm is used in business) or using causal forecasting technique (such as regression) would help. If the data is stationary, i.e., C.1 and C.2 are satisfied, but nei-

	S	T	U	V	W	Z	AB	AD	AG	AH
1	point	violation	test 1	test2	test3	Test 4	test 5	test 6	test 7	test 8
2	1	0	0							
3	2	0	0							
4	3	1	0				1			
5	4	0	0				0			
6	5	1	0				1	0		
7	6	0	0		0		0	0		
8	7	0	0		0		0	0		
9	8	0	0		0		0	0		0
10	9	0	0	0	0		0	0		0
11	10	0	0	0	0		0	0		0
12	11	0	0	0	0		0	0		0
13	12	0	0	0	0		0	0		0
14	13	0	0	0	0		0	0		0
15	14	0	0	0	0	0	0	0		0
16	15	0	0	0	0	0	0	0	0	0
17	16	0	0	0	0	0	0	0	0	0
18	17	0	0	0	0	0	0	0	0	0
19	18	0	0	0	0	0	0	0	0	0
20	19	0	0	0	0	0	0	0	0	0
21	20	0	0	0	0	0	0	0	0	0
22	21	0	0	0	0	0	0	0	0	0
23	22	0	0	0	0		0	0	0	0
24	23	0	0	0	0		0	0	0	0

Figure 4.9   Detailed results of Nelson's eight tests.

ther C.3 and/or C.4 are satisfied, then one of the smoothing techniques (moving average or exponential), differencing, or Box-Jenkins technique, would be useful.

References

Cryer, J.D. and R.B. Miller. *Statistics for Business: Data Analysis and Modeling.* 2nd ed. Wadsworth, Belmont, CA: 1994.

Hanke, J.E., D.W. Wichern, and A.G. Reitsch. *Business Forecasting.* 7th ed. Prentice-Hall, Upper Saddle River, NJ: 2001.

Klimberg, R.K. and S. Ratick. "A New Measure of Relative Forecast Error." *INFORMS Fall 2000 Meeting*, San Antonio, November 2000.

Lewis, C.D. "Industrial and business forecasting methods: A Radical guide to exponential smoothing and curve fitting." Butterworth Scientific, London; Boston: 1982.

Makridakis, S., S.C. Wheelwright, and R.J. Hyndman. *Forecasting Methods and Applications.* 3rd ed. John Wiley & Sons, New York: 1998.

Middleton, M.R. *Data Analysis Using Mircosoft Excel.* 1st ed. Duxbury Press, 1997.

Moore, G.H. and J. Shiskin. "Early Warning Signals for the Economy." In *Statistics: A Guide to Business and Economics*, edited by J. M. Tanur et al. Holden-Day, San Francisco: 1976.

Nelson, L.S. "The Shewhart Control Chart—Test for Special Causes." *Journal of Quality Technology* 16 (1984): 237–239.

Roberts, H.V. *Data Analysis for Managers with MINITAB.* 2nd ed. Scientific Press, Redwood City, CA: 1991.

Chapter 5

Advanced Time Series Forecasting Techniques

5.1 Introduction

This chapter will first examine other advanced time series techniques that expand on the basic moving average and exponential methods discussed in Chapter 3. These advanced techniques consider either a trend and/or a seasonal component. Time series data in general is correlated with itself, i.e., the actual value in time period t is/could be related to the actual value in time period t–1 . . . and is/could be related to the actual value in time period t–k. This lagged correlation is called autocorrelation. Section 5.3, first examines autocorrelation and discusses its relationship to a group of time series models called auto-regressive integrated moving average (ARIMA) models. The chapter ends with a section exploring index numbers and how they are calculated. A list of time series methods arranged by their trend and seasonal time—seasonal components is shown in Table 5.1. Chapter 3 discussed the widely used time series methods of moving average and exponential smoothing. As Table 5.2 demonstrates, these methods do not have a trend or seasonal component. The time series should be stationary.

Table 5.1   Classification of Time Series Models and their Notation

		No Seasonal S_O	Seasonal Additive S_A	Seasonal Multiplicative S_M
		Seasonal Component		
Trend Component	No Trend T_0	$T_O S_O$ Moving Average	$T_O S_O$ Exponential Smoothing ⟶ $T_O S_A$	$T_0 S_M$
	Trend—Additive T_A	$T_A S_O$ Double Moving Average	$T_A S_O$ Double Exponential Smoothing ⟶ $T_A S_A$	$T_A S_M$

5.2   Advanced Time Series Techniques

5.2.1   Double Moving Average

The concept underlying moving averages is that the k most recent time periods is a good predictor of the current and next period values. Taking these averages removes some of the non-randomness in the data. The moving average technique is a good forecasting approach to use if the data is stationary. As shown in Chapter 3, the formula for a moving average forecast of order k, MA(k), is:

$$F_{t+1} = \frac{\sum\limits_{i=t-k+1}^{t} Y_i}{k} = \frac{Y_t + Y_{t-1} + Y_{t-2} + \bullet \bullet \bullet + Y_{t-k+1}}{k} \quad (5.1)$$

where:

  F_{t+1} = is the forecast for period t+1

  Y_t = is the actual value for period t.

This process is called moving averages because each average is calculated by dropping the oldest observation, t–k+1, and including the next observation, t+1.

The actual moving average, of order k, for time period t, L_t', is defined as the average of the k most recent observations, i.e.:

$$L_t' = \frac{\sum\limits_{i=t-k+1}^{t} Y_i}{k} = \frac{Y_t + Y_{t-1} + Y_{t-2} + \bullet \bullet \bullet + Y_{t-k+1}}{k} \quad (5.2)$$

As can be seen, $F_{t+1} = L_t'$, which implies that the moving average forecast (one period ahead) is equal to the moving average for time period t. As a result, the moving average forecast lags the series by one period, thus being one period behind in capturing any trend component.

The example in Figure 5.1 includes 12 observations with a slope of 6 (each period increases by exactly 6). The moving average forecasts, F_{t+1}, and actual moving average, L_t' of order 5, are computed in column (3) and in column (5) respectively. With the constant trend, the forecast is consistently off by 18 for each time period, column (4). Part of this error is the result of the moving average, L'_t, lagging behind one period, (column (6)—lag1). This lag is the trend of one period. The remaining error, (column (7)—lag2) is due to the fact that F_{t+1} cannot be calculated until the end of period t and is based upon L'_t. In general, L'_t is actually centered at time period [t − (k−1)/2] and not time period t (k is equal to the order of the moving average). As a result, L'_t lags by t − [t − (k−1)/2] = (k−1)/2 periods. So, in general,

$$lag2 = L'_t - L'_{t - \left(\frac{(k-1)}{2}\right)}$$

In the order five moving average example, L'_t for period 5 is really centered at [t − (k−1)/2] = 5 − (5−1)/2 = 5 − 2 = 3 – the third period. Thus, the five-period moving average: $lag2 = L'_t - L'_{t-2}$ and in particular the lag 2 for period 5, is $lag2 = L'_5 - L'_3$. It can be seen altogether that the forecast error, column (4), is comprised of a trend lag, column (6), and a centering lag, column (7).

A method to eliminate this constant error, i.e., capture the effects of the linear trend, is to use a forecasting technique called double moving averages. As its name implies, the double moving average method calculates a second moving average using the data calculated from the first moving average—taking a moving average of the moving average. Double moving averages are designated as MA(m x k), where k is the number of periods in the first moving average, and m is the number of periods in the second moving average. Both moving averages often have the same order, m = k.

The double moving average is defined as:

$$L''_t = \frac{\sum_{i=t-m+1}^{t} L'_i}{m} = \frac{L'_t + L'_{t-1} + L'_{t-2} + \bullet \bullet \bullet + L'_{t-m+1}}{m} \quad (5.3)$$

	A	B	C	D	E	F	G
				(4)		(6)	(7)
1	(1)	(2)	(3)	(2) - (3)	(5)	(2) - (5)	(5(t) - 5(t-2))
2	Period	Actual	F_{t+1} Forecast MA(5)	Forecast Error	L'_t Moving Average	Lag1	Lag2
3	1	100					
4	2	106					
5	3	112					
6	4	118					
7	5	124			112		
8	6	130	112	18	118	6	
9	7	136	118	18	124	6	12
10	8	142	124	18	130	6	12
11	9	148	130	18	136	6	12
12	10	154	136	18	142	6	12
13	11	160	142	18	148	6	12
14	12	166	148	18	154	6	12

Figure 5.1 Moving averages and lags for data on a line.

The double moving average forecast (one period ahead) is equal to:

$$F_{t+1} = L'_t + [L'_t - L''_t] + b_t \quad (5.4)$$

or in other words $F_{t+1} = MA(period\ t) + lag2 + lag1$.

The trend lag, lag1 or b_t, is estimated as:

$$b_t = \frac{2}{k-1}(MA(k)\ \ MA(m \times k)) = \frac{2}{k-1}(L'_t - L''_t) \quad (5.5)$$

Equation 5.5 shows that the trend lag is measured as the difference between the first and second moving averages. The trend lag is adjusted to calculate a one-period trend and not a multi-period trend by multiplying the trend lag by:

$$\frac{2}{k-1}$$

For example, Figure 5.2 demonstrates the double moving average of MA (5 x 5) for the data in Table 5.1. For period 9,

$$L_9' = \frac{\sum\limits_{i=9-5+1}^{9} Y_i}{5}$$

$$= \frac{Y_9 + Y_8 + Y_7 + \bullet \bullet \bullet + Y_5}{5}$$

$$= \frac{148 + 142 + 136 + 130 + 124}{5}$$

$$= 136$$

$$L_9'' = \frac{\sum\limits_{i=9-5+1}^{9} L_i'}{5}$$

$$= \frac{L_9' + L_8' + L_7' + \bullet \bullet \bullet + L_5'}{5}$$

$$= \frac{136 + 130 + 124 + 118 + 112}{5}$$

$$= 124$$

$$b_t = \frac{2}{k-1}(L_t' - L_t'') = \frac{2}{4}(136 - 124) = 6$$

So,

$$F_{t+1} = L_t' + [L_t' - L_t''] + b_t$$

$$= F_{10}$$

$$= L_9' + [L_9' - L_9''] + b_9$$

$$= 136 + [136 - 124] + 6$$

$$= 154$$

I	J	K	L	M	N	O	P
				(5)			
(1)	(2)	(3)	(4)	(3)-(4)	(6)	(7)	(8)
Period	Actual	L_t'	L_t''	Lag2	Trend	Forecast	Error
1	100						
2	106						
3	112						
4	118						
5	124	112					
6	130	118					
7	136	124					
8	142	130					
9	148	136	124	12	6		
10	154	142	130	12	6	154	0
11	160	148	136	12	6	160	0
12	166	154	142	12	6	166	0

Figure 5.2   Double moving average (5x5) with a straight line.

Generalizing and simplifying F_{t+m} such that:

$$F_{t+m} = a_t + b_t m \tag{5.6}$$

where

$$a_t = L_t' + \left[L_t' - L_t''\right] = 2L_t' - L_t'' \tag{5.7}$$

$$b_t = \frac{2}{k-1}(L_t' - L_t'') \tag{5.8}$$

and m is number of periods ahead to be forecast.

The double moving average model in Figure 5.3 is further illustrated by using the data from Chapter 3, in Figure 3.19, with a MA(3 × 3) model. Overall, the double moving average method is relatively good if the major time series component of the data is mostly a trend.

5.2.2 Double Exponential Smoothing

Another approach to forecasting data with a linear trend and some randomness uses exponential smoothing and is called double exponential smoothing (DES). Similar to double moving average, double exponential smoothing smoothes the exponentially smoothed data. To apply exponential smoothing, as demonstrated in Chapter 3, a smoothing factor, α, is needed, which can range from 0 to 1. The simple exponential smoothed value is:

$$L'_t = \alpha Y_t + (1 - \alpha)L'_{t-1} \tag{5.9}$$

Large values of α assign more weight to recent values, and small values of α assign more even weights to many recent values. Double exponential smoothing smoothes the data twice, so it is necessary to estimate two αs. Two approaches to estimating these αs will be examined. One approach uses the same α for both smoothing operations. This approach is called Brown's double exponential smoothing method. The other approach employs two different coefficients for the two smoothing operations, called α and β. This two-coefficient approach is called Holt's double exponential smoothing method.

	A	B	C	D	E	F	G	H
	(1)	(2)	(3)	(4)	(5) (3)-(4)	(6)	(7)	(8)
1								
2	Period	Actual	L'_t	L''_t	Lag2	Trend	Forecast	Error
3	1	144						
4	2	151						
5	3	134	143					
6	4	151	145.3333					
7	5	145	143.3333	143.8889	-0.55556	-0.55556		
8	6	145	147	145.2222	1.777778	1.777778	142.2222	2.777778
9	7	141	143.6667	144.6667	-1	-1	150.5556	-9.55556
10	8	166	150.6667	147.1111	3.555556	3.555556	141.6667	24.33333
11	9	151	152.6667	149	3.666667	3.666667	157.7778	-6.77778
12	10	164	160.3333	154.5556	5.777778	5.777778	160	4
13	11	151	155.3333	156.1111	-0.77778	-0.77778	171.8889	-20.8889
14	12	176	163.6667	159.7778	3.888889	3.888889	153.7778	22.22222
15	13	170	165.6667	161.5556	4.111111	4.111111	171.4444	-1.44444
16	14	180	175.3333	168.2222	7.111111	7.111111	173.8889	6.111111
17	15	156	168.6667	169.8889	-1.22222	-1.22222	189.5556	-33.5556
18	16	187	174.3333	172.7778	1.555556	1.555556	166.2222	20.77778
19	17	166	169.6667	170.8889	-1.22222	-1.22222	177.4444	-11.4444
20	18	182	178.3333	174.1111	4.222222	4.222222	167.2222	14.77778
21	19	154	167.3333	171.7778	-4.44444	-4.44444	186.7778	-32.7778
22	20	169	168.3333	171.3333	-3	-3	158.4444	10.55556

Figure 5.3 Double Moving Average (3x3) using the data from Chapter 3.

5.2.3 Brown's Double Exponential Smoothing

Similar to the double moving averages method, Brown's double exponential smoothing (DES) approach adds a smoothed value to measure the trend. Hence, Brown's double exponential smoothing forecast is:

$$F_{t+m} = a_t + b_t m \tag{5.10}$$

where

$$a_t = L'_t + \left[L'_t - L''_t\right] = 2L'_t - L''_t \tag{5.11}$$

$$b_t = \frac{\alpha}{1-\alpha}(L'_t - L''_t) \tag{5.12}$$

a_t = is the smoothed value at the end of period t

b_t = is an estimate of the trend at the end of period t

m = is the number of periods ahead to be forecast

The double exponential smoothed value is:

$$L_t^{''} = \alpha L_t^{'} + (1-\alpha)L_{t-1}^{''} \qquad (5.13)$$

Using the data from Chapter 3 and Figure 3.22, Brown's DES method is illustrated with an α of 0.5 in Figure 5.4. In particular, for period 9,

$$L_9^{'} = \alpha Y_9 + (1-\alpha)L_8^{'} = 0.5*151 + 0.5*154.55 = 152.78$$

$$L_9^{''} = \alpha L_9^{'} + (1-\alpha)L_8^{''} = 0.5*152.78 = 0.5*149.33 = 151.05$$

$$a_9 = 2L_9^{'} - L_9^{''} = 2*152.78 - 151.05 = 154.5$$

$$b_9 = \frac{\alpha}{1-\alpha}(L_9^{'} - L_9^{''}) = \frac{0.5}{0.5}(152.78 - 151.05) = 1.72$$

so,

$$F_{10} = F_{9+1} = a_9 + b_9 *1 = 154.5 + 1.72 = 156.22$$

As with simple exponential smoothing, to start the calculating process, starting values for the first period must be identified. So, the following definitions are used:

$$
\begin{aligned}
L_1^{'} &= L_1^{''} = Y_1 \\
a_1 &= Y_1 \\
b_1 &= \frac{(Y_2 - Y_1) + (Y_4 - Y_3)}{2}
\end{aligned}
\qquad (5.14)
$$

Therefore, in the example in Figure 5.4,

$$L_1^{'} = L_1^{''} = Y_1 = a_1 = 144$$

and $b_1 = 12$.

	A	B	C	D	E	F	G	H
1	Brown's DES	alpha	0.5					
2								
3	Period	Actual	$L_t^{'}$	$L_t^{''}$	a_t	b_t	Ft+1	error
4	1	144.00	144.00	144.00	144.00	12.00		
5	2	151.00	147.50	145.75	149.25	1.75	156.00	-5.00
6	3	134.00	140.75	143.25	138.25	-2.50	151.00	-17.00
7	4	151.00	145.88	144.56	147.19	1.31	135.75	15.25
8	5	145.00	145.44	145.00	145.88	0.44	148.50	-3.50
9	6	145.00	145.22	145.11	145.33	0.11	146.31	-1.31
10	7	141.00	143.11	144.11	142.11	-1.00	145.44	-4.44
11	8	166.00	154.55	149.33	159.78	5.22	141.11	24.89
12	9	151.00	152.78	151.05	154.50	1.72	165.00	-14.00
13	10	164.00	158.39	154.72	162.06	3.67	156.22	7.78
14	11	151.00	154.69	154.71	154.68	-0.01	165.72	-14.72
15	12	176.00	165.35	160.03	170.67	5.32	154.67	21.33
16	13	170.00	167.67	163.85	171.50	3.82	175.99	-5.99
17	14	180.00	173.84	168.84	178.83	4.99	175.32	4.68
18	15	156.00	164.92	166.88	162.96	-1.96	183.82	-27.82
19	16	187.00	175.96	171.42	180.50	4.54	160.99	26.01
20	17	166.00	170.98	171.20	170.76	-0.22	185.04	-19.04
21	18	182.00	176.49	173.84	179.13	2.64	170.54	11.46
22	19	154.00	165.24	169.54	160.94	-4.30	181.78	-27.78
23	20	169.00	167.12	168.33	165.91	-1.21	156.64	12.36

Figure 5.4 Example of Brown's Double Exponential Smoothing model with $\alpha = 0.5$.

5.2.4   Holt's Double Exponential Smoothing

Holt's double exponential smoothing (DES) approach extends the simple exponential smoothing method to consider a trend by using two parameters, α and β (both of which must be between 0 and 1). These two parameters are used to smooth the level (α) and the trend (β). The level is calculated as:

$$L_t = \alpha Y_t + (1-\alpha)(L_{t-1} + b_{t-1}) \qquad (5.15)$$

Equation 5.15 is similar to the simple exponential smoothing Equation 5.12 except that the second term in 5.15 is adjusted for the trend of the previous time period. The other parameter, β, is used to smooth the estimate of the trend which is calculated as:

$$b_t = \beta(L_t - L_{t-1}) + (1 - \beta)\, b_{t-1} \qquad (5.16)$$

Equation 5.15 estimates the level of the data by smoothing the randomness in the data such that the difference $L_t - L_{t-1}$ provides an estimate of the trend. Equation 5.16 adds this estimate of the trend, $L_t - L_{t-1}$, to the previous period's trend, b_{t-1}, to provide a smoothed estimate of the trend. Holt's DES forecast is:

$$F_{t+m} = L_t + b_t m \qquad (5.17)$$

where m is number of periods ahead to be forecast.

Returning to the sales data in Figure 5.4 and Chapter 3, Holt's DES is applied, using an $\alpha = 0.5$ and a $\beta = 0.9$ in Figure 5.5. For period 9,

$$L_9 = \alpha Y_9 + (1 - \alpha)(L_8 + b_8)$$
$$= 0.5*151 + 0.5*(152.7879 + 9.405172)$$
$$= 156.5965$$

$$b_9 = \beta(L_9 - L_8) + (1 - \beta)\, b_8$$
$$= 0.9 * (156.5965 - 152.7879) + 0.1 * 9.405172$$
$$= 4.38285$$

so,

$$F_{10} = F_{9+1} = L_9 + b_9 * 156.5965 + 4.38285 = 162.1931$$

As with Brown's DES method, Holt's DES requires determination of initial first period values. In Figure 5.5, the same approach, Equation 5.14, was used as for Brown's DES method.

	A	B	C	D	E	F
1	Holt's DES	alpha	0.5	beta	0.9	
2						
3	Period	Actual	L_t		Ft+1	error
4	1	144.00	144	12		
5	2	151.00	153.5	9.75	156	-5
6	3	134.00	148.625	-3.4125	163.25	-29.25
7	4	151.00	148.1063	-0.80813	145.2125	5.7875
8	5	145.00	146.1491	-1.84228	147.2981	-2.29812
9	6	145.00	144.6534	-1.53033	144.3068	0.693219
10	7	141.00	142.0615	-2.48571	143.1231	-2.12306
11	8	166.00	152.7879	9.405172	139.5758	26.42418
12	9	151.00	156.5965	4.368285	162.1931	-11.1931
13	10	164.00	162.4824	5.734113	160.9648	3.035174
14	11	151.00	159.6083	-2.01332	168.2165	-17.2165
15	12	176.00	166.7975	6.268954	157.5949	18.40506
16	13	170.00	171.5332	4.889063	173.0664	-3.06642
17	14	180.00	178.2111	6.499039	176.4223	3.577725
18	15	156.00	170.3551	-6.42054	184.7102	-28.7102
19	16	187.00	175.4673	3.958913	163.9345	23.06545
20	17	166.00	172.7131	-2.08287	179.4262	-13.4262
21	18	182.00	176.3151	3.033529	170.6302	11.36978
22	19	154.00	166.6743	-8.37336	179.3486	-25.3486
23	20	169.00	163.6505	-3.55879	158.301	10.69904

Figure 5.5 Example of Holt's Double Exponential Smoothing model with $\alpha = 0.5$ and $\beta = 0.9$.

Lastly, Holt's DES method can produce exactly the same forecasts as Brown's DES method. If given Brown's α_B, Holt's α_H and β_H can be calculated as:

$$\alpha_H = 2\alpha_B - \alpha_B^2 \qquad \beta_H = \frac{\alpha_B}{2 - \alpha_B}$$

Advantage—models both the level and trend

Disadvantage—does not consider seasonality

5.2.5   Exponential Smoothing with a Seasonal Component and with/without a Trend

Looking back, the moving average and exponential smoothing techniques for modeling data with no trend or seasonal components, i.e., stationary data, were introduced and discussed in Chapter 3. Earlier in this chapter, data with a linear trend was examined and a moving average approach (double moving average), was again applied. Subsequently, two exponential smoothing approaches (Holt's and Brown's double exponential smoothing) were also discussed. These approaches will now be expanded to consider data with a seasonal component. This expansion will no longer focus on the moving average approaches, which although easy to understand, are not as flexible nor as computationally efficient as the exponential smoothing approaches.

In addressing a seasonal component, both additive and multiplicative models are considered. An additive model is most likely to be advantageous if the seasonal factors are constantly the same above or below, e.g., the first and third quarters may be consistently $1 million higher, and the second and fourth quarters may be consistently $1 million lower. On the other hand, with a multiplicative seasonal model, the seasonal effects are not a constant plus or minus. In this situation, the seasonal effects are a constant percentage above or below, e.g., the first and third quarters may consistently be 10 percent higher and the second and fourth quarters consistently 10 percent lower. When should one or the other be used? Unless the graph of the data clearly illustrates a familiar pattern, both additive and multiplicative models should be run to see which one gives the best result.

Trend effects can also have an additive or multiplicative model. A multiplicative trend model would have a similar pattern to the curvilinear graph in Figure 5.6. Generally speaking, a seasonal component is made up of several elements, e.g., four quarters, twelve months, and so on, while a trend component is composed of one element, the trend. Because the trend consists of one element, a curvilinear trend can easily be transformed into a linear growth or decay by simply taking the natural log of the data.

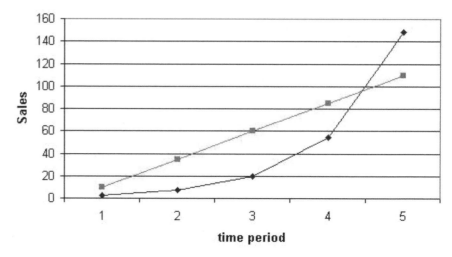

Figure 5.6   Linear and Exponential growth (additive versus multiplicative).

In Table 5.1, a notation is structured for the different additive and multiplicative models with and without a seasonal component. Note that in Table 5.1, notation-wise there is no difference between moving average or exponential smoothing, which are both T_0S_0. This condition is similarly true for the T_AS_0 models of double moving average and double exponential smoothing.

In 1969, C. C. Pegels developed a general framework to classify exponential smoothing models with (additive or multiplicative) or without a trend and with (additive or multiplicative) or without seasonal components, as shown in Table 5.2. First notice that Pegels did break down the trend models into additive (row B) and multiplicative (row C).

The models in Table 5.1 and Pegels' classification in Table 5.2 can easily be cross referenced:

$$T_0S_0 = A1 \qquad T_OS_A = A2 \qquad T_OS_M = A3$$
$$T_AS_0 = B1 \qquad T_AS_A = B2 \qquad T_AS_M = B3$$

So for example, T_0S_A and A2 both are additive seasonal models with no trend. Note that because Pegels addressed only exponential smoothing methods, in the above cross reference T_0S_0 and T_AS_0 do not imply the moving average methods. They only identify the corresponding exponential smoothing methods.

Pegels additionally developed the following simplified set of equations for each of the nine exponential smoothing models in Table 5.2:

$$L_t = \alpha U_t + (1 - \alpha)V_t \qquad (5.18a)$$

$$b_t = \beta W_t + (1 - \beta)b_{t-1} \qquad (5.18b)$$

$$S_t = \gamma_t + (1 - \gamma)S_{t-s} \qquad (5.18c)$$

where U_t, V_t, W_t, X_t and F_{t+m} (m is the number of periods ahead to forecast) vary from model to model and are defined in Table 5.3. For example, two models earlier discussed are the simple exponential smoothing model, T_0S_0 or A1, and Holt's DES model, T_AS_0 or B1. Using the equations in Table 5.3 for the simple exponential smoothing model, and substituting into Equation 5.18a, gives:

$$L_t = \alpha Y_t + (1 - \alpha)L_{t-1}$$

which is the simple exponential smoothing Equation 3.2. In Figure 5.7, Pegels' notation is applied to develop the simple exponential smoothing model, T_0S_0, with $\alpha = 0.1$ for the data in Figure 3.22.

Similarly, Holt's DES model, gives:

$$L_t = \alpha Y_t + (1 - \alpha)(L_{t-1} - b_{t-1})$$

$$b_t = \beta(L_t - L_{t-1}) + (1 - \beta)b_{t-1}$$

Table 5.2 Pegels' Classification

	1 no seasonal effect	2 additive seasonal effect	3 multiplicative seasonal effect
A. no trend effect	A1	A2	A3
B. additive effect	B1	B2	B3
C. multiplicative trend	C1	C2	C3

Table 5.3 Equations for Pegels' Nine Exponential Smoothing Models

Trend	Seasonal None	Additive	Multiplicative
None	T_0S_0 $U_t = Y_t$ $V_t = L_{t-1}$ $F_{t+m} = L_t$	T_0S_A $U_t = Y_t - S_{t-s}$ $V_t = L_{t-1}$ $X_t = Y_t - L_t$ $F_{t+m} = L_t + S_{t+m-s}$	T_0S_M $U_t = Y_t/S_{t-s}$ $V_t = L_{t-1}$ $X_t = Y_t/L_t$ $F_{t+m} = L_t * S_{t+m-s}$
Additive	T_AS_0 $U_t = Y_t$ $V_t = L_{t-1} + b_{t-1}$ $W_t = L_t - L_{t-1}$ $F_{t+m} = L_t + mb_t$	T_AS_A $U_t = Y_t - S_{t-s}$ $V_t = L_{t-1} + b_{t-1}$ $W_t = L_t - L_{t-1}$ $X_t = Y_t - L_t$ $F_{t+m} = L_t + mb_t + S_{t+m-s}$	T_AS_M $U_t = Y_t/S_{t-s}$ $V_t = L_{t-1} + b_{t-1}$ $W_t = L_t - L_{t-1}$ $X_t = Y_t/L_t$ $F_{t+m} = (L_t + mb_t) * S_{t+m-s}$
Multiplicative	$U_t = Y_t$ $V_t = L_{t-1} * b_{t-1}$ $W_t = L_t/L_{t-1}$ $F_{t+m} = L_t * b_t^m$	$U_t = Y_t - S_{t-s}$ $V_t = L_{t-1} * b_{t-1}$ $W_t = L_t/L_{t-1}$ $X_t = Y_t - L_t$ $F_{t+m} = L_t * b_t^m + S_{t+m-s}$	$U_t = Y_t/S_{t-s}$ $V_t = L_{t-1} * b_{t-1}$ $W_t = L_t/L_{t-1}$ $X_t = Y_t/L_t$ $F_{t+m} = L_t * b_t^m * S_{t+m-s}$

which corresponds exactly to the two Holt's DES Equations 5.15 and 5.16. Similarly, Pegels' notation is applied in Figure 5.8 to develop Holt's Double Exponential Smoothing model with $\alpha = 0.5$ and $\beta = 0.9$ for the data in Figure 5.5.

As with Brown's DES method, Holt's DES requires that initial first period values be determined. In Figure 5.5 the same approach, Equation 5.14, was used as was employed for Brown's DES method.

Nevertheless, it should be noted that several alternative approaches can be used to decide on the initial values of L_1 and b_1, e.g., assigning values, averaging values to more sophisticated approaches using least-squares regression, decomposition, or backcasting. These initialization approaches are summarized by Gardner (1985). In Figure 5.9, a regression approach is used to find initial values for b_0 and L_0 using Holt's DES model with the data in Figure 5.8. A simple trend line regression was used, taking the time period as the independent variable and the actual values as the dependent variable. The value of b_0 is equal to b_1 (the slope of the regression equation – cell L19) and L_0 is equal to b_0 (the y-intercept of the regression equation – cell L18). There is no real initialization standard. In general, the influence of the initial values has little effect on fits and forecasts after the first several periods, i.e., if there are more than fifteen to twenty observations the recent fits and forecasts should be relatively close regardless of the approach to estimating the initial values.

In similar fashion, for each of the remaining models in Pegel's framework, use can be made of the equations in the matching cells in Table 5.3, then they can be simply substituted into the 5.18a–c equations. In particular, take a look at the additive trend and multiplicative seasonal model, cell B3 or $T_A S_M$. Using the equations in Table 5.3 and substituting into 5.18a–c we get:

$$L_t = \alpha Y_t / S_{t-s} + (1 - \alpha)(L_{t-1} - b_{t-1})$$

$$b_t = \beta(L_t - L_{t-1}) + (1 - \beta)b_{t-1}$$

	A	B	C	D	E	F	G	H
1			Exponential					
2	U(t)	Y(t)				L(t) = αU(t) + (1 - α)V(t)		
3	V(t)	L(t-1)				b(t) = βW(t) + (1- β)b(t-1)		
4	F(t+1)	L(t)				S(t) = γX(t) + (1 - γ)S(t-s)		
5	α	0.1						
6								
7	Period	Actual	U(t)	V(t)	L(t)	F(t+1)		
8	1	144.00	144.00	144	144	144		
9	2	151.00	151.00	144	144.7	144		
10	3	134.00	134.00	144.7	143.63	144.7		
11	4	151.00	151.00	143.63	144.367	143.63		
12	5	145.00	145.00	144.367	144.4303	144.367		
13	6	145.00	145.00	144.4303	144.4873	144.4303		
14	7	141.00	141.00	144.4873	144.1385	144.4873		
15	8	166.00	166.00	144.1385	146.3247	144.1385		
16	9	151.00	151.00	146.3247	146.7922	146.3247		
17	10	164.00	164.00	146.7922	148.513	146.7922		
18	11	151.00	151.00	148.513	148.7617	148.513		
19	12	176.00	176.00	148.7617	151.4855	148.7617		
20	13	170.00	170.00	151.4855	153.337	151.4855		
21	14	180.00	180.00	153.337	156.0033	153.337		
22	15	156.00	156.00	156.0033	156.003	156.0033		
23	16	187.00	187.00	156.003	159.1027	156.003		
24	17	166.00	166.00	159.1027	159.7924	159.1027		
25	18	182.00	182.00	159.7924	162.0132	159.7924		
26	19	154.00	154.00	162.0132	161.2118	162.0132		
27	20	169.00	169.00	161.2118	161.9907	161.2118		

Figure 5.7 Using Table 5.3 notation, simple exponential smoothing model, $T_0 S_O$, with $\alpha = .1$ for the data in Figure 3.22.

$$S_t = \gamma Y_t / L_t + (1 - \gamma)S_{t-s}$$

and the m period ahead forecast is

$$F_{t+m} = (L_t + mb_t)\, S_{t+m-s}$$

Pegels' notation is applied in Figure 5.10 to develop the $T_A S_M$ model with $\alpha = 0.5$, $\beta = 0.9$ and $\gamma = 0.2$, for the data in Figure 5.5.

To initialize this model, initial values are needed for L_t, b_t, and S_t. The level, L_s, (calculated in cell K13 and equal to cell I15) is initialized by calculating the average of the actual values for the first season, i.e.:

$$L_s = \frac{\sum_{i=1}^{s} Y_i}{s}$$

The initial trend, b_s, (calculated in cell L13 and equal to cell E15) is given by:

$$b_s = \frac{1}{s}\left[\frac{Y_{s+1}-Y_1}{s}+\frac{Y_{s+2}-Y_2}{s}+\cdots+\frac{Y_{s+s}-Y_s}{s}\right]$$

The seasonal indices are initialized by taking the ratio of the actual to the mean of the first year, L_s:

$$S_i = \frac{Y_i}{L_s} \qquad i=1,2,....,s$$

	A	B	C	D	E	F	G	H
1				Holt's double exponential				
2	U(t)	Y(t)				L(t) = αU(t) + (1 - α)V(t)		
3	V(t)	L(t-1)+b(t-1)				b(t) = βW(t) + (1- β)b(t-1)		
4	F(t+1)	L(t)+1(bt)				S(t) = γX(t) + (1 - γ)S(t-s)		
5	α	0.5				W(t) = L(t)-L(t-1)		
6	β	0.9						
7								
8	Period	Actual	U(t)	V(t)	b(t)	W(t)	L(t)	F(t+1)
9	1	144.00	144.00	144	12		144	
10	2	151.00	151.00	156	9.75	9.5	153.5	156
11	3	134.00	134.00	163.25	-3.4125	-4.875	148.625	163.25
12	4	151.00	151.00	145.2125	-0.80813	-0.51875	148.1063	145.2125
13	5	145.00	145.00	147.2981	-1.84228	-1.95719	146.1491	147.2981
14	6	145.00	145.00	144.3068	-1.53033	-1.49567	144.6534	144.3068
15	7	141.00	141.00	143.1231	-2.48571	-2.59186	142.0615	143.1231
16	8	166.00	166.00	139.5758	9.405172	10.72638	152.7879	139.5758
17	9	151.00	151.00	162.1931	4.368285	3.808631	156.5965	162.1931
18	10	164.00	164.00	160.9648	5.734113	5.885872	162.4824	160.9648
19	11	151.00	151.00	168.2165	-2.01332	-2.87415	159.6083	168.2165
20	12	176.00	176.00	157.5949	6.268954	7.189207	166.7975	157.5949
21	13	170.00	170.00	173.0664	4.889063	4.735742	171.5332	173.0664
22	14	180.00	180.00	176.4223	6.499039	6.677926	178.2111	176.4223
23	15	156.00	156.00	184.7102	-6.42054	-7.85605	170.3551	184.7102
24	16	187.00	187.00	163.9345	3.958913	5.112186	175.4673	163.9345
25	17	166.00	166.00	179.4262	-2.08287	-2.75418	172.7131	179.4262
26	18	182.00	182.00	170.6302	3.033529	3.602018	176.3151	170.6302
27	19	154.00	154.00	179.3486	-8.37336	-9.64079	166.6743	179.3486
28	20	169.00	169.00	158.301	-3.55879	-3.02384	163.6505	158.301

Figure 5.8 Holt's Double Exponential Smoothing model with α = 0.5 and β = 0.9 for the data in Figure 5.5.

5.3 Autoregressive Integrated Moving Average (ARIMA) Models

5.3.1 Autocorrelation

Often, and especially with time series data, the data is correlated with itself, i.e., it is correlated with its lagged values. A lagged value is the value of the data one or more prior time periods before the current time period. For example, sales in this time period are related to sales in the previous time period, or sales in this time period are related to sales three time periods earlier. The correlation between the lag values and the data itself is called autocorrelation.

The formula to estimate the theoretical autocorrelation between observations k periods apart (or lagged k periods) is:

$$\rho_k = \frac{\sum_{t=k+1}^{n}(Y_t - \overline{Y}_k^{+})(Y_{t\,k} - \overline{Y}_k^{-})}{\sqrt{\sum_{t=k+1}^{n}(Y_t - \overline{Y}_k^{+})^2 \sum_{t=k+1}^{n}(Y_{t-k} - \overline{Y}_k^{-})^2}}$$

where:

ρ_k = theoretical estimate of autocorrelation coefficient for lag of k periods

Y_t = actual value in time period t

$$\overline{Y_k}^{\,+} = \frac{\sum_{t=k+1}^{n} Y_t}{n-k}$$

$$\overline{Y_k}^{\,-} = \frac{\sum_{t=1}^{n-k} Y_t}{n-k}$$

n = total number of time periods

For convenience, often in practice the mean of the entire series,

$$\overline{Y} = \frac{\sum_{t=1}^{n} Y_t}{n}$$

is used to estimate the partial means, $\overline{Y_k}^{\,+}, \overline{Y_k}^{\,-}$, and the sum of the square of the entire series is substituted for the partial sum of the squares. As a result, the equation to compute the sample autocorrelation coefficient of lag k is:

$$r_k = \frac{\sum_{t=k+1}^{n} (Y_t - \overline{Y})(Y_{t-k} - \overline{Y})}{\sum_{t=1}^{n} (Y_t - \overline{Y})^2}$$

where:

r_k = sample autocorrelation coefficient for lag of k periods

Y_t = actual value in time period t

$\overline{Y}$ = average of the actual values

n = total number of time periods

	A	B	C	D	E	F	G	H	K	L
1			Holt's double exponential						SUMMARY OUTPUT	
2	U(t)	Y(t)				L(t) = αU(t) + (1 - α)V(t)				
3	V(t)	L(t-1)+b(t-1)				b(t) = βW(t) + (1- β)b(t-1)			Regression Statistics	
4	F(t+1)	L(t)+1(bt)				S(t) = γX(t) + (1 - γ)S(t-s)			Multiple R	0.70162536
5	α	0.5				W(t) = L(t)-L(t-1)			R Square	0.49227815
6	β	0.9							Adjusted R Square	0.46407138
7									Standard Error	10.9393158
8	Period	Actual	U(t)	V(t)	b(t)	W(t)	L(t)	F(t+1)	Observations	20
9	0				1.77218		140.542			
10	1	144.00	144.00	142.314	2.53075	2.61504	143.157	142.314		
11	2	151.00	151.00	145.688	4.9212	5.1868	148.344	145.688	ANOVA	
12	3	134.00	134.00	153.265	-3.74812	-4.71137	143.633	153.265		df
13	4	151.00	151.00	139.884	1.25388	1.80965	145.442	139.884	Regression	1
14	5	145.00	145.00	146.696	0.49063	0.40582	145.848	146.696	Residual	18
15	6	145.00	145.00	146.339	-0.11178	-0.17871	145.669	146.339	Total	19
16	7	141.00	141.00	145.558	-2.16268	-2.39056	143.279	145.558		
17	8	166.00	166.00	141.116	9.03507	10.2793	153.558	141.116		Coefficients
18	9	151.00	151.00	162.593	3.81817	3.23851	156.797	162.593	Intercept	140.542105
19	10	164.00	164.00	160.615	5.34154	5.5108	162.307	160.615	Period	1.77218045
20	11	151.00	151.00	167.649	-2.15047	-2.98291	159.324	167.649		
21	12	176.00	176.00	157.174	6.32124	7.26254	166.587	157.174		
22	13	170.00	170.00	172.908	5.01254	4.86712	171.454	172.908		
23	14	180.00	180.00	176.467	6.60254	6.77921	178.233	176.467		
24	15	156.00	156.00	184.836	-6.3736	-7.81539	170.418	184.836		
25	16	187.00	187.00	164.044	3.95645	5.10423	175.522	164.044		
26	17	166.00	166.00	179.479	-2.10893	-2.78286	172.739	179.479		
27	18	182.00	182.00	170.63	3.0074	3.57588	176.315	170.63		
28	19	154.00	154.00	179.323	-8.38777	-9.6539	166.661	179.323		
29	20	169.00	169.00	158.274	-3.56085	-3.02453	163.637	158.274		

Figure 5.9 Holt's Double Exponential Smoothing model with α = 0.5 and β = 0.9 for the data in Figure 5.5 using Linear Regression for initial values.

	A	B	C	D	E	F	G	H	I	J	K	L	M	N
1			Holt's-Winters exponential											
2	U(t)	Y(t)/S(t-4)				L(t) = αU(t) + (1 - α)V(t)								
3	V(t)	L(t-1)+b(t-1)				b(t) = βW(t) + (1- β)b(t-1)								
4	F(t+1)	(L(t)+1(bt))*s(t+1-4)				S(t) = γX(t) + (1 - γ)S(t-4)								
5	X(t)	Y(t)/L(t)				W(t) = L(t)-L(t-1)								
6	α	0.5												
7	β	0.9												
8	γ	0.2												
9														
10	Period	Actual	U(t)	V(t)	b(t)	x(t)	s(t)	W(t)	L(t)	F(t+1)			0.25	
11	0												-1.50	
12	1	144.00					0.9931				Ls	bs	1.75	
13	2	151.00					1.04138				145.00	1.0625	3.75	S
14	3	134.00					0.92414							0.9931
15	4	151.00			1.0625		1.04138		145					1.04138
16	5	145.00	146.01	146.063	1.0375	0.992915	0.993066	1.03472	146.035	145.05				0.92414
17	6	145.00	139.24	147.072	-2.4877	1.012886	1.035681	-2.8794	143.155	152.32				1.04138
18	7	141.00	152.57	140.668	2.87045	0.961662	0.931643	3.4658	146.621	131.052				
19	8	166.00	159.40	149.492	7.33103	1.074797	1.048063	7.82665	154.448	156.677				
20	9	151.00	152.05	161.779	2.95505	0.962295	0.986911	2.46883	156.917	159.661				
21	10	164.00	158.35	159.872	2.2703	1.030728	1.03469	2.19421	159.111	165.418				
22	11	151.00	162.08	161.381	2.58448	0.933654	0.932045	2.61939	161.73	150.414				
23	12	176.00	167.93	164.315	4.21086	1.059464	1.050343	4.39157	166.122	172.587				
24	13	170.00	172.25	170.333	5.07573	0.992448	0.988019	5.17183	171.294	168.292				
25	14	180.00	173.97	176.369	3.99384	1.027589	1.03327	3.87363	175.167	182.237				
26	15	156.00	167.37	179.161	-1.3104	0.900342	0.925704	-1.8997	173.267	165.85				
27	16	187.00	178.04	171.957	1.4256	1.068589	1.053992	1.7296	174.997	181.241				
28	17	166.00	168.01	176.423	-2.3588	0.963895	0.983194	-2.7792	172.218	173.458				
29	18	182.00	176.14	169.859	0.46758	1.052026	1.037021	0.78161	172.999	176.147				
30	19	154.00	166.36	173.467	-2.7307	0.906344	0.921832	-3.086	169.913	159.908				
31	20	169.00	160.34	167.183	-5.8087	1.031981	1.04959	-6.1507	163.763	175.473				

Figure 5.10 The T_AS_M model with α = 0.5, β = 0.9 and γ = 0.2, for the data in Figure 5.5.

The difference between the theoretical estimate and the sample autocorrelation estimate is relatively small if the number of observations in the time series is large, compared to the number of periods lagged, k. For example, using the sales data in Figure 5.3, the theoretical estimate and sample autocorrelation coefficients of lag 1 are calculated, as shown in Figure 5.11 (also in Excel file Autocorrelation2, worksheet Autocorrelation), as:

$$\rho_1 = \frac{\sum_{t=2}^{20}(Y_t - \overline{Y}_1^{+})(Y_{t-1} - \overline{Y}_1^{-})}{\sqrt{\sum_{t=2}^{20}(Y_t - \overline{Y}_1^{+})^2 \sum_{t=2}^{20}(Y_{t-1} - \overline{Y}_1^{-})^2}}$$

$$= \frac{\sum_{t=2}^{20}(Y_t - 159.9)(Y_{t-1} - 158.6)}{\sqrt{\sum_{t=2}^{20}(Y_t - 159.9)^2 \sum_{t=2}^{20}(Y_{t-1} - 158.6)^2}}$$

$$= \frac{1151.6}{\sqrt{(4000.9)^2(4140.4)^2}}$$

$$= 0.283$$

$$r_1 = \frac{\sum_{t=2}^{20}(Y_t - \overline{Y})(Y_{t-1} - \overline{Y})}{\sum_{t=1}^{n}(Y_t - \overline{Y})^2} = \frac{\sum_{t=2}^{20}(Y_t - 159.15)(Y_{t-1} - 159.15)}{\sum_{t=1}^{n}(Y_t - 159.15)^2}$$

$$= \frac{1143.78}{4242.55}$$

$$= 0.2696$$

	Sales (Y_t)	(Y_t - Ȳ⁻)	(Y_t - Ȳ⁻)²	Lagged Sales (Y_{t-1})	(Y_t - Ȳ⁺)	(Y_t - Ȳ⁺)²	(Y_t - Ȳ⁺)(Y_{t-1} - Ȳ⁺)	(Y_t - Ȳ)	(Y_{t-1} - Ȳ)	(Y_t - Ȳ)²	(Y_t - Ȳ)(Y_{t-1} - Ȳ)
2	144	-14.63158	214.0831	151	-8.94737	80.0554017	130.9141274	-8.15	-15.15	229.5225	123.4725
3	151	-7.631579	58.240997	134	-25.9474	673.265928	198.0193906	-25.15	-8.15	66.4225	204.9725
4	134	-24.63158	606.71468	151	-8.94737	80.0554017	220.3878116	-8.15	-25.15	632.5225	204.9725
5	151	-7.631579	58.240997	145	-14.9474	223.423823	114.0720222	-14.15	-8.15	66.4225	115.3225
6	145	-13.63158	185.81994	145	-14.9474	223.423823	203.7562327	-14.15	-14.15	200.2225	200.2225
7	145	-13.63158	185.81994	141	-18.9474	359.00277	258.2825485	-18.15	-14.15	200.2225	256.8225
8	141	-17.63158	310.87258	166	6.052632	36.634349	-106.7174515	6.85	-18.15	329.4225	-124.3275
9	166	7.368421	54.293629	151	-8.94737	80.0554017	-65.92797784	-8.15	6.85	46.9225	-55.8275
10	151	-7.631579	58.240997	164	4.052632	16.4238227	-30.92797784	4.85	-8.15	66.4225	-39.5275
11	164	5.368421	28.819945	151	-8.94737	80.0554017	-48.033241	-8.15	4.85	23.5225	-39.5275
12	151	-7.631579	58.240997	176	16.05263	257.686981	-122.5069252	16.85	-8.15	66.4225	-137.1275
13	176	17.36842	301.66205	170	10.05263	101.055402	174.598338	10.85	16.85	283.9225	182.8225
14	170	11.36842	129.241	180	20.05263	402.108033	227.966759	20.85	10.85	117.7225	226.2225
15	180	21.36842	456.60942	156	-3.94737	15.5817175	-84.34903047	-3.15	20.85	434.7225	-65.6775
16	156	-2.631579	6.9252078	187	27.05263	731.844875	-71.19113573	27.85	-3.15	9.9225	-87.7275
17	187	28.36842	804.76731	166	6.052632	36.634349	171.7036011	6.85	27.85	775.6225	190.7725
18	166	7.368421	54.293629	182	22.05263	486.31856	162.4930748	22.85	6.85	46.9225	156.5225
19	182	23.36842	546.0831	154	-5.94737	35.3711911	-138.9806094	-5.15	22.85	522.1225	-117.6775
20	154	-4.631579	21.451524	169	9.052632	81.9501385	-41.92797784	9.85	-5.15	26.5225	-50.7275
21	169									97.0225	
22 Sum	3183							15.15	-9.85	4242.55	1143.7775
24 Average Avg(all)					Avg+						
25	159.15		4140.4211	159.9474			4000.94737	1151.631579			
26 Avg-											
27	158.6315789										
28 Theoretical								Sample			
29 Autocorrelation	0.28295							Autocorrelation 0.269597			

Figure 5.11 Steps to calculating the theoretical and sample autocorrelation of lag of 1 with the data from Figure 5.3.

A graphical display of autocorrelations of various lags is called a correlogram. The Excel file called Autocorrelation2, contains two worksheets—Theoretical and Sample—that respectively calculate and graph the estimated theoretical and sample autocorrelation for several lags. To produce the autocorrelation coefficients and correlograms, simply copy the data into column B (starting in row 2). Figure 5.12 illustrates the estimated theoretical autocorrelations and corresponding correlogram of the data in Figure 5.11.

Like correlation, an autocorrelation coefficient can range from −1 to 1 and the closer the autocorrelation coefficient is to −1 or 1, the stronger the relationship. (Note that the autocorrelation coefficient of lag of 0 is equal to 1.) Theoretically, each autocorrelation coefficient for a random series is equal to zero. A particular autocorrelation coefficient is significantly different from zero if n, the number of time periods, is large. (When time series data is analyzed using regression in Chapters 6 and 7, the Durbin-Watson test is used to test whether or not the error term in time period t is significantly related to the error term in time period t−1, i.e., whether the first autocorrelation is significant or not.) As a result, the sampling distribution of autocorrelations can be assumed to be approximately normal with a mean of zero, and with a standard deviation of

$$ \frac{1}{\sqrt{n}} $$

In the correlograms in the Autocorrelation2 theoretical and sample worksheets as shown in Figure 5.12, the 95 percent confidence limits are drawn in red. Autocorrelation coefficients outside these limits may be considered to be significantly different from zero.

Statistically, when it is necessary to test whether one autocorrelation coefficient is equal to zero or not, there is a probability α of being incorrect. In determining the critical limits in the correlogram, a level of confidence of 95 percent is used. So there is a 5-percent chance of incorrectly deciding that an autocorrelation coefficient is non-zero. However, when this test is applied repeatedly to several autocorrelations, the likelihood of incorrectly deciding that at least one autocorrelation coefficient is non-zero can be rather significant. For example, if 20 autocorrelations are being tested there is about a 64 percent chance of at least one false rejection. A statistical test to test all the autocorrelations for all lags up to lag k is equal to zero is the Ljung-Box statistic. (Tests of this kind are known as portmanteau tests.) The equation for the Ljung-Box statistic is:

$$ Q_h = n(n+2)\sum_{k=1}^{h}(n-k)^{-1}r_k^2 $$

where h is the number of autocorrelation coefficients being tested. The Ljung-Box statistic follows a $\chi 2$ distribution with h degrees of freedom. The Ljung-Box statistic for 5 lags, as shown in Autocorrelation2 file and in Figure 5.12, cell K18, equals 33.33.

	A	B	C	D	E	F	G–L
1	T	Data	Z	n	Lag	ACF	Correlogram
2	0.28295	144	-1.01386	20	1	0.28295	
3	0.753985	151	-0.54541	5	2	0.753985	
4	0.203939	134	-1.68307		3	0.203939	
5	0.771506	151	-0.54541		4	0.771506	
6	0.068121	145	-0.94693		5	0.068121	
7	0	145	-0.94693		6		
8	0	141	-1.21462		7		
9	0	166	0.45841		8		
10	0	151	-0.54541		9		
11	0	164	0.324568		10		
12	0	151	-0.54541		11		
13	0	176	1.127621		12		
14	0	170	0.726094		13		
15	0	180	1.395306		14		
16	0	156	-0.2108		15		
17	0	187	1.863754		16		
18	0	166	0.45841		17		Ljung-Box 33.33172
19	0	182	1.529148		18		
20	0	154	-0.34464		19		χ^2 11.0705
21	0	169	0.659173		20		p-value 3.23E-06

Figure 5.12   The estimated theoretical autocorrelations and correlogram for the data in Figure 5.3.

The critical $\chi 2$ value, using a 0.05 level of significance, is in cell K20 (or the p-value for the Ljung-Box statistic is in cell K21). If the Ljung-Box statistic is greater than the critical $\Pi 2$ value or the p-value is less than 0.05, the conclusion is that one or more of the autocorrelations is non-zero (Reject H_0). Otherwise, it can be assumed that all the autocorrelation coefficients up to lag h are not significantly different from zero. In this example the Ljung-Box statistic is greater than the $\chi 2$ value, i.e., 33.33 > 11.07 (or 3.3E-06 < 0.05), so it can be concluded that one or more of the first five autocorrelations is non-zero.

The pattern and significance of the autocorrelation coefficients can be very useful in identifying significant components of the time series data. If the time series data is/has:

Random: All the autocorrelation coefficients are statistically equal to zero.

Stationary: The low-order autocorrelations (first several lags) are large, but higher-order lags decrease rapidly.

Trend: The low-order autocorrelations are large and decrease slowly as the lag increases.

Seasonal: A significant autocorrelation coefficient occurs at the appropriate time lag, i.e., at lag 4, 8, 12 if there is a quarterly season, or lag 12, 24, 36 if there is a monthly season.

5.3.2 Differencing

Several approaches to identify, measure, and remove the trend and seasonal components of the time series data were discussed in Chapter 3. Another approach is the method of differencing. The k difference data measures the amount of change between the time t and time t–k, that is,

$$Y_t^k = Y_t - Y_{t-k}$$

The first difference, $Y_t^1 = Y_t - Y_{t-1}$, is one way to capture and remove the effect of the trend. Figure 5.13 shows the sample auto-correlations and the corresponding correlogram for the data in Figure 5.3. The p-value for the Ljung-Box statistic is significantly small, so one or more of the autocorrelations is non-zero. The first difference of this data, $Y_t^1 = Y_t - Y_{t-1}$, is calculated in column B in Figure 5.14, and the sample autocorrelations and correlogram of the first differences, Y_t^1, are displayed in Figure 5.15. Examining the Ljung-Box statistic in Figure 5.15, the p-value is now even smaller, 1.26E-10, implying even more strongly that one or more of the autocorrelations is significantly non-zero.

Differencing can also be applied to capture the seasonal component by performing a seasonal difference. In particular, using the data in Figure 5.3, a quarterly seasonal difference can be taken, yielding $Y_t^4 = Y_t - Y_{t-4}$. These seasonal differences are calculated in column C of Figure 5.14 and the corresponding sample autocorrelations and correlogram are shown in Figure 5.16. The p-value

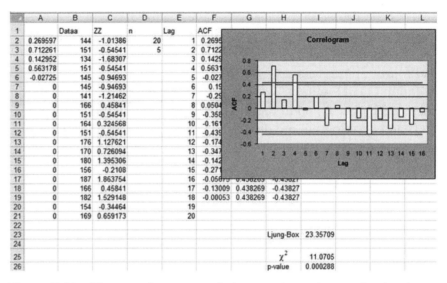

Figure 5.13 The sample autocorrelations and correlogram for the data in Figure 5.3.

	Sales	$Y_t - Y_{t-1}$ $(1-B)Y_t$	$Y_t - Y_{t-4}$ $(1-B)^4Y_t$	Column C(Column B) $(1-B)(1-B)^4Y_t$
	Sales	**(1-B)Y_t**	**(1-B)⁴Y_t**	**(1-B)(1-B)⁴Y_t**
3	144			
4	151	7		
5	134	-17		
6	151	17		
7	145	-6	1	
8	145	0	-6	-7
9	141	-4	7	13
10	166	25	15	8
11	151	-15	6	-9
12	164	13	19	13
13	151	-13	10	-9
14	176	25	10	0
15	170	-6	19	9
16	180	10	16	-3
17	156	-24	5	-11
18	187	31	11	6
19	166	-21	-4	-15
20	182	16	2	6
21	154	-28	-2	-4
22	169	15	-18	-16

Figure 5.14 Differencing of the data in Figure 5.3.

now for the Ljung-Box statistic is significantly large, 0.234, implying that autocorrelations are now significantly different from zero.

If necessary, the trend and seasonal difference, that is, the first and fourth difference, can both be applied to the data. For instance, in column D in Figure 5.14 the first difference of the seasonal difference is calculated, and in Figure 5.17 the corresponding autocorrelations and correlogram are displayed. The p-value for the Ljung-Box statistic is not as large, 0.10, implying one or more of the autocorrelations may be non-zero.

A helpful notation tool especially when discussing differencing, is the backward shift operator B which is defined as $BY_t = Y_{t-1}$. As such, the effect of B is to shift the data back one period.

The first difference can then be expressed as

$$Y_t^1 = Y_t - Y_{t-1} = Y_t - BY_t = (1 - B)Y_t$$

Further, a seasonal difference can be written as $(1 - B)^s Y_t$. The backward shift operator B can also be useful in expressing the seasonal difference followed by a first difference calculated in column D in Figure 5.14, which can be written as $(1 - B)(1 - B)^4 Y_t$.

5.3.3   Autoregressive and moving average models

Starting in Chapter 6 and further expanded in Chapter 7, is a discussion of the forecasting method of regression. The form of the regression equation is

$$Y_t = b_0 + b_1 X_1 + b_2 X_2 \cdot \cdot \cdot \cdot + b_p X_p + \varepsilon \qquad (5.19)$$

where

Y_t = the forecast variable

X_i = explanatory variable i

b_0, b_i = regression coefficients

ε = error term

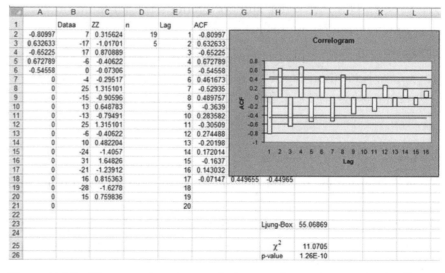

Figure 5.15   The sample autocorrelations and correlogram for the first difference (column B in Figure 5.14).

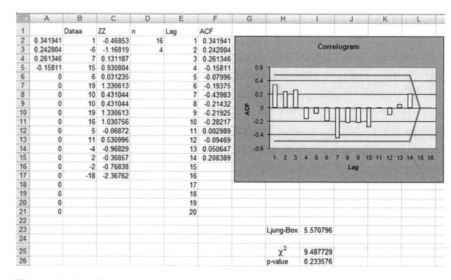

Figure 5.16   The sample autocorrelations and correlogram for the seasonal difference of 4 (column C in Figure 5.14).

Instead of utilizing explanatory variables like GNP or advertising, each explanatory variable can be defined as a time lagged value, i.e.,

$$X_1 = Y_{t-1}$$

$$X_2 = Y_{t-2}$$

$$\bullet$$

$$\bullet$$

$$\bullet$$

$$X_p = Y_{t-p}$$

Equation 5.19 becomes

$$Y_t = b_0 + b_1 Y_{t-1} + b_2 Y_{t-2} \cdots + b_p Y_{t-p} + \varepsilon_t \qquad (5.20)$$

Forecasting models such as Equation 5.20, in which the forecast variable is a function of time lagged values, is called an autoregressive model of order p. Similarly as lagged values of the time series are regressed, the lagged values of the errors can be used as explanatory variables;

$$Y_t = b_0 + b_1 \varepsilon_{t-1} + b_2 \varepsilon_{t-2} \cdots + b_q \varepsilon_{t-q} + \varepsilon_t \qquad (5.21)$$

Equation 5.21 is called a moving average model of order q. The autoregressive model, 5.20, and the moving average model, 5.21, can be grouped together to form a family of models called autoregressive moving average (ARMA) models. The ARMA models are only useful if the data is stationary. So, these ARMA models are extended to consider non-stationary data, and they are called autoregressive integrated moving average (ARIMA) models. Differencing is used to reduce non-stationary issues.

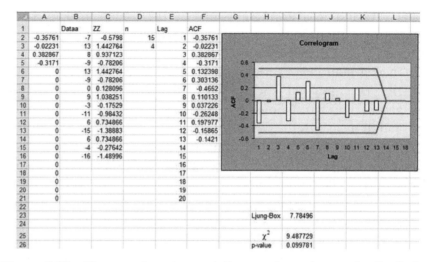

Figure 5.17 The sample autocorrelations and correlogram for the first and seasonal difference of 4 (column D in Figure 5.14).

5.3.4 ARIMA models

A standard notation to identify the type of ARIMA model is ARIMA(p, d, q), where:

p = order of autoregression
d = order of integration (differencing)
q = order of moving average

For example, Equation 5.20 is an AR(p) model and Equation 5.21 is a MA(q) model.

In their 1970 book, Box and Jenkins describe a three-stage iterative methodology of model selection, parameter estimation, and model checking to forecast univariate ARIMA models:

Step 1: Model Selection

The first step in model selection is to generate graphs and statistics of the time series data. If the series is identified as being non-stationary, various transformations can be performed to convert the data into a stationary series. Often the process used to convert the data into a stationary process is differencing.

Once a stationary series has been obtained, the form of the model to be employed is identified by the autocorrelations (ACFs) and partial autocorrelations (PACFs) of the series. A partial autocorrelation measures the degree of association between Y_t and Y_{t-k}, after removing the effects of other lags. (The PACFs can be estimated by using either regression or the Yuke-Walker equations (DeLurgio).) The unique pattern of the data's ACFs and PACFs are compared with corresponding theoretical patterns of ARIMA models to identify the form of the model. In particular, Table 5.4 lists the expected patterns for the pure AR and MA models. Similarly, patterns of the ACFs and PACFs are used to identify the higher-order models. During this model identification process, an overarching theme should be the principle of parsimony, i.e., building a significant model with the least number of variables—simple models are preferred to complex ones.

Step 2: Parameter Estimation

After the model selection step, parameter estimates must be determined. The methods of least squares or maximum likelihood are employed to estimate the model coefficients (Farnum and Stanton).

Step 3: Model checking

Given the estimation of the model parameters, the adequacy of the selected model is evaluated by performing various statistical tests on the residuals to see if they are random. In particular, a portmanteau test such as the Ljung-Box statistic, discussed earlier in this chapter, is performed. If the portmanteau test is significant, the model is deemed to be inadequate and the analyst should go back to

Table 5.4   Expected Patterns of ACF and PACF

Model	ACF	PACF
AR(p)	Exponential decay or damped sine-wave pattern	Significant spikes at lags 1 to p; greater than p significantly small
MA(q)	Significant spikes at lags 1 to p; greater than p significantly small	Exponential decay or damped sine-wave pattern

Step 1 and select a different model. On the other hand, if the portmanteau test is not significant, the model is viewed as adequate and forecasts can be made.

Recent extensions of their methodology have expanded Box-Jenkins' initial three-stage iterative process, which includes either an initial data preparation step and/or a final step of model forecasting. The success of the Box-Jenkins approach, now often called simply the Box-Jenkins methodology, is synonymous with general univariate ARIMA modeling.

One of the statistical assumptions of the regression techniques is statistical independence, i.e., any particular error term is statistically independent of any other error term. This independence assumption is often violated when time series data is analyzed. One significant advantage of the ARIMA or Box-Jenkins models is that this assumption of independence of the residual (error) terms can be violated. The Box-Jenkins approach has been shown to be a powerful forecasting tool and to be especially accurate for short-range forecasting. As a rule of thumb, these ARIMA models should have at least forty to fifty observations. On the other hand, recent research has shown that the regression models using time series data provide accurate forecasts, even though the independence assumption is violated.

5.4 Index Numbers

Numerous business and economic series are collected over time. Decision-makers attempt to interpret the data patterns and identify significant variations over time, e.g., sales are increasing or decreasing. As was discussed in Chapter 3, several time series techniques can be utilized to examine the trend, seasonal, and cyclical components. Besides understanding the data patterns, decision-makers want to identify significant variations over time. For example, total sales revenue may have increased by 10 percent from the previous period, which may be interpreted as meaning that the number of units sold has also increased by 10 percent. This conclusion may or may not be true, i.e., the 10 percent increase could mostly be the result of a significant increase in price. To interpret the actual revenue activity correctly, the total revenue must be adjusted by an index number to remove the effects of any price changes. We will now examine what a simple index number is, how to calculate it, how to deflate a data set, and when to use aggregate index numbers.

An index number, a price or quantity index number, is expressed as a percentage that measures the relative change usually in price(s) and/or quantity(s) from one time period to another time period. One period is designated as the base period. This base period is the time period with which all other time period's values are compared. Index numbers and their variation over time can be extremely helpful in identifying and interpreting economic and business conditions.

A simple index number is defined as:

$$\text{Index number for time period i} = \frac{\text{Value in time period i}}{\text{Value in base time period}} * 100$$

For example, listed in Table 5.5 are the United States retail gasoline prices during the first week of September for the years 1990 to 2001, and these gasoline prices are graphed in Figure 5.18. The year-to-year changes do not really demonstrate any significant

Table 5.5 Gasoline Prices (Regular) (1st Week in September, Except in 2001—as of July 2001)

Year	Gasoline Prices (cents/gallon)	Year to Year Change	Difference from 1990	Price Relative (Base
1990	124.2	n/a	0	100.00
1991	112.7	-11.5	-11.5	90.74
1992	112.1	-0.6	-12.1	90.26
1993	105.5	-6.6	-18.7	84.94
1994	115.6	10.1	-8.6	93.08
1995	111.3	-4.3	-12.9	89.61
1996	119.7	8.4	-4.5	96.38
1997	124.3	4.6	0.1	100.08
1998	100.7	-23.6	-23.5	81.08
1999	124.2	23.5	0	100.00
2000	153	28.8	28.8	123.19
2001	148.8	-4.2	24.6	119.81

increases or decreases except for the years 1998 to 2000. Looking at the differences in Table 5.5, it can be seen that since 1990 gasoline prices decreased as much as 18.7 cents in 1993 and have increased as much as 28.8 cents in 2000. For the most part, these absolute values really do not illustrate any significant changes in gasoline prices.

It is now possible to see what the index numbers might indicate. Using 1990 as the base year, the first step is to calculate the price indices in the last column of Table 5.5. Specifically, the price index for 1993 is:

$$\text{Index number for 1993} = \frac{\text{Gasoline Price in 1993}}{\text{Gasoline Price in 1990}} * 100$$

$$= \frac{105.5}{124.2} * 100$$

$$= 89.6.$$

This index number or relative price of 89.6 implies that gasoline prices decreased by 10.4 percent from 1990 to 1993. Conversely, the index number for 2000 is 123.2, which means gasoline prices have now risen by 23.2 percent from 1990 to 2000. This dramatic swing in gasoline prices does not mean gasoline prices have increased by 23.2 – (–10.4) = 33.7 percent from 1993 to 2000. Percentage comparisons can only be made with the base year. It can only be said that in 1993, gasoline prices were 10.4 percent lower, and in 2000 gasoline prices were 23.2 percent higher than in 1990.

What if you must know the relative change in gasoline prices from 1993 to 2000? In order to answer this question, it is necessary to change the base year of the index from 1990 to 1993, which can be accomplished in two ways. If the actual data, that is, the gasoline prices, is available, it is a simple matter to calculate a new price index by using 1993 as the base year, as in column C in Table 5.6. For example,

$$\text{Index number for 2000} = \frac{\text{Gasoline Price in 2000}}{\text{Gasoline Price in 1993}} * 100$$

$$= \frac{153}{105.5} * 100$$

$$= 145.02.$$

These new price indices can also be calculated with the new base year of 1993 without using the gasoline price data by using only the old price indices with 1990 as the base year. That is, in general:

$$\text{New index value for i} = \frac{\text{Old Index number for i}}{\text{Index value of the new base period}} * 100$$

and in particular:

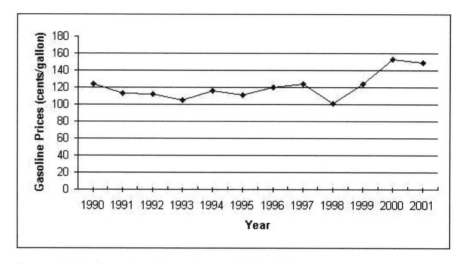

Figure 5.18   Gasoline Prices from 1990 to 2001.

$$\text{New index value for 2000} = \frac{\text{Old Index number for 2000}}{\text{Index value of 1993}} * 100$$

$$= \frac{123.19}{84.94}$$

$$= 145.02$$

As a result, it can now be said that gasoline prices increased by 45 percent from 1993 to 2000.

This procedure of changing the base year is very valuable when comparing two or more indices over the time in which these indices are likely not to have the same base year, i.e., they can easily be converted to a similar base year. Using the same base year, it is possible to compare how these prices (or quantities) have changed over time.

5.4.1   Deflating data

Thus far, in this examination of gasoline prices from 1990 to 2001, gasoline prices were seen to go down by almost nineteen cents and to increase by about twenty-nine cents, or correspondingly, using price indices, prices decreased by 10 and increased by 23 percent. Were these changes significant? Should people have been happy with the nineteen cents decrease and upset with the twenty-nine cents increase or were these just minor changes? The key depends on what happened to purchasing power during this time period—can the purchasing power of $1.242 per gallon of gasoline in 1990 be compared to $1.055 /gal in 1993 or $1.53 /gal in 2000?

When analyzing time series data it is often necessary to adjust the raw data to a given point in time. Earlier in Chapter 3, seasonal indices were used to adjust the quarterly data or the data were deseasonalized. (Note that the sum of the four indices added to four.) In addition to seasonal effects, it may be desirable to remove any effects of price changes, i.e., the data may need to be deflated.

Table 5.7 lists the gasoline prices and corresponding consumer price indices (CPIs) for the period 1990 to 2001. The CPI is one of the primary measures of the cost of living in the United States, and is published monthly by the U. S. Bureau of Labor Statistics. The CPI is computed with a 1982–1984 base of 100. In 1990 the CPI was 130.7. This index implies that the cost of living has increased by 30.7 percent since the base period of 1982–1984. Gasoline prices are deflated by dividing the gasoline price in each year by the corresponding CPI value and multiplying by 100, e.g., for 1993 the deflated gasoline price is:

$$\text{Deflated Gasoline Price in 1990} = \frac{\text{Gasoline Price in 1990}}{\text{CPI in 1990}} * 100$$

$$= \frac{124.2}{130.7} * 100$$

$$= 95.03$$

Table 5.6   Price Relatives for One Gallon of Gasoline

	A	B	C
Year	Gasoline Prices (cents/gallon)	Price Relative (Base 1990)	Price Relative (Base 1993)
1990	124.2	100.00	117.73
1991	112.7	90.74	106.82
1992	112.1	90.26	106.26
1993	105.5	84.94	100.00
1994	115.6	93.08	109.57
1995	111.3	89.61	105.50
1996	119.7	96.38	113.46
1997	124.3	100.08	117.82
1998	100.7	81.08	95.45
1999	124.2	100.00	117.73
2000	153	123.19	145.02
2001	148.8	119.81	141.04

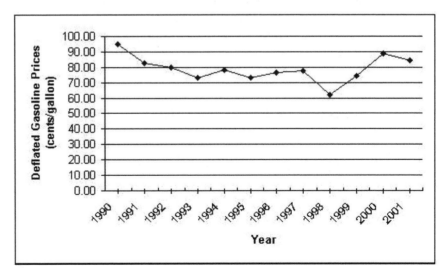

Figure 5.19   Deflated gasoline prices.

Table 5.7   Gasoline Prices, CPI, and Deflated Gasoline Prices

Year	Gasoline Prices (cents/gallon)	CPI (1982 - 1984 Base)	Deflated Gasoline Prices
1990	124.2	130.7	95.03
1991	112.7	136.2	82.75
1992	112.1	140.3	79.90
1993	105.5	144.5	73.01
1994	115.6	148.2	78.00
1995	111.3	152.4	73.03
1996	119.7	156.9	76.29
1997	124.3	160.5	77.45
1998	100.7	163	61.78
1999	124.2	166.6	74.55
2000	153	172.2	88.85
2001	148.8	176.6	84.26

The deflated gasoline prices are listed in the last column in Table 5.6 and are graphed in Figure 5.19. In relation to the base period dollars of 1982–1984, during 1990 to 2001 gasoline cost slightly less and its price has actually decreased. By deflating the gasoline prices it is possible to identify and understand the real dollar changes that are occurring over time.

5.4.2   Aggregate Index numbers

If more than one item is being examined, e.g., gasoline, food, and clothing, it would be nice to have an index that measures the price change for the group of items. An unweighted aggregate index, I_t, in period t for a group of n items is defined as:

$$I_t = \frac{\sum_{i=1}^{n} P_{it}}{\sum_{i=1}^{n} P_{i0}} * 100$$

where

P_{it} = price of item i in period t

P_{i0} = price of item i in base period 0.

However, what if the number of units consumed differs from item to item? For example, let's just say one item, a relatively expensive item, is consumed significantly more than the other items. In such a situation, the unweighted aggregate index would not be a good measure. Because most of the variation is in the quantities consumed, the unweighted aggregate index is not widely used. Instead, analysts use what is called a weighted aggregate index that does consider amounts of quantities consumed. The weighted aggregate index, I_t, in period t for a group of n items is defined as:

$$I_t = \frac{\sum_{i=1}^{n} P_{it}Q_i}{\sum_{i=1}^{n} P_{i0}Q_i} * 100$$

where Q_i is the number of units consumed of item i.

Notice in the equation above that the quantity term does not have a subscript for time period. It is assumed that the quantities are fixed and do not vary, although the prices do. Two extensions of the weighted aggregate index do consider that the quantities vary from time period to time period. One extension calculates a fixed-weighted aggregate index from base-year quantities, i.e.:

$$I_t = \frac{\sum_{i=1}^{n} P_{it}Q_{i0}}{\sum_{i=1}^{n} P_{i0}Q_{i0}} * 100$$

This fixed-weighted aggregate index is called a Laspeyres index. The other extension revises each period by the quantities used, i.e.:

$$I_t = \frac{\sum\limits_{i=1}^{n} P_{it} Q_{it}}{\sum\limits_{i=1}^{n} P_{i0} Q_{it}} * 100$$

This weighted aggregate index is known as a Paasche index. The CPI and producer price index (PPI), two well-known consumer indices, are calculated by using the Laspeyres method.

The National Bureau of Economic Research (NBER) studies the cyclical nature of U.S. business and economic activities and is the source of three major economic indices:

- Index of Leading Indicators: A composite index that attempts to anticipate turning points in the economy.

- Index of Coincident Indicators: A composite index of how the economy is currently performing.

- Index of Lagging Indicators: A composite index that tends to lag behind the economy.

References

Box, G.E.P. and G.M. Jenkins. *Times Series Analysis: Forecasting and Control*. Holden-Day, San Francisco: 1970.

DeLurgio, Stephen A. *Forecasting Principles and Applications*. Irwin/McGraw-Hill, 1998: 326–329.

Farnum, Nicholas R. and LaVerne W. Stanton. *Quantitative Forecasting Methods*. PWS-Kent, Boston: 1989: 475–479.

Gardner, E.S. "Exponential Smoothing: The State of the Art." *Journal of Forecasting* 4 (1985): 1–28.

Pegels, C.C. "Exponential Forecasting: Some New Variations." *Management Science* 12, no. 5 (1969): 311–315.

Chapter 6

Simple Linear Regression Analysis in Forecasting

6.1 Introduction

In this chapter is developed the concept of forecasting in which the forecast variable could be related to another explanatory independent variable. Typically, regression modeling is interested in how variables are related. For instance, a firm may be interested in describing the relationships between its levels of sales revenue and the amount it spends on advertising. It is important for the firm, in its marketing decision making, to be able to identify the effects that differing levels of marketing expenditures have on the sales revenue. The process of explaining this relationship will be described here through the development of a simple linear regression model. In the particular example, the firm's sales will be represented by y, and the level of the firm's marketing effort by x. The y variable will be referred to as the dependent variable, and the x variable, as the independent variable.

6.2 The Simple Linear Regression Model

In the simple linear regression model, the variable to be forecast, y, is referred to as the dependent variable. The value of this variable will depend on another variable, x, the independent variable. When these values are plotted on a graph, the simplest model to relate the dependent variable to the independent variable is a straight-line model. The straight-line model is given by:

$$y = b_0 + b_1 x_1 + e \qquad (6.1)$$

where

    y = dependent variable (the forecast variable)
    x_1 = independent variable (the predictor variable of y)
    b_0 = y intercept
    b_1 = slope of the line
    e = random error

The process of fitting the model may be described as a procedure for estimating the model from a given set of data. The most common statistical estimation technique is the method of ordinary least squares.

In the method of ordinary least squares, the model form is calculated by deciding how well a straight-line model fits the data set, with the object of determining how well the observed data fits the predicted values of y. The least squares line is the one that has the smallest sum of squares of errors compared with any other simple straight-line models. The deviations are the vertical distances between the observed and the predicted values of y.

The sum of squares of the deviations of the y values is given by the following for all n data points.

$$SSE = \sum_{i=1}^{n} [(y_i - b_0 + b_1 x_1]^2 \qquad (6.2)$$

b_0 is the estimate of b_0
b_1 is the estimator of b_1

$$b_1 = \frac{\sum_{i=1}^{n} x_i y_i - \sum_{i=1}^{n} x_i \sum_{i=1}^{n} y_i}{\sum_{i=1}^{n} x_i^2 [\sum_{i=1}^{n} x_i]^2} \qquad (6.3)$$

$$b_0 = \sum_{i=1}^{n} y_i - b_1 \sum_{i=1}^{n} x_i \qquad (6.4)$$

$$y = b_0 + b_1 x_1 \text{ (estimated simple regression model)} \qquad (6.5)$$

6.3 Assumptions Underlying the Simple Linear Regression Model

Listed below are some basic assumptions underlying the general form of the probability distribution of the random error term, e, of the simple linear regression model:

Assumption 1: The mean of the probability distribution of e is 0. This assumption states that the mean value of y for a given value of x is given by $b_0 + b_1 x_1$.

Assumption 2: The variance of the probability distribution of e is constant for all levels of the independent variable, x. That is, the variance of e is constant for all values of x.

Assumption 3: The probability distribution of e is normal.

Assumption 4: The errors that are associated with two different observations are independent of each other.

6.4 Standard Error of the Estimate

An estimator of the variance is a most important quantity in defining test statistics and confidence intervals. The best estimate of the variance is given by s^2, which is obtained by dividing the sum of the squares of the residuals

$$SSE = \frac{\sum_{i=1}^{n}(y_i - y_i)^2}{n-2} \tag{6.6}$$

by the number of degrees of freedom associated with this quantity $(n-2)$. The square root of this quantity is referred to as the standard error of the estimate. This quantity measures the standard amount by which the actual y differs from the estimated (y). The standard error measures the vertical distance from the sample data points to the regression line, and it is used to measure the best-fit regression line. When it is assumed that the data points are normally distributed, the quantity is used as an estimate of that normal distribution.

6.5 Predicting Y

To get a point prediction for a given value of y for a given value of x, the simple linear regression equation is used. The value of x is substituted into the equation and the value of y is calculated.

The standard error of the forecast (SF) is a quantity that measures the variability of predicted values of y around the true value of y given for a value of x, where

$$SF = SSE\sqrt{\frac{1}{n} + \frac{(X_i - \bar{X})^2}{\sum_{i=1}^{n}X_i^2 - n\bar{X}^2}} \approx \frac{SSE}{\sqrt{n}} \tag{6.7}$$

Thus, the forecast error depends upon the value of x for which the forecast is described. The prediction interval for y, when the sample size is greater than 30 or when the sample size is less than 30, is given by y ± zSF or y ± tSF (t distribution with n − 2 df), respectively.

6.6 Correlation

The correlation coefficient is a statistical measure of the association between two variables. The correlation r_{xy} ranges from +1.0 to −1.0. If the value of r_{xy} equals +1.0, then there exists a perfect positive linear relationship between x and y. If the value of r_{xy} equals −1.0, then there is a perfect negative linear relationship between x and y. If r_{xy} equals 0, then there is no relationship between x and y. The correlation coefficient measures the magnitude of the linear relationship as well as the direction of the relationship.

The correlation coefficient between two variables x and y is given by:

$$r_{xy} = \frac{\sum_{i=1}^{n}(x_i - \bar{x})(y_i - \bar{y})}{\sum_{i=1}^{n}(x_i - \bar{x})^2 \sum_{i=1}^{n}(y_i - \bar{y})} \tag{6.8}$$

The simple correlation coefficient is a standardized measure of covariance. A quite important notion is that correlation is not a measure of causation. There must be a true relationship between the variables for causation to exist. Without such a theoretical basis, the variables are said to be spuriously related.

6.7 Coefficient of Determination

To determine the proportion of variance in y that is explained by x, the coefficient of determination is calculated by squaring the correlation coefficient, r_{xy}. Thus,

$$r^2_{xy} = \text{Explained variation/Total variance}$$

6.8 Residuals

The total deviation is given by:

$$\sum_{i=1}^{n}(y_i - \bar{y})^2 \qquad (6.9)$$

In other words, total deviation refers to the sum of squared residuals around the mean of y. The term $(y_i - \bar{y})$ is referred to as the residual.

To determine the error or residual of any observation, the predicted value of y is calculated first. Then the predicted value is subtracted from the actual value.

The total deviation can be partitioned into two parts:

$$(y_i - \bar{y}) = (y_i - \bar{y}) + (y_i - y_i) \qquad (6.10)$$

That is, total deviation equals the deviation explained by the regression deviation plus that unexplained by the regression (residual error). Now let:

$\bar{Y}$ = mean of the total group
Y_i = value predicted with the regression equation
Y_i = actual data

If these values are summed over all values of Y_i (all observations) and squared, then these deviations will provide an estimate of the variation of Y explained by regression and thus unexplained by the regression equation:

$$\sum_{i=1}^{n}(Y_i - \bar{Y}) = \sum_{i=1}^{n}(Y_i - \bar{Y})^2 + \sum_{i=1}^{n}(Y_i - Y_i)^2 \qquad (6.11)$$

Total variation explained = Explained variation + Unexplained variation (Residual).

Thus, it is seen that the residuals represent what cannot be explained with the regression model. After the process of fitting the data to a straight line (least squares regression line), it is of great value to examine the residuals to see that the regression model is appropriate and adequate for the data. To study the residuals, it is quite worthwhile to view a scatterplot of residuals versus the explanatory variable x. If it is seen that a straight line regression is appropriate, then the residuals will not have a relationship with the independent variable x. Thus, the residual plot will show only a random pattern. Residuals that are large in magnitude from the vast majority of the observations are referred to as outliers. Typically an observation is an extreme value with regard to the x variable. These observations are typically called influential observations. If these observations are left out of the fitting process, then the values of the regression parameters will be significantly altered. Influential observations often have small residuals and are usually outliers.

6.9 Statistical Inference on the Slope of the Regression Model

Tests for statistical significance are tests of whether the computed values of the regression coefficients are significantly different from zero (null hypothesis). To determine the statistical significance, regression analysis requires a *t* test be undertaken for each parameter estimate.

The existence of a significant statistical relationship between the x and y variables can be determined by testing whether b_1 (the slope) is equal to zero. If this hypothesis is rejected, then it is concluded that there is evidence of a linear relationship.

The null hypothesis is given as:

H_0: $B_1 = 0$ (There is no linear relationship.)

The alternative hypothesis is given as:

H_1: $B_1 \neq 0$ (There is a linear relationship.)

How is the *t* statistic for testing a hypothesis for a population slope, B_1, using the *t*-test determined? The *t* statistic for this test equals the difference between the sample slope and the hypothesized population slope, divided by the standard error of the slope.

$$t = \frac{b_1 - B_1}{S_{b_1}} \tag{6.12}$$

$$S_{b1} = S_{yx} / \text{SQRT} (SS_x) \tag{6.13}$$

$$SS_x = \sum_{i=1}^{n} (X_i - X)^2 \tag{6.14}$$

$$S_{yx} = \text{SQRT} (MSE) \tag{6.15}$$

$$MSE = \frac{\sum_{i=1}^{n} (Y_i - Y_i)}{(n-2)} \tag{6.16}$$

The test statistic, *t*, follows a *t* distribution with (n − 2) df.

An alternative to the *t* statistic is the F statistic for testing whether the slope is significant. If so, the F statistic is equal to the regression mean squares (MSR) divided by the error mean square, where

$$MSR = \frac{SSR}{k} \tag{6.17}$$

and

$$MSE = \frac{SSE}{(n-k-1)} \tag{6.18}$$

Here, k is the number of explanatory variables in the regression.

The F-test statistic follows an F distribution with k and n-k-1 df. Using a level of significance, α, the decision rule for this hypothesis is:

Reject H_0 if F > F_0. Here, F_0 is the upper tailed critical value from the F distribution with k and n-k-1 df. Otherwise, do not reject H_0.

The ANOVA table for testing the significance of the regression slope parameter is given by Table 6.1.

Table 6.1   The ANOVA Table for Testing The Significance of the Regression Slope Parameter

Source of Variation	Df	Sum of Squares	MS	F
Explained by Regression	K	$SSR = \sum_{i=1}^{n} (Y_i - \bar{Y})^2$	$MSR = \dfrac{SSR}{k}$	$F = \dfrac{MSR}{MSE}$
Error	n-k-1	$SSE = \sum_{i=1}^{n} (Y_i - Y_i)^2$	$MSE = \dfrac{SSE}{(n-k-1)}$	
Total	n-1	$SST = \sum_{i=1}^{n} (Y_i - \bar{Y})^2$		

6.10 Testing for First-Order Autocorrelation

One of the basic assumptions of regression modeling is the independence of errors. This assumption is violated when the data underlying the modeling process are from sequential periods. A residual at any one point in time may be similar to residuals at adjacent points in time. Negative residuals are more likely to be followed by other negative residuals and similarly, positive residuals are followed by positive residuals. These patterns of residuals are referred to as autocorrelation. In the presence of significant levels of autocorrelation in a set of data, the validity of a fitted regression model is highly questionable.

When the error term in the regression model has a positive degree of autocorrelation, the ordinary least squares procedures are significantly affected.

1. The regression coefficients are no longer minimum variance.

2. The MSE typically seriously under-estimates the variance of the error terms.

3. The estimated value of the standard deviation of the regression coefficients under-estimates the standard deviation of the estimated regression parameters.

4. The applicability of the statistical tests of significance is under serious question.

It is quite important that the presence of autocorrelated errors be deleted. The simple linear regression model for one variable, when the random error terms follow a first-order autoregressive process, is given by

$$y_t = b_0 + b_1 + e_e \tag{6.19}$$

$$e_e = pe_{t-1} + u_i \tag{6.20}$$

where p is a parameter such that $|p| < 1$ and u_i are independently distributed normal random variables, $N(0,\sigma^2)$. The parameter p is called the autocorrelated parameter.

6.10.1   The Durbin-Watson Statistic

In addition to using a graphical view of the residual plots, autocorrelation can be detailed and measured by using the Durbin-Watson statistic. The Durbin-Watson test for autocorrelation assumes the first-order autoregressive error model, with the values of the independent variable fixed. The statistical test determines whether or not the autocorrelation parameter is zero. When the error terms are zero, the distance term u_t is independent.

The hypotheses are as follows:

H_0: p = 0

H_1: p ≠ 0

The Dubin-Watson statistic D is defined as follows:

$$D = \frac{\sum_{i=1}^{n}(e_i - e_{i-1})^2}{\sum_{i=1}^{n}e_i^2} \qquad (6.21)$$

where e_i is the residual at the time period i.

If the successive residuals are positively autocorrelated, the value of D will be close to 2. If there is a negative autocorrelation, then D will be greater than 2 and could even approach its maximum value of 4.

The exact critical values of the Durbin-Watson test are difficult to obtain. However, lower and upper bounds, d_L and d_U, can be obtained from a table (at various levels of significance) such that a value of D outside these bounds leads to a definite decision with regard to the hypothesis. The specific decision rule is:

If $D > d_U$, then conclude H_0.

If $D < d_L$, then conclude H_0.

If $d_L \leq D \leq d_U$, then the test is not conclusive.

Small values of the D statistics indicate that p > 0 (since the adjacent error terms e_t and e_{t-1} are of the same size when they are positively autocorrelated.

Hence the difference in the residuals $e_t - e_{t-1}$ would tend to be small when p > 0, and this is a small value of the Durbin-Watson test statistic.

6.11 An Example of Simple Linear Regression

Consider the data charted in Table 6.2. The data are for 10 months with

    x = advertising expenditure
    y = sales

Table 6.2   Advertising Expenditure versus Sales

Observation	x	y	x^2	y^2	xy
1	10	11	100	121	110
2	7	10	49	100	70
3	10	12	100	144	120
4	5	6	25	36	30
5	8	10	64	100	80
6	8	7	64	49	56
7	6	9	36	81	54
8	7	10	49	100	70
9	9	11	81	121	99
10	10	10	100	100	100
Total	80	96	668	952	789

The firm wishes to determine the relationship between sales and advertising. With:

$$\bar{x} = 80/10 = 8$$

$$\bar{y} = 96/10 = 9.6$$

$$S_{xx} = 668 - 10(8)^2 = 668 - 640 = 28$$

$$S_{xy} = 789 - 10(9.6) = 789 - 768 = 21$$

$$S_{yx} = 952 - 10(9.6)^2 = 952 - 921.6 = 30.4$$

$$r_{xy} = \frac{21}{\sqrt{28 * 30.4}} = 21/29 = 0.724 \text{ or } r_{xy}^2$$

$$\beta = S_{xy}/S_{xx} = 21/28 = 0.75$$

$$\bar{\alpha} = y - \beta x = 9.6 - 0.75(0.8) = 3.6$$

Hence, the regression of y on x is

$$y = 3.6 + 0.75x$$

Because x is advertising budget and y is sales, the slope coefficient 0.75 measures the marginal value of advertising. The intercept, 3.6, means that sales will be 3.6 when advertising is zero! Clearly this does not make sense. However, this anomaly merely illustrates the point made earlier, that one should not try to get predicted values of y too far out of the range of sample values. Here, x ranges from 5 to 10.

As for the reverse regression:

$$\beta = S_{xy}/S_{yy} = 21/30.4 = 0.69 \text{ and:}$$

$$\bar{\alpha} = x \, \beta \, y = 8.0 - 9.6(0.69) = 1.37.$$

Therefore the regression of x on y is:

$$x = 1.37 + 0.69y$$

Per the calculation of standard errors, consider the data above. Earlier, the regression equation of y on x was obtained as:

$$y = 3.6 + 0.75x$$

The standard errors of α and β are obtained by:

1. Computing the variances of α and β in terms of σ^2.

2. Substituting $\sigma^2 = RSS/(n-2)$ for σ^2.

3. Taking the square root of the resulting expressions gives:

$$\bar{V}(\alpha) = \sigma^2 \left(\frac{1}{n} + \frac{x^2}{S_{xx}} \right) = \sigma^2 \left(\frac{1}{10} + \frac{64}{28} \right) = 2.39 \, \sigma^2$$

$$V(\beta) = \frac{\sigma^2}{S_{xx}} = \frac{\sigma^2}{28} = 0.036 \, \sigma^2$$

$$\sigma^2 = \frac{1}{n} \left(\frac{S_{yy} - S_{xy}^2}{S_{xx}} \right) = \frac{1}{8} \left(\frac{30.4 - 21^2}{28} \right) = 1.83$$

$$SE(\alpha) = \sqrt{(2.39)(1.83)} = 2.09$$

$$SE(\beta) = \sqrt{(0.036)(1.83)} = 0.256$$

The standard errors are usually presented in parentheses under the estimates of the regression coefficients. Confidence intervals for α, β, and σ^2 can also be calculated:

Given that $(\alpha - \alpha)/SE(\alpha)$ and $(\beta - \beta)/SE(\beta)$ have *t*-distributions with n–2 df, using the table of the *t*-distribution with n–2 = 8 df, gives:

$$\text{Prob}[\,-2.306 < (\alpha - \alpha)/SE(\alpha) < 2.306\,] = 0.95$$

$$\text{Prob}[\,-2.306 < (\beta - \beta)/SE(\beta) < 2.306\,] = 0.95$$

These expressions give confidence intervals for α and β. Simplifying the expressions gives the 95-percent confidence limits of α and β as $(-1.22, 8.42)$ and $(0.16, 1, 34)$, respectively. Note that the 95-percent confidence limits for α are $\alpha \pm 2.306\ SE(\alpha)$, and for β are $\beta \pm 2.306\ SE(\beta)$. Although it is not often used, the procedure of finding a confidence interval for σ^2 will also be illustrated. It is known that RSS/σ^2 has a X^2-distribution with (n–2) df, so the tables of the X^2-distribution can be used to acquire any required confidence interval. Suppose that a 95-percent confidence interval is desired.

$$\text{Then } RSS = (n-2)\ \sigma^2$$

From the tables of the X^2-distribution with 8 degrees of freedom, it is found that the probability of obtaining a value <2.18 is 0.025 and of obtaining a value >17.53 is 0.025. Hence,

$$\text{Prob}[2.18 < 8\sigma^2/\sigma^2 < 17.53] = 0.95$$

or

$$\text{Prob}[8\sigma^2/17.53 < \sigma^2 < 8\sigma^2/2.18] = 0.95$$

With $\sigma^2 = 1.83$, substituting this value gives the 95-percent confidence limits for σ^2 as $(0.84, 6.72)$.

Note that the confidence intervals for α and β are symmetric around α and β, respectively, because the *t*-distribution is a symmetric distribution., which it is not with the confidence interval for σ^2.

The confidence intervals obtained for α, β, and σ^2 are all very wide. Narrower intervals can be produced by reducing the confidence coefficient. For instance, the 80-percent confidence limits for β are

$$\beta \pm 1.397\ SE(\beta)$$

$\text{Prob}(-1.397 < t < 1.397) = 0.80$ from the t-tables with 8 df, so the 80-percent confidence limits for β are:

$$0.75 \pm 1.397(0.256) = (0.39, 1.11).$$

The confidence intervals here constructed are two-sided intervals. Sometimes, upper and lower limits are needed for β, so one-sided intervals are constructed. For instance, the t-tables with 8 df, gives:

$$\text{Prob}\ (t < 1.86) = 0.95$$

and

$$\text{Prob}\ (t > -1.86) = 0.95$$

Hence, for a one-sided confidence interval, the upper limit for β is

$$\beta + 1.86\ SE(\beta) = 0.75 + 1.86(0.256) = 0.75 + 0.48 = 1.23.$$

The upper 95-percent confidence interval is then $(-\infty, 1.23)$. Similarly, the lower limit for β is

$$\beta - 1.86\ SE(\beta) = 0.75 - 1.86(0.256) = 0.75 - 0.48 = 0.27.$$

Thus, the lower 95-percent confidence interval is $(0.27, +\infty)$.

Further examples of the use of one-sided intervals will be given after a discussion of tests of hypotheses.

6.12 Hypothesis Testing

Turning to the problem of hypothesis testing, suppose it is necessary to test the hypothesis that the true value of β is 1.0. It is known that:

$$t_0 = (\hat{\beta} - \beta) / SE(\hat{\beta})$$

has a *t*-distribution with $(n-2)$ degrees of freedom.

Let t_0 be the observed t-value. If the alternative hypothesis is $\beta \neq 1$, then $|t_0|$ is considered as the test statistic. Hence, if the true value of β is 1.0, then:

$$t_0 = \frac{0.75 - 1.0}{0.256} = -0.98$$

Hence, $|t_0| = 0.98$. The t-tables for 8 degrees of freedom show that:

$$Prob\,(t > 0.706) = 0.25$$

$$Prob\,(t > 1.397) = 0.10$$

Thus, the probability that $t > 0.98$ is roughly 0.19 (by linear interpolation) or the probability that $|t_0| = 0.98$ is 0.38. This probability is not very low, and the hypothesis that β equals 1.0 is not rejected. It is customary to use 0.05 as a low probability and to reject the suggested hypothesis if the probability of obtaining an extreme t-value as the observed t_0 is less than 0.05. Here, either the suggested hypothesis is not true or it is true, but an improbable event has occurred.

Note that for 8 degrees of freedom, the 5-percent probability points are ± 2.306 for a two-sided test and ± 1.86 for a one-sided test. Thus, if both high and low t-values are to be considered as evidence against the suggested hypothesis, it is rejected if the observed t_0 is > 1.86 or < –1.86, depending on the suggested direction of deviation.

Although it is customary to use the 5-percent probability level for rejection of the suggested hypothesis, there is nothing sacred about this number. The theory of significance tests with the commonly used significance levels of 0.05 and 0.01 owes its origins to the famous British statistician Sir R. A. Fisher (1890 – 1962). He is considered the father of modern statistical methods, and the numbers 0.05 and 0.01 suggested by him have been adopted universally.

Another point to note is that the hypothesis being tested (here, $\beta = 1$) is called the null hypothesis. Again, the terminology is misleading and owes its origin to the fact that the initial hypotheses tested were that some parameters were zero. Thus, a hypothesis $\beta = 0$ can be called a null hypothesis but not a hypothesis $\beta = 1$. For the present the standard terminology will be continued, the hypothesis tested will be called the null hypothesis, and the standard significance levels of 0.05 and 0.01 will be used.

Finally, it should be noted that there is a correspondence between the confidence intervals derived earlier and tests of hypotheses. For instance, the 95-percent confidence interval we derived earlier for $\beta = \beta_0$, where β_0 is in this interval, will not be rejected at the 5-percent level for a two-sided test. However, the hypothesis $\beta = 1.35$ or $\beta = 0.10$ will be rejected. For one-sided tests, one-sided confidence intervals are considered to be suitable.

It is also customary to term some regression coefficients as "significant" or "not significant" depending on the t-ratios, and asterisks are attached to them if they are significant. This procedure should be avoided. For instance, in our illustrative example, the regression equation is sometimes presented as:

$$y = 3.6 + 0.75^* x$$
$$(2.09) \ (0.256)$$

The * on the slope coefficient indicates that it is "significant" at the 5-percent level. However, this statement means "it is significantly different from 'zero'", and this statement is meaningful only if the hypothesis being tested is $\beta = 0$. Such a hypothesis would not be meaningful in many instances. For instance, if x = advertising expenditure and y = sales, then a hypothesis $\beta = 0$ does not make any sense. Similarly, if y is a post-training score and x is a pre-training score, a hypothesis $\beta = 0$ would mean that the pre-training score has no effect on the post-training score, and no one would be interested in testing such an extreme hypothesis.

6.13 Example Problems in Excel 2007 for Simple Linear Regression Forecasting

In this section, three examples of the use of simple linear regression using the tools of Excel 2007 are given. The first example uses specific Excel functions, which include intercept, slope, R-square, forecast, and trend in the regression computation. These functions use the LINEST Command. The second example makes use of the regression analysis of Excel 2007. The third example makes use of the linear trend line feature of Excel 2007.

6.13.1 Regression Analysis—Problem 1 in Excel 2007

Imagine that your job in the sales and marketing department includes marketing analysis, such as developing regression models to predict sales of products based on various levels of advertising. You believe that one particular product's sales are significantly influenced by the amount of radio advertising conducted. You have 12 months of past history, i.e. radio spots aired relative to sales, charted in Table 6.3.

Part 1

1. Determine the intercept, slope, R-square, and standard error of estimate.

2. Predict the sales revenue for 50, 70, 90, and 110 radio spots.

Table 6.3   Sales History

Sales ($100,000's)	Radio Spots
1260	50
1286	70
1279	60
1310	90
1450	120
1428	80
1315	111
1463	107
1370	47
1426	106
1315	93
1304	86

Part 2

Use the LINEST function to determine the following statistical summary measures:

1. Slope

2. Standard error of the slope

3. R-square

4. F-statistic

5. Sum of the squares of the regression

6. Intercept

7. Standard error of the intercept

8. Standard error of the estimate

9. Degrees of freedom

10. Sum of the squares of the residuals

6.13.2   Solution of Problem 1

Part 1 (refer to Figure 6.1)

Enter the data into the Excel spreadsheet in cells A2:B13 (as shown).

1. The intercept, slope, R-square, and standard error of estimate can be determined by use of the following functions:

$$=INTERCEPT(A2:A13,B2:B13)$$

$$=SLOPE(A2:A13,B2:B13)$$

$$=RSQ(A2:A13,B2:B13)$$

$$=STEYX(A2:A13,B2:B13)$$

Note that the syntax for these functions, as well as the others to be used below, requires the dependent (y) variable's values be stated first, followed by the independent (x) variable's values. That is, the syntax is =FUNCTION(known y-values, known x-values). These functions are entered into cells F2:F5. See Figure 6.1.

2. Sales revenue can be predicted in three different ways.

A. The regression model is of the form $y = b_0 + b_1x$, so the slope (b_1) and intercept (b_0) values can be used from part (a). Enter the value of the independent variable (x), the number of radio spots, into cell D9. In Figure 6.1, the value 90 is used. Then enter the formula:

$$=F2+F3*D9 \text{ into cell F9.}$$

B. The second means of predicting sales is with the forecast function. Enter the value of the independent variable into cell D11. Then enter the formula:

$$=FORECAST(D11,A2:A13,B2:B13)$$

into cell F11. The syntax requires the value of the independent variable used for the prediction to precede the values of the known dependent and independent variables. It should be noted that the forecast function can only be used for simple linear regression.

C. The third approach is to use the trend function. This is an array function, and the steps outlined here must be followed in sequence for the function to work. First, enter the four levels of radio advertising into cells D13:D16 that are to be used to predict sales dollars. Then enter the formula:

$$=TREND(A2:A13,B2:B13,D13:D16,1)$$

into cells F13:F16. Here, the syntax is slightly different, with the values of the independent variable that are used for the forecast following the values of the known dependent and independent variables. Also, the last term is used to either include, or not include an intercept value. Placing 1 in this position, or omitting a value, includes the intercept and placing a 0 does not (i.e. the regression is forced through the origin). Here, the intercept term is to be included. The last step is to select (highlight) cells F13:F16, press F2 (edit), simultaneously hold down Control and Shift and press Enter. The predicted values will then appear in their respective cells. Brackets will also be seen around the trend function in the formula bar, which indicates that the input was entered properly. Note that this function can be used for multiple regression problems (two or more independent variables).

Part 2 (refer to Figure 6.2)

The LINEST function determines the statistics for a line. The function uses the "least squares" method to calculate the best straight-line fit of the data, returning an array that describes the line. The function must, therefore, be entered as an array similar to the TREND function in Part 1. The LINEST function can also be used for multiple regression analysis. The syntax for this function is =LINEST(known y's, known x's, constant, statistics). The y's and x's are (as usual) the known values of the dependent and independent variables, respectively. The constant is a logical value; 1 (includes a constant, b_0) or 0 (forces regression line through the origin). The statistics are also logical values, which allows the user to specify whether additional summary statistics are to be calculated. If this logical value is 0 or is omitted, the function only returns the slope and intercept (if appropriate). For a more detailed description of the function, refer to Microsoft Excel Help.

	A Sales ($100,000's)	B Radio Spots	C	D	E	F Value	G	H Function (column F)
2	1260	50				1207.3289		=INTERCEPT(A2:A13,B2:B13)
3	1286	70				1.6844		=SLOPE(A2:A13,B2:B13)
4	1279	60				0.3137		=RSQ(A2:A13,B2:B13)
5	1310	90				63.3257		=STEYX(A2:A13,B2:B13)
6	1450	120						
7	1428	80						
8	1315	111		Radio Spots		Predicted Sales ($100,000)		Function (column F)
9	1463	107		90		1359		=F2+F3*D9
10	1370	47						
11	1426	106		90		1359		=FORECAST(D11,A2:A13,B2:B13)
12	1315	93						
13	1304	86		50		1292		{=TREND(A2:A13,B2:B13,D13:D16,1)}
14				70		1325		{=TREND(A2:A13,B2:B13,D13:D16,1)}
15				90		1359		{=TREND(A2:A13,B2:B13,D13:D16,1)}
16				110		1393		{=TREND(A2:A13,B2:B13,D13:D16,1)}

Figure 6.1 Values and formulas for Problem 1, Part 1.

	A Sales ($100,000's)	B Radio Spots	C	D Function Description	E
2	1260	50		Slope	Intercept
3	1286	70		Std Error of Slope	Std Error of Intercept
4	1279	60		R-square	Std Error of Estimate
5	1310	90		F	df
6	1450	120		SS Regression	SS Residuals
7	1428	80			
8	1315	111		Function Syntax	
9	1463	107		{=LINEST($A$2:$A$13,$B$2:$B$13,1,1)}	{=LINEST($A$2:$A$13,$B$2:$B$13,1,1)}
10	1370	47		{=LINEST($A$2:$A$13,$B$2:$B$13,1,1)}	{=LINEST($A$2:$A$13,$B$2:$B$13,1,1)}
11	1426	106		{=LINEST($A$2:$A$13,$B$2:$B$13,1,1)}	{=LINEST($A$2:$A$13,$B$2:$B$13,1,1)}
12	1315	93		{=LINEST($A$2:$A$13,$B$2:$B$13,1,1)}	{=LINEST($A$2:$A$13,$B$2:$B$13,1,1)}
13	1304	86		{=LINEST($A$2:$A$13,$B$2:$B$13,1,1)}	{=LINEST($A$2:$A$13,$B$2:$B$13,1,1)}
14					
15				Function Value	
16				1.6844	1207
17				0.7879	69.4205
18				0.3137	63.3257
19				4.5703	10
20				18328	40101

Figure 6.2 Values and formulas for Problem 1, Part 2.

To obtain the desired information:

- Enter the data into the Excel spreadsheet in cells A2:B13.

- Enter =LINEST($A$2:$A$13, $B$2:$B$13,1,1) in cell D16. The dollar signs ($) are used to freeze rows and columns so that the formulas can be copied and pasted.

- Copy and paste the formula so that it appears in cells D16:E20.

- Select (highlight) cells D16:E20, press F2 (edit), then simultaneously hold down Control and Shift and press Enter. The predicted values will appear in their respective cells. Brackets will again appear around the linest function in the formula bar just as they did with the trend function.

- The summary statistics will appear in the sequence: slope, intercept, standard error slope, standard error intercept, R-square, standard error estimate, F-statistic, degrees of freedom, sum of squares regression, and sum of squares residuals.

6.13.3 Regression Analysis—Problem 2 in Excel 2007

As an analyst in the sales and marketing department, assume you have been asked to perform a regression analysis of advertising expenditure versus market share. This analysis is to be presented to the VP of sales and marketing, who will very likely pass it along to the executive committee of the corporation. You have decided to examine the last 11 quarters of data, given in Table 6.4.

The regression analysis can be performed, using the regression analysis tool. The corresponding regression charts (residual and linear fit plots should be included). Then the forecast market share for an advertising budget of five million dollars is to be determined.

6.13.4 Solution of Problem 2

Regression Analysis—Summary Output and Residuals

The regression analysis tool performs simple or multiple linear regression analysis using the least squares method to fit a line through the data set. This problem is one of simple linear regression, i.e., one independent variable. An outline for using this tool is given below.

Table 6.4   Expenditure versus Market Share

Market Share (%)	Advertising Expense ($MM)
7.0	6.0
6.6	4.7
7.3	9.1
7.5	7.5
6.6	3.2
6.7	6.8
5.9	2.8
5.6	4.2
6.2	7.9
6.9	8.5
6.3	3.8

1. Enter the data in columns on the spreadsheet (Figure 6.3).

2. From the Tools menu, choose Data Analysis, which brings up a dialogue box listing several options. Scroll down and select Regression by highlighting it and then clicking OK. This sequence will bring up the Regression dialogue box, shown in Figure 6.4.

3. Enter the range of cells containing the dependent variable's values ("Input Y Range:"), including the column heading. This range is B1:B12, and entry can be accomplished by placing the cursor in the range edit box and either (1) manually entering this vector of cells, (2) clicking on the collapse button to the right of the range edit box and then highlighting (or entering) the vector of cells, or (3) simply highlighting the vector of cells directly.

4. Similarly, enter the range of cells containing the independent variable's values (including the column heading), A1:A12.

5. Check the "Labels" box, because the column headings of the variables to be used have been included. If the headings had not been included this option would be deselected.

6. Make sure for this problem that the "Constant is Zero" box is deselected because it is not proposed that the regression line be forced through zero.

7. The default confidence level is 95 percent. If another confidence level were desired, this option could be selected and the level changed.

8. The Output options can be a range on the current worksheet, another (new) worksheet, or a new workbook (file). The output is seven columns wide, not including any plots that might be requested. The output is also 18 rows deep, and would increase with addition of more independent variables. Residual information also increases the number of rows required. For this example, the output is to be placed on the same worksheet as the data, beginning in cell D1, which is entered as the "Output Range".

9. Select "Residuals" to obtain the fitted values (predicted y's) and residuals.

10. Select "Standardized Residuals". Standardized residuals are simply scaled (divided) by the standard deviation of the residuals. This step usually helps to more readily identify potential outliers in the data set.

11. Select "Residual Plots". This graph is helpful in assessing whether the functional form of the fitted line is appropriate. The plot of residuals should exhibit a random pattern; otherwise additional modeling may be necessary.

	A	B
1	Adv Exp ($MM)	Mkt Share (%)
2	6.0	7.0
3	4.7	6.6
4	9.1	7.3
5	7.5	7.5
6	3.2	6.6
7	6.8	6.7
8	2.8	5.9
9	4.2	5.6
10	7.9	6.2
11	8.5	6.9
12	3.8	6.3

Figure 6.3 Data in Excel, Problem 2.

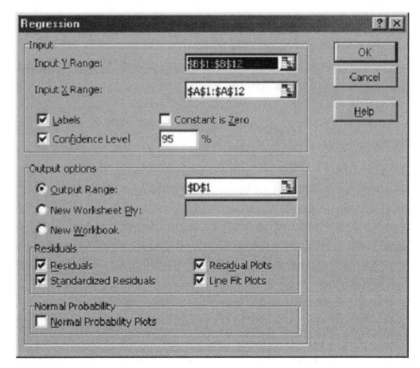

Figure 6.4 Regression dialog box.

12. Select "Line Fit Plots". This option generates a scatter plot of the x and y variables plus the fitted (predicted) y values.

13. Do not select "Normal Probability Plots" because this option is improperly implemented.

14. Finally, click "OK". The summary output and charts should appear. Note that in certain instances the error message "Cannot add chart to a shared workbook" may be received. To deal with this message, click "OK" and change the output options to a new workbook. The results can always be copied (cut) and pasted into the original workbook afterward.

15. Not all of the output will be visible, e.g. cell D6 contains the heading "Adjusted R-square" but the cell width is too small to see the data in full. The column widths can be changed so that all the output is visible. The cells that are too small are D6, E24, F16, G24, I11, and J16:L16. To enlarge the cells, click on D6, then hold down the Control key while clicking on the other seven cells. From the Format menu select "Column" and then "Autofit Selection." The summary output after being formatted is shown in Figure 6.5.

16. The residual output is automatically placed below the summary output. This arrangement is somewhat inconvenient for comparison with the original data (observations), but the residual output can easily be moved or copied and inserted beside the data. To move the residual output, select columns C:E and choose "Insert" from the shortcut menu. The shortcut menu is made visible by holding the Shift key and pressing F10. The columns could also have been inserted (after highlighting C:E) by clicking on the "Insert" menu and selecting "Columns." Now, select the residual output, excluding the observation numbers but including the labels, cells H24:J39. Choose Cut or Copy from the menu bar, select cell C1, and choose Paste. The widths of columns C:E can be adjusted as in step 15. The num-

ber of decimal places displayed in these cells can also be reduced. See Figure 6.6.

Just as in Problem 1 in the previous section for sales revenue, market share can be predicted in three different ways. The FORECAST or TREND functions could be used. However, the regression model, which is of the form $y = b_0 + b_1x$ is already available, and the slope (b_1) and intercept (b_0) values can be used to determine the forecast. The value of the slope (b_1) is contained in cell E18 and the intercept value is in cell E17 of Figure 6.5. Enter the value of the independent variable (x), the \$5MM advertising budget, into cell A13. Then enter the formula =E17+E18*A13 in cell B13. The resulting calculated value in cell B13 is a predicted market share of 6.5 percent.

6.13.5   Regression Charts

For simple linear regression (one independent variable), the regression analysis tool provides the option of creating two charts; residual plot and line fit plot, which were selected in steps 11 and 12 (above). The charts are placed toward the top and just to the right of the summary output (in the ongoing problem, cells M1:S12).

The line fit plot is shown in Figure 6.7. It is similar to a scatter plot but it also includes the predicted values. To reformat this chart so that it shows a scatter plot of the data but the predicted values are transformed to a fitted trend line, follow the steps below:

1. Select the data series for "Predicted Mkt Share (%)" by clicking one of the square markers. The series could also be selected by clicking on any chart object and using the up/down arrow keys to toggle. After making the selection, the points are highlighted and

"=SERIES("Predicted Mkt Share (%)",'2'!\$A\$2:\$A\$12,'2'!\$E\$25:\$E\$35,2)"

	A	B	C	D	E	F	G	H	I	J
1	Adv Exp ($MM)	Mkt Share (%)		SUMMARY OUTPUT						
2	6.0	7.0								
3	4.7	6.6		*Regression Statistics*						
4	9.1	7.3		Multiple R	0.645340425					
5	7.5	7.5		R Square	0.416464265					
6	3.2	6.6		Adjusted R Square	0.351626961					
7	6.8	6.7		Standard Error	0.462561459					
8	2.8	5.9		Observations	11					
9	4.2	5.6								
10	7.9	6.2		ANOVA						
11	8.5	6.9			*df*	*SS*	*MS*	*F*	*Significance F*	
12	3.8	6.3		Regression	1	1.374332073	1.374332073	6.42322	0.032003111	
13				Residual	9	1.925667927	0.213963103			
14				Total	10	3.3				
15										
16					*Coefficients*	*Standard Error*	*t Stat*	*P-value*	*Lower 95%*	*Upper 95%*
17				Intercept	5.627915137	0.408124639	13.78969707	2.34E-07	4.704672358	6.55115791
18				Adv Exp ($MM)	0.165781915	0.065412501	2.53440722	0.032003	0.017808444	0.31375539
19										
20										
21										
22				RESIDUAL OUTPUT						
23										
24				*Observation*	*Predicted Mkt Share (%)*	*Residuals*	*Standard Residuals*			
25				1	6.622606625	0.377393375	0.860010144			
26				2	6.407090136	0.192909864	0.439606127			
27				3	7.13653056	0.16346944	0.37251681			
28				4	6.871279497	0.628720503	1.432738479			
29				5	6.158417264	0.441582736	1.006285901			
30				6	6.755232156	-0.055232156	-0.125863934			
31				7	6.092104498	-0.192104498	-0.437770845			
32				8	6.324199178	-0.724199178	-1.650316832			
33				9	6.937592263	-0.737592263	-1.68083721			
34				10	7.037061411	-0.137061411	-0.312337767			
35				11	6.257886412	0.042113588	0.095969126			

Figure 6.5 Summary output for Problem 2.

appears in the formula bar. Choose "Format", "Selected data series…" then click on the Patterns tab. Select Automatic for Line and None for Marker, and click OK.

2. Select the x-axis by clicking on the horizontal line at the bottom of the plot area. A square handle will appear at each end of the x-axis. Choose "Format", "Selected axis…" and click the Scale tab. Clear the Auto checkbox for all the options. Set the Minimum value to 2 in the edit box. Similarly, set the Maximum to 10, the Major Unit to 2, and the Minor Unit to 0.2. Click on the Number tab and set the decimals to 1, and then click OK.

3. To format the y-axis, click the vertical line and follow the procedure outlined in step 2. Set the Maximum and Minimum to 8 and 5, respectively. Set the Major and Minor Units to 1 and 0.2, respectively. Click on the Number tab and set the decimals to 1 and then click OK.

4. The chart's title and axis labels can be edited by double clicking on them. The text can then be modified, including font style and size, color, etc. The chart can also be resized by clicking on its border and stretching (or shrinking) it or by clicking on the box points with the mouse and dragging. See Figure 6.8.

The residual plot (Figure 6.9) simply needs to be resized. It has been enlarged (Figure 6.10) from approximately 6 standard columns wide by 10 rows high to 17 rows high (no change in width).

6.13.6   Regression Analysis—Problem 3 in Excel 2007

In a manner similar to that in Problem 1 where a regression analysis was performed on the effect of radio advertising spots relative to sales, here it is proposed to consider total advertising expenses relative to monthly sales. Table 6.5 contains 15 months of data, though

	A	B	C	D	E
1	Adv Exp ($MM)	Mkt Share (%)	Predicted Mkt Share (%)	Residuals	Standard Residuals
2	6.0	7.0	6.62	0.38	0.86
3	4.7	6.6	6.41	0.19	0.44
4	9.1	7.3	7.14	0.16	0.37
5	7.5	7.5	6.87	0.63	1.43
6	3.2	6.6	6.16	0.44	1.01
7	6.8	6.7	6.76	-0.06	-0.13
8	2.8	5.9	6.09	-0.19	-0.44
9	4.2	5.6	6.32	-0.72	-1.65
10	7.9	6.2	6.94	-0.74	-1.68
11	8.5	6.9	7.04	-0.14	-0.31
12	3.8	6.3	6.26	0.04	0.10

Figure 6.6   Reformatted summary output for Problem 2.

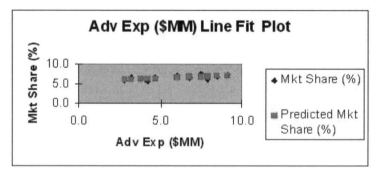

Figure 6.7   Unmodified line fit plot.

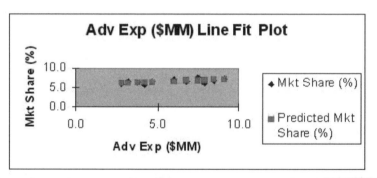

Figure 6.8   Formatted line fit plot.

it should be noted that the months are not regarded as having any effect, i.e. there is no seasonality, so the only explanatory variable will be advertising expense.

Table 6.5   Data for Scatter Plot

Month	Sales ($)	Advertising Expense ($)
1	50,000	1,000
2	60,000	1,790
3	65,000	1,610
4	70,000	1,690
5	75,000	2,001
6	80,000	2,004
7	100,000	2,300
8	108,000	2,770
9	120,000	3,430
10	130,000	3,750
11	154,000	4,750
12	150,000	4,982
13	159,000	6,900
14	168,000	7,940
15	171,000	8,020

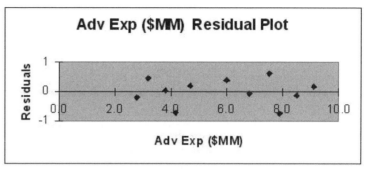

Figure 6.9   Unmodified residual plot.

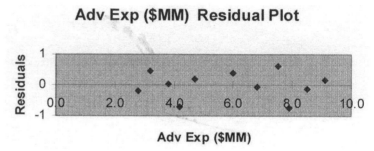

Figure 6.10   Resized residual plot

6.13.7   Solution of Problem 3

Nonlinearity of the Data

A scatter plot can be used to confirm the nonlinear nature of the data set. To construct a scatter plot, enter the data from Table 6.5 into the spreadsheet as shown below in Figure 6.11.

In Figure 6.12, the independent variable, which is total advertising expenses, is entered to the left of the dependent variable, which is sales. Next, highlight cells B1:C16 and click on the chart wizard (or from the tool bar, click on "Insert" and select "Chart"). To use the wizard, select XY (Scatter) chart type, and click "Next" (Step 1, as shown in Figure 6.13). Make sure that the data range is correct and that it specifies that the data is in columns (Step 2 in Figure 6.14).

It is apparent from simply examining the data that it is questionable whether a simple linear model will be appropriate. It is proposed to demonstrate that this is so, then the data will be evaluated, using a polynomial, logarithmic, power, and an exponential model. First it is necessary to decide which model is most appropriate for the given data, then using a $4,000 level of advertising expenditures to make a prediction for sales with each model.

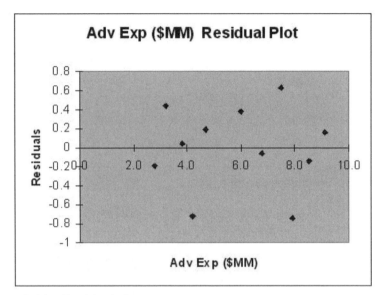

Figure 6.11   Residual plot.

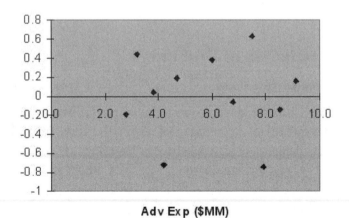

Figure 6.12   Data in Excel for Problem 3.

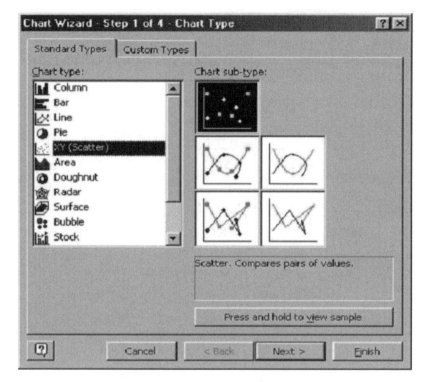

Figure 6.13   Chart wizard dialogue box—Step 1.

The chart title, along with the X and Y-axis labels, can be specified at Step 3 of the wizard under "Chart Options" (see Step 3 in Figure 6.15).

Finally, Step 4 of the Wizard, shown in Figure 6.16, allows the user to specify the chart's location. Use the default, i.e. as an object in Sheet 1 (the current worksheet). Click "Finish."

The chart (scatter plot) can then be viewed on the worksheet, as shown in Figure 6.17.

As can be seen from the scatter plot in Figure 6.18, it appears that a simple linear model may not be as appropriate as a nonlinear model.

Based on the scatter plot, which of the four simple nonlinear models will provide the best fit to the data? To initially help answer this question trend lines can be inserted on the scatter plot by clicking

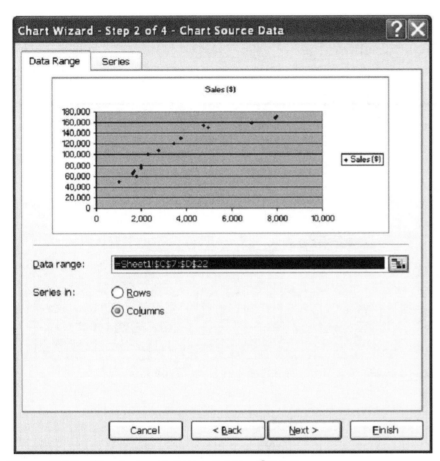

Figure 6.14 Chart wizard dialogue box—Step 2.

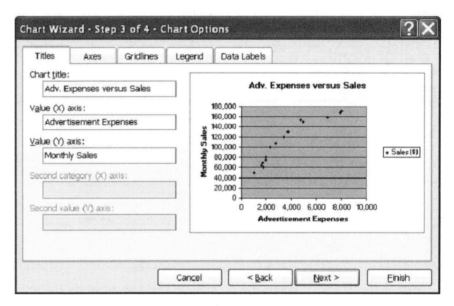

Figure 6.15 Chart wizard dialogue box—Step 3.

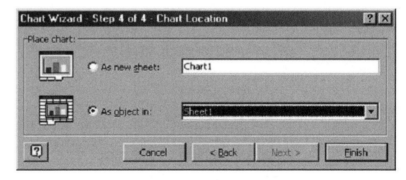

Figure 6.16 Chart wizard dialogue box—Step 4.

on a data point on the scatter plot to select the data series. Then choose "Add Trendline" from the Chart menu (this step can also be done via the shortcut menu, which is activated by right-clicking the mouse). From the Add Trendline dialogue box shown in Figure 6.19, sequentially select the four options being considered (and a linear trendline can be viewed as well). Also, under the "Options" tab of the Add Trendline dialogue box, choose whether to add the linear equation and the R^2-value to the chart, as in Figure 6.20. The scatter plots with the added trendlines are shown in Figures 6.21 through 6.25.

Just from visual inspection it can be said with certainty that neither the linear (as expected) nor the exponential models are the best fit. Of the other three, the logarithmic and polynomial are both better fits than the power model. Visually, it is difficult to determine whether the logarithmic or polynomial provide a better model. However, the polynomial model has the higher R^2-value (0.9804).

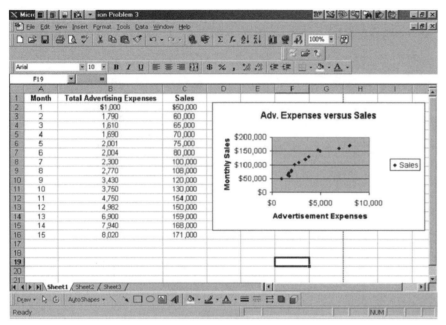

Figure 6.17   Screen view of worksheet.

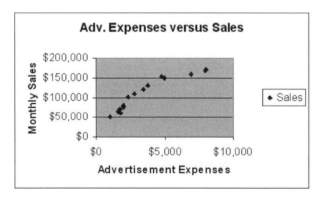

Figure 6.18   Scatter plot.

To obtain more complete regression results of the four nonlinear models, follow the steps outlined for each model below. The data set, A1:C16 will need to be copied to a new worksheet as each of the four models is constructed.

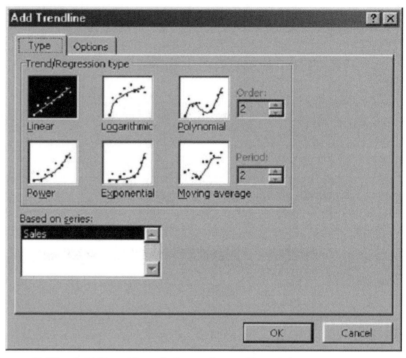

Figure 6.19   Add Trendline dialogue box—Type tab.

6.13.8   Polynomial Model

To construct a polynomial model, specifically a quadratic model, for the data set:

1. Insert an additional column to the left of "Sales". With the active cell as C1 (the title of this column), choose Insert and Columns. Then enter the header title of this new C column as "Advertisement Expenses^2".

2. Select cell C2 and enter the formula =C2^2. Copy this formula down through cell C16. This can be done in a number of ways, the most efficient being to left click and hold on the fill handle when cell C2 is the active cell and then drag the box down

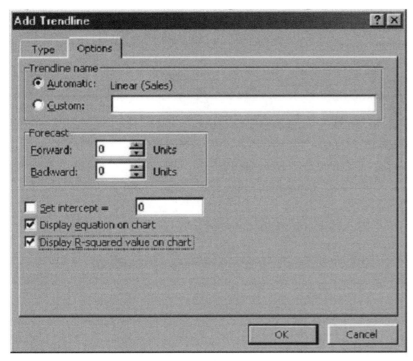

Figure 6.20   Add Trendline dialogue box—Options tab.

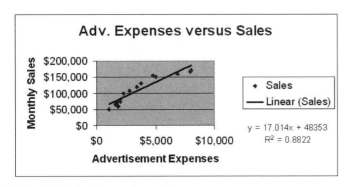

Figure 6.21   Plot with linear trendline.

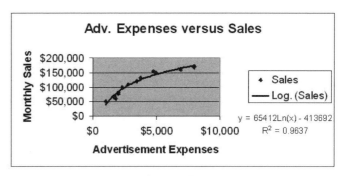

Figure 6.22   Plot with logarithmic trendline.

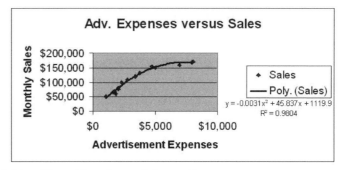

Figure 6.23   Plot with polynomial trendline.

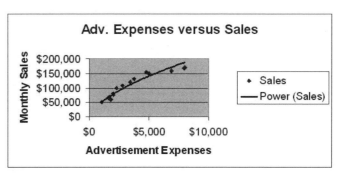

Figure 6.24   Plot with power trendline.

through cell C16. The squared values will appear in cells C2:C16, as shown in Figure 6.26.

3. From the Tools menu, choose "Data Analysis", which brings up a dialogue box listing several options. Scroll down and select "Regression" by highlighting it and then clicking "OK". This brings up the Regression dialogue box.

4. Enter the range of cells containing the values of the dependent variable. ("Input $\underline{Y}$ Range:"), including the column heading. This range is D1:D16.

5. Similarly, enter the range of cells containing the values for the independent variable (including the column heading), B1:C16.

6. Check the "Labels" box, because the column headings of the variables have been included. If the headings had not been included, this option would be deselected.

7. Make sure for this problem that the "Constant is Zero" box is deselected because it is not intended to force the regression line through zero.

8. The default confidence level is 95 percent. If another confidence level was desired, this option could be selected and the level changed, or simply deselected.

9. The Output options can be varied from a range on the current worksheet, another (new) worksheet, or a new workbook (file). The output is to be placed on the same worksheet as the data, beginning in cell E1, which is entered as the "Output Range".

10. Select "Residuals" to obtain the fitted values (predicted y's) and residuals.

11. Select "Standardized Residuals". Standardized residuals are simply scaled (divided) by the standard deviation of the residuals. This action usually helps to more readily identify potential outliers in the data set.

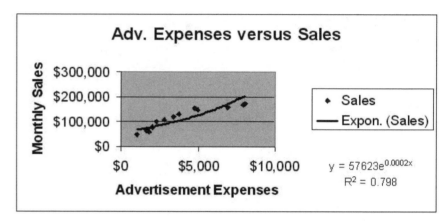

Figure 6.25   Plot with exponential trendline.

	A	B	C	D
1	Month	Total Advertising Expenses	(Total Advertising Expenses)^2	Sales
2	1	1,000	1,000,000	50,000
3	2	1,790	3,204,100	60,000
4	3	1,610	2,592,100	65,000
5	4	1,690	2,856,100	70,000
6	5	2,001	4,004,001	75,000
7	6	2,004	4,016,016	80,000
8	7	2,300	5,290,000	100,000
9	8	2,770	7,672,900	108,000
10	9	3,430	11,764,900	120,000
11	10	3,750	14,062,500	130,000
12	11	4,750	22,562,500	154,000
13	12	4,982	24,820,324	150,000
14	13	6,900	47,610,000	159,000
15	14	7,940	63,043,600	168,000
16	15	8,020	64,320,400	171,000

Figure 6.26   Worksheet with data for quadratic model.

12. Select "Residual Plots". This graph is helpful in assessing whether the functional form of the fitted line is appropriate. The plot of residuals should exhibit a random pattern; otherwise additional modeling may be necessary.

13. Select "Line Fit Plots". This option generates a scatter plot of the x and y variables plus the fitted (predicted) y values.

14. Do not select "Normal Probability Plots" because this option is improperly implemented.

15. Finally, click "OK". The summary output and charts should appear. Note that you could sometimes receive the error message, "Cannot add chart to a shared workbook." To deal with this event, click "OK" and change the output options to a new workbook. The results can always be copied (cut) and pasted into the original workbook afterward.

16. Not all the output will be visible because the cell width is too small to see it in full. However, the column widths can be changed so that all the output is visible.

17. The residual output is automatically placed below the summary output. This arrangement is somewhat inconvenient for comparison with the original data (observations). The residual output can be easily moved or copied and inserted beside the data. The number of decimals displayed in these cells may also be reduced.

The regression output (excluding the plots and residuals) is shown in Figure 6.27. The four nonlinear models can be compared after they have been generated. If the analyst wanted to make a prediction of sales based on a specific advertising expenditure level using this quadratic model, the level could be entered into cell B17 and the formula squaring this value copied down from cell C16 into C17. Then the formula = -0.0031*C17+45.837*B17+1119.9 (which corresponds to the regression equation shown on the plot in Figure 6.23), is entered in cell D17. The predicted sales for a $4,000 advertising expenditure is $134,259 with this model.

If a scatter plot revealed data with an S-shape, a cubic model might be appropriate, i.e. instead of just having x and x^2 as explanatory variables, a third would be added, x^3. Note, though, that the Add Trendline feature may give erroneous results for a third-order model, so it would be recommended to simply use the Regression tool. As an additional exercise, try fitting a cubic model to the data.

	E	F	G	H	I	J	K	L	M
1	SUMMARY OUTPUT								
2									
3	*Regression Statistics*								
4	Multiple R	0.9902							
5	R Square	0.9804							
6	Adjusted R Square	0.9772							
7	Standard Error	6442.8							
8	Observations	15							
9									
10	ANOVA								
11		*Df*	*SS*	*MS*	*F*	*Significance F*			
12	Regression	2	24971221161	12485610581	300.7903348	5.59574E-11			
13	Residual	12	498112172	41509347.67					
14	Total	14	25469333333						
15									
16		*Coefficients*	*Standard Error*	*t Stat*	*P-value*	*Lower 95%*	*Upper 95%*	*Lower 95.0%*	*Upper 95.0%*
17	Intercept	1119.9	6851.075563	0.163464458	0.872873487	-13807.30373	16047.11843	-13807.30373	16047.11843
18	Total Advertising Expenses	45.837	3.78302775	12.11645711	4.34223E-08	37.59438422	54.07940273	37.59438422	54.07940273
19	(Total Advertising Expenses)^2	-0.0031	0.000404101	-7.765421913	5.09236E-06	-0.004018478	-0.002257556	-0.004018478	-0.002257556

Figure 6.27 Regression output for quadratic model.

6.13.9 Logarithmic Model

The logarithmic model creates a trendline using the equation $y = c * Ln(x) + b$. Refer back to Figure 6.23. Ln is the natural log function with base e (approximately 2.718). The log function is defined *only* for positive values of x, therefore the values of the independent variable must be positive. If any x values are nonpositive (either zero or negative), the Logarithmic icon on the Add Trendline Type tab will be grayed out. If this had happened with the data set used here, a constant could have been added to to each x value.

Construction of a logarithmic model for the data set is almost identical to that for the quadratic model:

1. Insert an additional column to the left of "Sales". With the active cell as C1 (the title of this column), choose Insert and Columns. Then enter the header title of this new C column as "Ln(Advertisement Expenses)".

2. Select cell C2 and enter the formula =LN(C2). Copy this formula down through cell C16. The values will appear in cells C2:C16, as shown in Figure 6.28.

3. From the Tools menu, choose "Data Analysis", and select "Regression"to bring up the Regression dialogue box.

4. Enter the range of cells containing the values for the dependent variable ("Input Y Range:"), including the column heading. This range is D1:D16.

5. Similarly, enter the range of cells containing the values of the independent variable (including the column heading), C1:C16.

6. Check the "Labels" box, because the column headings of the variables have been included.

7. Make sure for this problem that the "Constant is Zero" box is deselected because it is not necessary to force the regression line through zero.

	A	B	C	D
1	Month	Total Advertising Expenses	Ln(Total Advertising Expenses)	Sales
2	1	1,000	6.90776	50,000
3	2	1,790	7.48997	60,000
4	3	1,610	7.38399	65,000
5	4	1,690	7.43248	70,000
6	5	2,001	7.60140	75,000
7	6	2,004	7.60290	80,000
8	7	2,300	7.74066	100,000
9	8	2,770	7.92660	108,000
10	9	3,430	8.14032	120,000
11	10	3,750	8.22951	130,000
12	11	4,750	8.46590	154,000
13	12	4,982	8.51359	150,000
14	13	6,900	8.83928	159,000
15	14	7,940	8.97967	168,000
16	15	8,020	8.98969	171,000

Figure 6.28   Worksheet with data for logarithmic model.

8. The default confidence level is 95 percent. If another confidence level were desired, this option could be selected and the level changed, or simply deselected.

9. For the Output options, the output is to be placed on the same worksheet as the data, beginning in cell E1, which is entered as the "Output Range".

10. Select "Residuals", "Standardized Residuals", "Residual Plots", and "Line Fit Plots", but not "Normal Probability Plots".

11. Format the output, as shown in Figure 6.29, as before.

Again, the four nonlinear models will be compared after they have all been generated. Here, if the analyst wanted to make a prediction of sales based on a specific advertising expenditure level using the logarithmic model, the level could be entered into cell B17 and the natural log formula copied down from cell C16 into C17. Then the formula =F18* C17+F17 (which corresponds to the regression equation shown on the plot in Figure 6.22) could be entered in cell D17. The forecast sales for a $4,000 level of advertising expense is $128,838.

	E	F	G	H	I	J	K	L	M
1	SUMMARY OUTPUT								
2									
3	*Regression Statistics*								
4	Multiple R	0.9817							
5	R Square	0.9637							
6	Adjusted R Square	0.9610							
7	Standard Error	8427.9							
8	Observations	15							
9									
10	ANOVA								
11		*Df*	*SS*	*MS*	*F*	*Significance F*			
12	Regression	1	24545957742	24545957742	345.57709	9.53686E-11			
13	Residual	13	923375591	71028892					
14	Total	14	25469333333						
15									
16		*Coefficients*	*Standard Error*	*t Stat*	*P-value*	*Lower 95%*	*Upper 95%*	*Lower 95.0%*	*Upper 95.0%*
17	Intercept	-413692	28291	-14.62286732	1.889E-09	-474810.1116	-352573.29	-474810.1116	-352573.29
18	Ln(Total Advertising Expense)	65412	3519	18.5897039	9.537E-11	57810.21481	73013.67217	57810.21481	73013.67217

Figure 6.29   Regression output for logarithmic model.

6.13.10 Power Model

The power model creates a trendline using the equation $y = c * x^b$. Refer back to Figure 6.24. Excel transforms the original x and y data to determine the fitted values. Therefore, both dependent and independent variables must be strictly positive. Again, if any x or y values are nonpositive a constant can be added.

The power trendline function does not find values of b and c that minimize the sum of squared deviations between actual y and predicted y ($= c * x^b$). Rather, standard linear regression is applied to the logarithm of both sides of the power formula, written as $Ln(y) = Ln(c) + b * Ln(x)$. That is, the intercept and slope that minimize the sum of squared deviations between actual $Ln(y)$ and predicted $Ln(y)$ are determined using the formula $Ln(y) = $ Intercept + Slope * $Ln(x)$. As can be seen in Figure 6.30, the Intercept and Slope correspond to $Ln(c)$ and b values, respectively.

Construction of a power model for the data set is fairly straightforward at this point, and the steps are outlined below:

1. Enter the label "Ln(Advertisement Expenses)" and "Ln(Sales)" in cells D1 and E1, respectively.

2. Select cell D2 and enter the formula =LN(B2). Copy this formula down through cell D16. Similarly, select cell E2 and enter the formula =LN(C2). Copy this formula down through cell E16. See Figure 6.30.

3. From the Tools menu, choose "Data Analysis", and select "Regression" to bring up the Regression dialogue box.

4. Enter the range of cells containing the values for the dependent variable ("Input Y Range:"), including the column heading. This range is E1:E16.

5. Similarly, enter the range of cells containing the values for the independent variable (including the column heading), D1:D16.

6. Check the "Labels" box, because the column headings of the variables have been included.

7. Make sure for this problem that the "Constant is Zero" box is deselected because it is not intended to force the regression line through zero.

8. The default confidence level is 95 percent. If another confidence level were desired, this option could be selected and the level changed, or simply deselected.

9. For the Output options, the election is to have the output placed on the same worksheet as the data, beginning in cell F1, which is entered as the "Output Range".

10. Select "Residuals", "Standardized Residuals", "Residual Plots", and "Line Fit Plots", but not "Normal Probability Plots".

11. Format the output, shown in Figure 6.31, as before.

To make a prediction of sales based on a specific advertising expenditure level with this power model, the value of c in the power formula $(y = c * x^b)$ must be determined. The value of c is determined by raising e to the power of the value of the intercept, $Ln(c)$. Therefore, to accomplish this on the worksheet, enter the formula

=EXP(G17) in cell D18. Cell D18 now contains the value of c. Now enter the expense level for which it is required to predict sales in cell B17. Then enter the formula =D18*(B17^G18) in cell C17. Cell C17 now contains the forecast sales level expected for an advertising expense of $4,000, which is $122,067 using this model.

	A	B	C	D	E
1	Month	Total Advertising Expenses	Sales	Ln(Total Advertising Expenses)	Ln(Sales)
2	1	1,000	50,000	6.90776	10.81978
3	2	1,790	60,000	7.48997	11.00210
4	3	1,610	65,000	7.38399	11.08214
5	4	1,690	70,000	7.43248	11.15625
6	5	2,001	75,000	7.60140	11.22524
7	6	2,004	80,000	7.60290	11.28978
8	7	2,300	100,000	7.74066	11.51293
9	8	2,770	108,000	7.92660	11.58989
10	9	3,430	120,000	8.14032	11.69525
11	10	3,750	130,000	8.22951	11.77529
12	11	4,750	154,000	8.46590	11.94471
13	12	4,982	150,000	8.51359	11.91839
14	13	6,900	159,000	8.83928	11.97666
15	14	7,940	168,000	8.97967	12.03172
16	15	8,020	171,000	8.98969	12.04942

Figure 6.30 Worksheet with data for power model.

	F	G	H	I	J	K	L	M	N
1	SUMMARY OUTPUT								
2									
3	*Regression Statistics*								
4	Multiple R	0.9687							
5	R Square	0.9384							
6	Adjusted R Square	0.9336							
7	Standard Error	0.1068							
8	Observations	15							
9									
10	ANOVA								
11		*df*	*SS*	*MS*	*F*	*Significance F*			
12	Regression	1	2.259813417	2.2598134	197.99155	3.03012E-09			
13	Residual	13	0.14837792	0.0114137					
14	Total	14	2.408191337						
15									
16		*Coefficients*	*Standard Error*	*t Stat*	*P-value*	*Lower 95%*	*Upper 95%*	*Lower 95.0%*	*Upper 95.0%*
17	Intercept	6.506736	0.3586243	18.143599	1.294E-10	5.731975027	7.281496122	5.731975027	7.281496122
18	Ln(Advertising Expenses)	0.627630	0.044604639	14.070947	3.03E-09	0.531267063	0.723991952	0.531267063	0.723991952

Figure 6.31 Regression output for power model.

6.13.11 Exponential Model

The equation for the exponential model is given by $y = c * e^{bx}$. Refer back to Figure 6.25. Excel uses a log transformation of the original dependent variable (y) data to calculate fitted values. Again, this transformation requires that the y values be positive. If any of these values is nonpositive, then the same workaround of adding a constant can be used.

The outline for developing this exponential model is shown below:

1. Enter the label "Ln(Advertisement Expenses)" in cell D1.

2. Select cell D2 and enter the formula **=LN(C2)**. Copy this formula down through cell D16. See Figure 6.32.

3. From the Tools menu, choose "Data Analysis", and select "Regression" to bring up the Regression dialogue box.

4. Enter the range of cells containing the values for the dependent variable ("Input Y Range:"), including the column heading. This range is D1:D16.

5. Similarly, enter the range of cells containing the values for the independent variable (including the column heading), B1:B16.

6. Check the "Labels" box, because the column headings of the variables have been included.

7. Make sure for this problem that the "Constant is Zero" box is deselected because the regression line does not need to be forced through zero.

8. The default confidence level is 95 percent. If another confidence level were desired, this option could be selected and the level changed, or simply deselected.

	A	B	C	D
1	Month	Total Advertising Expenses	Sales	Ln(Sales)
2	1	1,000	50,000	10.81978
3	2	1,790	60,000	11.00210
4	3	1,610	65,000	11.08214
5	4	1,690	70,000	11.15625
6	5	2,001	75,000	11.22524
7	6	2,004	80,000	11.28978
8	7	2,300	100,000	11.51293
9	8	2,770	108,000	11.58989
10	9	3,430	120,000	11.69525
11	10	3,750	130,000	11.77529
12	11	4,750	154,000	11.94471
13	12	4,982	150,000	11.91839
14	13	6,900	159,000	11.97666
15	14	7,940	168,000	12.03172
16	15	8,020	171,000	12.04942

Figure 6.32 Worksheet with data for exponential model.

9. For the Output options, the output is to be placed on the same worksheet as the data, beginning in cell E1, which is entered as the "Output Range".

10. Select "Residuals", "Standardized Residuals", "Residual Plots", and "Line Fit Plots", but not "Normal Probability Plots".

11. Format the output, shown in Figure 6.33, as before.

To determine the value of c for the exponential equation, e must be raised to the power of the intercept value. To accomplish this, enter the formula =EXP(F17) in cell F20. To make a prediction of sales using this exponential model, enter a value for the independent variable (x), advertisement expense, in cell B17. Then enter the formula =F20*EXP(F18*B17) in cell C18 to calculate the predicted sales. The predicted value for $4,000 advertisement expense with this model is $108,129.

Another means of developing an exponential regression model is with the LOGEST and GROWTH worksheet functions, which are similar to the LINEST and TREND functions, respectively. These functions use the equation $y = b * m^x$. Here, b and m corresponds to c and e^b, respectively, in the trendline exponential equation shown in Figure 6.25.

LOGEST provides regression coefficients, standard errors, and other summary measures, and it can be used for multiple regression (two or more independent, x, variables). It is an array function (as is GROWTH) with syntax

=LOGEST(known_y's,known_x's,constant,stats)

where, "const" and "stats" are true/false (1/0) argument values. If "const" is true (1), b is forced to equal 1 and "stats" just indicates whether summary statistics are desired. To obtain the results shown in Figure 6.34, enter the formula

=LOGEST($C$2:$C$16,$B$2:$B$16,1,1)

in cell D1 and then copy and paste it to cells D1:E5. With cells D1:E5 selected (highlighted) press F2. Then hold down the Shift and Control keys simultaneously and press Enter. The same values, except for m, appear as were obtained using the Regression analysis tool (Figure 6.33).

6.13.12 Comparison of the Models

Adjusted R-square comparison criteria are used for the four models, which are summarized in Table 6.6, along with the figures for a linear model. Based on the adjusted R-square values, the quadratic model provides the best fit for the data.

Table 6.6   Models and Adjusted R-square Criteria

Model	Adjusted R-square
Linear	0.8731
Polynomial (quadratic)	0.9772
Logarithmic	0.9610
Power	0.9336
Exponential	0.7824

6.14 Example Problems in Excel 2007 for Simple Linear Regression Forecasting

In this section Excel 2007 regression techniques are employed in simple linear regression. Section 6.14.1 explores the problem of autocorrelation, and section 6.14.2 explores the problem of heteroscedasticity, mentioned in earlier chapters.

6.14.1   Autocorrelation—A Common Problem with Time Series Data

In many regression applications utilizing time series data, the assumptions that the error terms are random and uncorrelated, i.e. independent, may not hold true. Often the error terms are correlated over time. When this is so, the terms are referred to as being auto-correlated. When it is determined that autocorrelation exists, the reliability of the regression model from the least squares fit, and any inferences drawn, are questionable. Some of the specific concerns with autocorrelation are

- the regression coefficients may be inefficient,

- their standard deviation may be underestimated,

	E	F	G	H	I	J	K	L	M
1	SUMMARY OUTPUT								
2									
3	*Regression Statistics*								
4	Multiple R	0.8933							
5	R Square	0.7980							
6	Adjusted R Square	0.7824							
7	Standard Error	0.19346							
8	Observations	15							
9									
10	ANOVA								
11		*df*	*SS*	*MS*	*F*	*Significance F*			
12	Regression	1	1.921624314	1.9216243	51.341572	7.31124E-06			
13	Residual	13	0.486567024	0.0374282					
14	Total	14	2.408191337						
15									
16		*Coefficients*	*Standard Error*	*t Stat*	*P-value*	*Lower 95%*	*Upper 95%*	*Lower 95.0%*	*Upper 95.0%*
17	Intercept	10.96168555	0.094676915	115.77992	5.591E-21	10.75714855	11.16622255	10.75714855	11.16622255
18	Total Advertising Expenses	0.000157349	2.19598E-05	7.1653034	7.311E-06	0.000109907	0.00020479	0.000109907	0.00020479

Figure 6.33   Regression output for exponential model.

	A	B	C	D	E
1	Month	Total Advertising Expenses	Sales	Function Description	Function Description
2	1	1,000	50,000	m	b
3	2	1,790	60,000	Std Error of m	Std Error of b
4	3	1,610	65,000	R Square	Std Error of Estimate
5	4	1,690	70,000	F	df
6	5	2,001	75,000	ssreg	ssresid
7	6	2,004	80,000		
8	7	2,300	100,000	Function Syntax	Function Syntax
9	8	2,770	108,000	=LOGEST($C$2:$C$16,$B$2:$B$16,1,1)	=LOGEST($C$2:$C$16,$B$2:$B$16,1,1)
10	9	3,430	120,000	=LOGEST($C$2:$C$16,$B$2:$B$16,1,1)	=LOGEST($C$2:$C$16,$B$2:$B$16,1,1)
11	10	3,750	130,000	=LOGEST($C$2:$C$16,$B$2:$B$16,1,1)	=LOGEST($C$2:$C$16,$B$2:$B$16,1,1)
12	11	4,750	154,000	=LOGEST($C$2:$C$16,$B$2:$B$16,1,1)	=LOGEST($C$2:$C$16,$B$2:$B$16,1,1)
13	12	4,982	150,000	=LOGEST($C$2:$C$16,$B$2:$B$16,1,1)	=LOGEST($C$2:$C$16,$B$2:$B$16,1,1)
14	13	6,900	159,000		
15	14	7,940	168,000	Function Value	Function Value
16	15	8,020	171,000	1.000157361	57623.48832
17				2.19598E-05	0.094676915
18				0.797953337	0.193463776
19				51.34157239	13
20				1.921624314	0.486567024

Figure 6.34   Worksheet with LOGEST function.

- the mean square error may underestimate the variance of the error terms, and

- any confidence intervals determined would be erroneous, along with any hypothesis tests using either the t or F test.

When autocorrelation is sufficient to make the model no longer reliable, there are remedial measures that can be taken. Remedial measures for autocorrelation include the addition of a predictor variable and transformation of the variables (which is only recommended when the addition of another variable is unsuccessful).

To make this thought a bit more tangible, consider the example below.

Example

Monthly sales for a product from its introduction to the marketplace to date are shown in Figure 6.35. A regression model needs to be constructed to predict next month's sales dollars.

Month	Sales ($000)	Month	Sales ($000)	Month	Sales ($000)
1	16.6	13	60.6	25	112.3
2	15.8	14	73.9	26	123.6
3	17.9	15	77.9	27	120.1
4	27.9	16	83.7	28	127.2
5	35.0	17	95.9	29	130.9
6	35.7	18	105.9	30	137.6
7	43.7	19	106.5	31	148.8
8	57.9	20	97.9	32	158.7
9	57.6	21	98.3	33	158.2
10	54.4	22	102.2	34	163.6
11	57.7	23	101.6	35	162.9
12	65.1	24	111.5	36	?

Figure 6.35   Monthly time series of sales.

The data is first entered, as shown in Figure 6.36, in EXCEL (range A4:B39) and then a time series scatter plot of the data is created. The plot is done via the chart wizard. The trend line is inserted after the scatter plot is created by right clicking on a data point and selecting "Add Trendline…". The plot with trendline is shown in Figure 6.36.

In addition to having a positive trend, the pattern has a cyclical component. A cyclical component results in alternating clustering on the positive and negative sides of the trend line.

Next, the regression analysis is performed, using the Regression Analysis Tool in EXCEL. To construct the model using the Regression Analysis Tool, select "Tools", "Data Analysis…", and "Regression." Complete the resulting dialogue box as shown in Figure 6.36.

6.14.2   Heteroscedasticity: Unequal Error Variance—Identification and Remedy

The condition of unequal error variance is known as heteroscedasticity (in contrast to homoscedasticity or equal error variance). This nonconstancy of error can either be increasing or decreasing systematically. In many business, social science, and biological science applications, heteroscedasticity is not uncommon and a scatter plot of the residuals reveals a megaphone type of pattern, either increasing or decreasing in error variance with the independent variable. Of course, more complex patterns are also possible. Heteroscedasticity is a concern because it causes problems in determining the confidence limits of predicted values. That is, attempts are being made to develop unbiased estimators of the regression coefficients with minimum variance. However, due to heteroscedasticity, the various dependent (y) variable values no longer have the same reliability, and observations with small variance provide more reliable information about the regression function than those with larger variance. There are formal tests for ascertaining whether the error terms have constant variance, such as the modified Levene test and the Breusch-Pagan test. However, simple residual plots can be used, which can include absolute values or squared values of the residuals against the predictor variable, x, or against the fitted values of the dependent variable, y. A means of remediation includes a transformation on the dependent variable, y. However, a simultaneous transformation on the independent variable, x, may be required, to either obtain or maintain a linear relationship. As a footnote, if an appropriate linear relationship already exists, an alternative to transformations is to use a technique known as weighted least squares. The following example shows how to use the residual plots to identify heteroscedasticity. The example then performs an appropriate transformation to remedy the condition.

Example

Data has been collected on the number of visual blemishes on the products from a production line. relative to line speed. Although these blemishes are cosmetically unaesthetic, they cause no disfunctionality in the product. However, it is a concern from a sales standpoint in that an unattractive product is difficult to sell. The object is to be able to predict the number of blemishes per unit at a given line speed. Given the data (Figure 6.37) below, the problem is to construct a simple linear regression model, taking into account any unequal error variance.

6.14.3   Solution of Heteroscedasticity Example

Before starting to build a regression model it might be advisable to visually examine the data using a xy-scatter plot. The steps to construct the scatter plot are outlined below.

1. Enter the data in columns in the spreadsheet as in Figure 6.37. Note that the independent variable, line speed, is entered to the left of the dependent variable, defects.

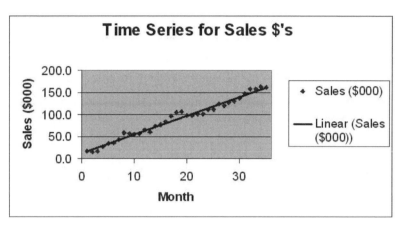

Figure 6.36   Scatter plot with trend line.

Speed	Defects	Speed	Defects	Speed	Defects	Speed	Defects
27	73	32	76	40	70	54	71
21	66	33	69	42	72	57	99
22	63	31	66	43	80	52	86
24	75	34	73	46	83	53	79
25	71	37	78	43	75	56	92
23	70	38	87	44	71	52	85
20	65	33	76	46	80	50	71
20	70	35	79	47	96	59	90
29	79	30	73	45	92	50	91
24	72	31	80	49	80	52	100
25	68	37	68	48	70	58	80
28	67	39	75	40	90	57	109
26	79	46	89	42	85		
38	91	49	101	55	76		

Figure 6.37   Defects versus line speed data.

2. Next, highlight cells A3:B57 and click on the chart wizard (or from the tool bar, click on "Insert" and select "Chart"). Using the wizard, select XY (Scatter) chart type and click "Next" to produce the menu seen in Figure 6.39). Make sure that the data range is correct and that it specifies that the data is in columns as in Figure 6.38.

The chart title, along with the X and Y-axis labels, can be specified at step 3 of the wizard under "Chart Options" (see Figure 6.40).

Finally, step 4 of the wizard allows the chart's location to be specified. Use the default, i.e. as an object in Sheet 1 (the current worksheet). See Figure 6.42. Click "Finish."

The chart (scatter plot) can then be viewed on the worksheet as shown in Figure 6.43.

As can be seen from the scatter plot in Figure 6.44, it appears that heteroscedasticity is a concern with this data set, with variability of the dependent variable (defects) increasing as the explanatory variable (line speed) increases. To remedy this problem, use a transformation on the y variable. The transformation to be employed is y' = 1/y, i.e. the reciprocal of the dependent variable. Note, though, that sometimes a simultaneous transformation of the independent variable is necessary to establish or maintain a linear relationship. Also, other transformations of y might be more appropriate if the relationship had of been curvilinear.

6.15 Regression Analysis—Summary Output and Residuals

For completeness it may be best to first develop the regression model without transforming the y variable. An outline for using the regression analysis tool is given below.

1. Having already entered the data in columns, from the Tools menu, choose "Data Analysis", which brings up a dialogue box listing several options. Scroll down and select "Regression" by highlighting it and then clicking "OK". This brings up the Regression dialogue box, shown in Figure 6.45.

2. Enter the range of cells containing the values for the dependent variable ("Input Y Range:"), including the column heading.

	A Line Speed	B Defects
3		
4	27	73
5	21	66
6	22	63
7	24	75
8	25	71
9	23	70
.	.	.
.	.	.
.	.	.
56	58	80
57	57	109

Figure 6.38   Worksheet with data.

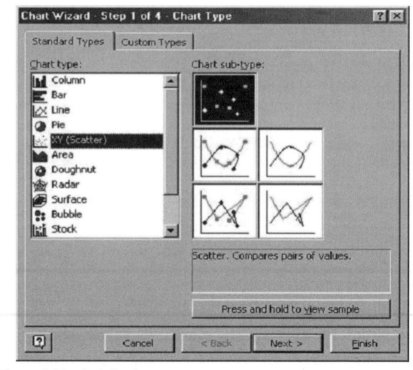

Figure 6.39   Specify chart type.

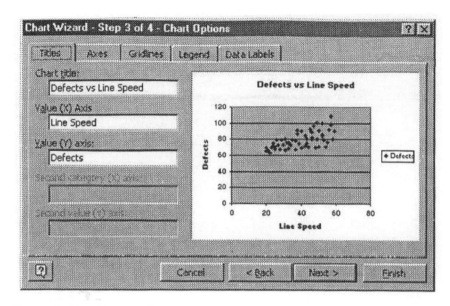

Figure 6.41   Chart options.

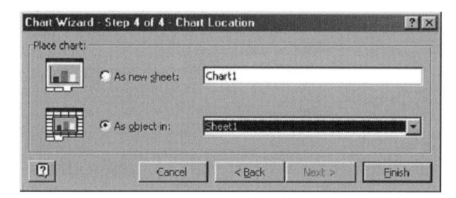

Figure 6.42   Specify chart location.

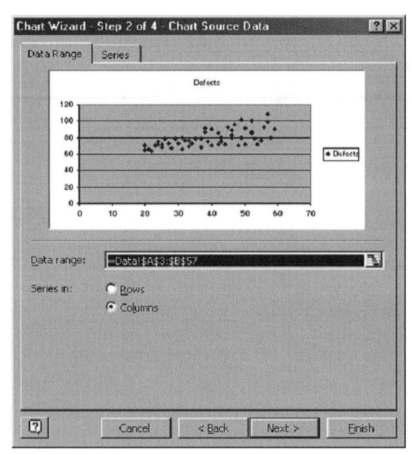

Figure 6.40   Specify data source.

This range is B3:B57. This entry can be accomplished by placing the cursor in the range edit box and either (1) manually entering this vector of cells, (2) clicking on the collapse button to the right of the range edit box and then highlighting (or entering) the vector of cells, or (3) simply highlighting the vector of cells directly.

3. Similarly, enter the range of cells containing the values for the independent variable (including the column heading), A3:A57.

4. Check the "Labels" box, because the column headings of the variables have been included. If the headings had not been included this option would be deselected.

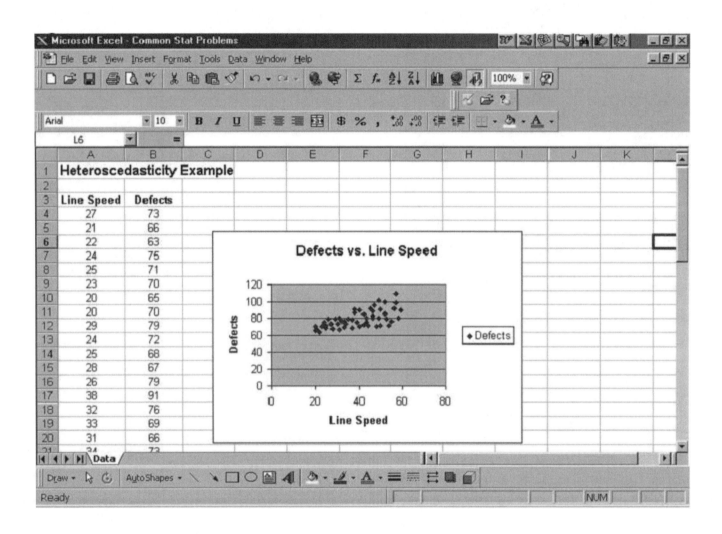

Figure 6.43   Worksheet with scatter plot.

5. Make sure for this problem that the "Constant is Zero" box is deselected because the regression line is not to be forced through zero.

6. Leave the confidence level box unselected because it is inappropriate for the nontransformed data.

7. The Output options can be varied from a range on the current worksheet, another (new) worksheet, or a new workbook (file). The output is to be placed on the same worksheet as the data, beginning in cell D3.

8. Select "Residuals" and "Standardized Residuals". Standardized residuals are simply scaled (divided) by the standard deviation of the residuals. This usually helps to more readily identify potential outliers in the data set.

9. Select "Residual Plots". This graph is helpful in assessing whether the functional form of the fitted line is appropriate. The plot of residuals should exhibit a random pattern; otherwise additional modeling may be necessary. Here, the pattern is not expected to be random.

10. Select "Line Fit Plots". This option generates a scatter plot of the x and y variables plus the fitted (predicted) y values.

11. Do not select "Normal Probability Plots" because this option is improperly implemented.

12. Finally, click "OK", and the summary output and charts should appear. Note that in certain instances the error message, "Cannot add chart to a shared workbook" might be received. To deal with this event, click "OK" and change the output options to a new workbook. The results can always be copied (cut) and pasted into the original workbook afterward.

13. If less than the whole output is visible, the cell widths may be adjusted. The graphs may also be made larger, and reformatted.

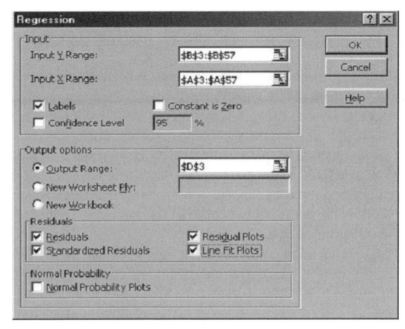

Figure 6.44 Regression dialogue box.

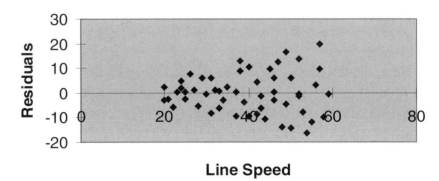

Figure 6.45 Residual plot.

As expected, the residual plot as shown in Figure 6.45, indicates increasing variance, and the R-square for this model is 0.4077.

The 13 steps outlined above are now repeated, using a transformed y variable. First, copy the original data to a new worksheet to avoid overwriting the summary output from the nontransformed model. Next, transform the y variable to its reciprocal. Enter a column heading of "1/Defects" in cell C3. Then enter the formula "=1/B4" in cell C4. Copy this formula down through cell C57. The range C3:C57 now becomes the new range of the dependent variable. Follow the outline above, making the appropriate substitution for the transformed data.

Figure 6.46 shows the residual plot from the transformed model. There is a substantial improvement (compare this plot to that of Figure 6.45). The R-square for this model is 0.4265, which is also an improvement from 0.4077 of the nontransformed model.

From the output summary, the regression equation for the transformed model is $y' = 0.016406 - (9*10-5)x$. To make a prediction using the transformed model, calculate y' for the x (independent variable, line speed) of interest. Then convert y' to y by taking its reciprocal, i.e. y = 1/y', the forecast number of defects occurring at the given line speed. For example, a line speed of 40 results in 78 expected defects.

Note, though that a confidence interval can now be provided for this prediction. A 95-percent confidence level was selected for the regression parameters, and a similar 95-percent confidence interval can be provided for the prediction. This selection is done by using the lower and upper 95-percent values for the slope and intercept. The lower and upper 95-percent values for the intercept are 0.01521 and 0.017602, respectively. The lower and upper 95-percent values for the slope are –0.00012 and –0.000061, respectively. To construct the interval, substitute the lower values for the parameters

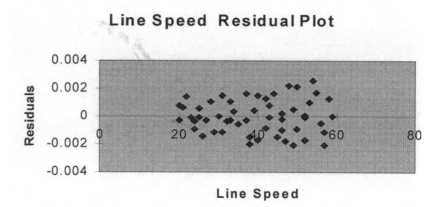

Figure 6.46   Residual plot/transformed model.

using the line speed of 40 and then repeat, using the upper values. The equations and solutions are shown below:

$$y' = b_0 + b_1xy = 1/y' \text{ equations}$$

$$0.010449 = 0.015210 - (11.9*10^{-5})4096 = 1/0.010449$$
$$\text{lower limit (defects)}$$

$$0.015164 = 0.017602 - (6.1*10^{-5})4066 = 1/0.015164$$
$$\text{upper limit (defects)}$$

Do not be confused by the lower limit being a higher value than the upper limit. This effect is simply due to the sign of the slope. Here, the slope is negative, so the lower limit is actually the upper limit in terms of magnitude (and vice versa for the other limit). Therefore, the expectation is that there will be 78 defects at a line speed of 40 but this prediction has a range of 66–96 defects at a confidence level of 95 percent. Stating this prediction a little plainer, for 95 percent of the time (on average) the defect level will fall within the given range at the particular line speed stated.

References

Abraham, B. and J. Ledolter. *Introduction to Regression Modeling.* Brooks/Cole, Belmont, CA: 2005.

Barreto, H. and F.M. Howland. *Introductory Econometrics.* Cambridge University Press, New York: 2006.

Bowerman, B.L., R.T. O'Connell, and A.B. Koehler. *Forecasting Time Series and Regression.* 4th ed. Brooks/Cole, Belmont, CA: 2005.

Weisberg, S. *Applied Linear Regression.* 3rd ed. Wiley, New York: 2005.

Chapter 7

Multiple Linear Regression Analysis in Forecasting

7.1 Introduction

This chapter extends the concepts of Chapter 6, which showed how a forecast variable can be related to a set of explanatory variables. Most situations require the use of a set of independent variables to predict a variable in an accurate fashion. When more than one independent variable is used, the problem becomes a multiple linear regression problem. A firm may be interested in describing the relationship between its sales revenue and the amount it spends on advertising, and the level of competition (the number of competing outlets in its market area). It is quite important for the firm's management to be able to see the effects that differing levels of marketing expenditures and the levels of competitive presence have upon the sales revenue.

7.2 The Multiple Regression Model

Multiple regression analysis modeling is an extension of the simple linear regression model. Although the computation is somewhat more complicated, it makes regression modeling more realistic because forecasting normally depends on multiple factors. The regression equation in multiple regressions has the following form:

$$Y = b_0 + b_1 X_1 + b_2 X_2 + ... + b_m X_m + e$$
$$Y = b_0 + b_1 X1$$

$$(7.1)$$

where

Y = dependent variable (forecast variable)

X_i = independent variable i

b_0 = y intercept

b_i = the slope for independent variable i

e_i = random error

This linear regression model is referred to as being linear in the coefficients. The parameters $b_0, b_1, ..., b_m$ are estimates of $B_0, B_1, ..., B_m$. These coefficients of the model are random variables. The random error e_i is assumed to be normally distributed with a mean of zero and an estimated variance denoted by S_e^2.

The assumptions underlying multiple linear regression models are as follows:

1. For each observation, error term e_i is normally distributed with a mean of zero and standard deviations S_e^2.

2. Each error term is independent of the error term associated with all other observations. The variables X_i are considered to be fixed quantities, but they also are considered to be random variables.

3. The X_i are independent of the error term e_i when it is assumed that X_i are fixed quantitative it is assumed that there is realization of m variables and that the only randomness is Y, which comes from the error term e_i.

7.3 The Multiple Regression Model in Matrix Terms

The following matrices are defined as:

$$Y_{nx1} = \begin{bmatrix} Y_1 \\ Y_2 \\ . \\ . \\ . \\ Y_n \end{bmatrix}$$

$$(7.2)$$

$$\begin{bmatrix} 1 & X_{11} & X_{12} & ... & X_{1m-1} \\ 1 & X_{21} & X_{22} & ... & X_{2m-1} \\ & & ... & & \\ 1 & X_{n1} & X_{n2} & ... & X_{nm-1} \end{bmatrix}$$

$$(7.3)$$

$$\begin{bmatrix} B_0 \\ B_1 \\ B_{...} \\ B_{m-1} \end{bmatrix} \qquad (7.4)$$

$$e_{mx1} = \begin{bmatrix} e_1 \\ e_2 \\ . \\ . \\ . \\ X_n \end{bmatrix} \qquad (7.5)$$

In matrix terms, the general linear regression model is:

$$Y_{nx1} = X_{nxm} + B_{nx1} + e_{nx1} \qquad (7.6)$$

where

y = a vector of responses
B = a vector of parameters
X = a matrix of constants
E = a vector of independent normal variables with expectation
E (e) = 0.

The vector Y has expectation $E_{nx1}(Y)$ = XB.

The least squares normal equations for the general linear equation are:

$$X'Xb = X'Y \qquad (7.7)$$

and the least squares estimates are

$$b_{nx1} = (X'X)^{-1}{}_{mxm}(X'Y)_{mx1} \qquad (7.8)$$

The fitted values are:

$$\hat{Y}_{nx1} = Xb \qquad (7.9)$$

and the residual term is given by:

$$e_{nx1} = Y - \hat{Y} = Y - X_b \qquad (7.10)$$

7.4 Analysis of Variance

In matrix terms, the sum of squares is given by the following

$$\text{SS Total} = Y' - h(1/n)Y'ky \qquad (7.11)$$

Where k is nxn matrix of all 1's

$$\text{SS Error} = Y'Y - b'X'Y = e'e \qquad (7.12)$$

$$\text{SS Regression} = b'X'Y - (1/n)\ Y'kY \qquad (7.13)$$

The analysis of variance for the multiple linear regression model is given in Table 7.1.

Table 7.1   Analysis of Variance

Source of Variation	SS	df	MS
Regression	SS Reg = b'X'Y–(1/n Y'kY)	p-1	SS Reg /p–1 = MSR
Error	SS Error = Y'Y– b'X'Y	n-p	SS Error/n–p = MSE
Total	SS Total = Y'Y–(1/n) Y'	kY	n–1

7.5   F Test for the Multiple Regression Model

To determine whether there is a significant relationship between the y variable and the set of x variables (independent explanatory) (X1… Xp),

The hypothesis is:

$$H_0 : B_1 = B_2 = ...B_{p-1} = 0 \qquad (7.14)$$

$$H_1 : B_1 \neq B_2 \neq ...B_{p-1} \neq 0 \qquad (7.15)$$

The F statistic F* = MS Regression/MS Error   (7.16)

If $F* \leq F(1-\alpha); p \ p-1, n-p$), then H_0 is significant   (7.17)

If $F* > F(1-\alpha); p \ p-1, n-p$), then H_0 is non significant   (7.18)

7.6   Coefficient of Multiple Determination

The coefficient measures the proportional reduction of total variation and is associated with the use of a set of explanatory variables $X_1,...,X_{p1}$. The coefficient is defined as follows:

R^2 = SS Regression / SS Total = [1-SS Error] / SS Total   (7.19)

And $0 \leq R^2 \leq 1$. When $R^2 = 0$, then all the regression coefficients $b_k = 0$. If R^2 is large, it does not imply that the fitted model is a good regression model. Also, adding more x variables may cause the R^2 to increase in magnitude, not reduce the sum of squared

error. It is sometimes suggested that an adjustment for the number of explanatory variables be made. The adjusted R^2_{adj} is defined as the following:

$$R^2_{adj} = \frac{1 - SSError / n - p}{SSTotal / n - 1} \qquad (7.20)$$

The R^2 is adjusted by the appropriate degrees of freedom.
The square root of R^2 is called the coefficient of multiple correlation.

7.7   Inference about the Regression Parameters

The variance covariance matrix is

$$\sigma^2(b)_{pxp} = \sigma^2(X'X)^{-1} \qquad (7.21)$$

The estimated variance covariance matrix is given by

$$\sigma^2(b)_{pxp} = MSE^2(X'X)^{-1} \qquad (7.22)$$

The confidence limits for B_k with $(1-\alpha)$ confidence is given by

$$B_k = t(1-\alpha; n-p) - s(b_k) \qquad (7.23)$$

Testing the hypothesis concerning each B_k, $H_0 : B_k = 0$ and $H_A : B_k \neq 0$. Use the test statistic:

$$t* = b_k / S(b_k) \qquad (7.24)$$

And the decision rule is as follows:

If $|t*| \leq (1 - \alpha/2; n - p)$, then H_0 is true; otherwise, it is not significant.

7.8   Estimation and Prediction

One needs to be very careful in estimation or prediction of a new observation in multiple regression to be sure that the estimation and forecasting do not fall outside the scope of the regression model. The specific danger is that the multiple regression may not be appropriate if it is extended outside the region of observation. The confidence region for a mean of the dependent (Y_m) is

$$\hat{Y}_m = t(1 - \alpha/2); n - p)s(\hat{Y}_m) \qquad (7.25)$$

Prediction of a new value y

$$\hat{Y}_{new} = t(1 - \alpha/2); n - p) + MSE(1 + X'_{new}(X'X)^{-1}X_{new)} \qquad (7.26)$$

7.9   Diagnostics and Their Use in Multiple Regression Models

Diagnostic techniques are important in evaluating multiple regression models, just as they are for simple linear regression. In fact, a number of the same procedures described in Chapter 6 can be applied directly to multiple regression models. These diagnostic techniques include scatter plots and residual plots.

7.9.1   Scatter Plots

The diagnostic procedure of scatter plots is a quite useful measure in regression modeling. Scatter plots of the response variable against each predictor variable aids in determination of the nature and strength of the relationships between each of the independent predicator variables and the dependent response variables. The scatter plot identifies gaps in the data points, as well as outlier points. Additionally, scatter plots of the predictor independent against each other are useful in studying the relationship amongst these variables as well as for finding gaps and detecting outliers.

7.9.2   Residual Plots

A plot of the residuals against the fitted values is useful in assessing appropriateness of the multiple regression function and the consistency of the variance of the error terms, as well as for providing information about outliers. A plot of the residuals against time or some other sequence provides diagnostics information about relationships between the error terms. Additionally, residuals should be plotted against each of the independent predictor variables. These plots provide information about the adequacy of the regression model and about possible variation in the magnitude of the error variance.

7.10 An Example Problem

Given the matrix of data in Table 7.2:

Y = Yearly sales of top stores from 15 cities (in millions of dollars)

X_1 = Number of employees (in 100's of employees)

X_2 = Size of stores (in 100's of square feet)

Find the multiple regression model $Y = b_0 + b_2 X_2$

$$X'X = \begin{bmatrix} 15 & 127 \\ 127 & 1157 \end{bmatrix}$$

$$\hat{B} = 1/1126 \begin{bmatrix} 1157 & -127 \\ 127 & 15 \end{bmatrix} \begin{bmatrix} 173 \\ 1611 \end{bmatrix} = \begin{bmatrix} -3.62 \\ 1.79 \end{bmatrix}$$

$$Y = -3.62 + 1.78 X_2$$

7.11 Another Example Problem

A company has five stores, which sell exercise equipment. The variable Y represents monthly sales in 100,000 dollars. X_1 is the number of people in each town (in 10,000s), and X_2 is the per capita income (in \$10,000s).

$$Y = \begin{bmatrix} 3 \\ 1 \\ 8 \\ 3 \\ 5 \end{bmatrix}$$

$$X = \begin{bmatrix} 1 & 5 & 5 \\ 1 & 1 & 4 \\ 1 & 5 & 6 \\ 1 & 2 & 4 \\ 1 & 4 & 6 \end{bmatrix}$$

Table 7.2   Example Problem Data

	Y	X_1	X_2
1	7	17	9
2	17	39	9
3	10	32	8
4	5	17	4
5	7	25	5
6	15	43	0
7	11	25	8
8	13	32	10
9	19	48	12
10	3	10	5
11	17	48	12
12	15	42	10
13	14	36	10
14	2	30	10
15	8	19	8

$$X'X = \begin{bmatrix} 5 & 15 & 25 \\ 15 & 55 & 81 \\ 25 & 91 & 129 \end{bmatrix}$$

$$X'Y = \begin{bmatrix} 20 \\ 76 \\ 109 \end{bmatrix}$$

$$B = \begin{bmatrix} 15 & 127 \\ 127 & 1157 \end{bmatrix}$$

$$Y = 4 + 2.5X_1 + 16.2X_2$$

$SS\ Total\ = 28$

$SS\ Regression\ = 1.5$

$SS\ Error = 26.5$

$R^2 = 0.95$

$n = 5$

$k = 3$

$Testing\quad H_0 : B_1 = B_2 = B_3 = 0$

$F = 17.67\quad F_{10,.95}(2,2) = 19.0$

Decision: Not significant

95% confidence for B_2

$b_2 = 2.5$

$S^2 = 0.75 = \mathrm{var}(b_2)$

$t_{0,.025}(2) = 4.303$

Confidence interval $2.5 \pm 4.303(.866) = 2.5 \pm .37$

7.12 Qualitative Variable

It is often necessary to determine that a dependent variable is related to an independent variable when a qualitative factor influences a particular situation. This relationship can be developed by using a dummy variable. Qualitative variables, unlike quantitative variables, cannot be measured on a numerical scale. Coded values of qualitative variables are referred to as levels. These coded variables are also referred to as dummy or indicator variables because the numbers assigned to the various levels are selected arbitrarily.

A convenient method of coding variables of two levels involves asssigning a value of 1 to one of the levels and a value of 0 to another.

For example,

$X = 0$ if male

$X = 1$ if female

as shown in Table 7.3.
The regression equation for the qualitative example is as follows:

Monthly sales = 50.1 + 16.2 (for a male)
Monthly sales = 3.85 (for a female)

$R^2 = 78.01$

$F = 25.75$

7.13 Polynomial Regression

Often the relationship between the dependent variable Y and a set of independent explanatory X variables is not a linear relationship. The nonlinear relationship between the variable Y and X can be expressed by the following

$$Y = B_0 + B_1 X + B_2 X^2 + B_3 X^3 + ... + B_m X^m + e$$

where m = the degree of the polynomial relation.

The multiple linear regression covers such situation. Typically, the lowest order polynomial that can be found that adequately relates Y and X should be used. Usually the degree of the polynomial is either (2) or (3). Higher degree models have serious

Table 7.3   Qualitative Variable Coding

Person	Monthly Sales	Sales Mode	Male/Female
1	8,440	200	0
2	7,740	171	0
3	7,570	145	0
4	8,590	176	1
5	7,911	193	0
6	7,044	121	1
7	7,580	154	1
8	8,590	193	1
9	7,850	159	1
10	7,920	150	1
11	8,670	190	1
12	7,930	138	1
13	7,450	155	0
14	8,380	190	1
15	7,680	160	

estimation problems. That is, quite small errors in the data cause very large errors in the estimated multiple regression model.

7.14 Nonlinear Multiple Regression Models

There are many situations in multiple regression data modeling where specific nonlinear model types can be used to process the data effectively by using appropriate transformations. Such models can be transformed. Linear models are referred to as intrinsically linear.

7.14.1   Multiplicative Model

A multiplicative model is given by the following:

$$Y = B_0 + B_1 X_1 B_2 X_2 B_3 X_3 B_m X_m + e \qquad (7.27)$$

The multiplicative model has four independent variables $X_1, X_2, X_3 \, and \, X_4$. The model parameters are $B_1, B_2, B_3 \, and \, B_4$. The multiplicative model can be transformed into a nonlinear model by taking a logarithmic transformation. After taking the logarithmic transformation of the multiplicative model, the following linear model is given in (7.27).

$$\log Y = \log B_0 + B_1 \log X_1 + B_2 \log X_2 + B_3 \log X_3 + ... + \log e (9.27)$$

The expression above is a multiple linear regression model. It is assumed that log e are normally distributed with mean 0 and a variance equal to σ^2, and that for successive observation, errors are independent of each other. Thus, the assumptions of multiple linear regression are satisfied so that significance tests can be performed. An antilog is taken to convert back to the original variables.

7.14.2   Exponential Model

Another transformable model is the exponential model, given in (7.28). Taking natural logarithms of both sides produces the following linear regression:

$$L_n \ Y = B_0 + B_1 X_1 + B_2 X_2 + B_3 X_3 + L_n e \qquad (7.28)$$

7.14.3   Reciprocal Model

The reciprocal model is given by:

$$Y = 1/(B_0 + B_1X_1 + B_2X_2 + B_3X_3 + B_4X_4 + Le) \qquad (7.29)$$

The model becomes a linear regression model by taking reciprocals of both sides.

7.15 Variance Stabilizing Transformation

One quite important assumption of multiple linear regression analysis is that errors have equal variance. The problem of heteroscedasticity occurs when the variances of the errors increase or decrease as one or more independent explanatory variables change. In the presence of heteroscedastic errors, there are serious estimation problems with the regression parameters. To correct this violation, the following sets of transformations of the dependent variables are frequently used. These transformations also tend to make error distributions approximately normal.

7.15.1   Square Root Transformation

$$Y = \sqrt{y} \qquad (7.30)$$

This is the least square transformation for variance stabilization.

7.15.2   Logarithmic Transformation

$$Y = \log y \qquad (7.31)$$

This is a stronger transformation for variance stabilization than the square root transformation

7.15.3   Reciprocal Transformation

$$Y = 1/y \qquad (7.32)$$

This is the most severe transformation.

7.16 Multiple Regression Models with Indicator Variables

This section will discuss the use of multiple regression models where the dependent variable Y can take on values of 0 or 1 (success or failure).

The logistic function is given by:

$$E(Y/X) = \frac{e^{B0+B1X1+B2X2}}{1+e^{B0+B1X1+B2X2}} \qquad (7.33)$$

One complication that usually arises in using normal multiple regression procedures is that the logistic transformation only linearizes the response function, but it does not eliminate the unequal variances in the error terms. To eliminate these unequal variances, a weighted least squares approach is needed.

The appropriate weighting is used (n is necessarily large):

$$W_j = n * \frac{\pi}{1-\pi} \qquad (7.34)$$

7.17 Multicollinearity

In regression analysis, the nature and significance of the relationship between the independent variables and the dependent variable is of concern. When the independent variables are correlated amongst themselves, multicollinearity exists.

In perfect correlation, regression analysis breaks down completely, and the regression coefficient estimates then have infinite variances. When the degree of colinearity is not very severe, variance of the regression estimates would be quite large, rather than infinite. As the degree of colinearity amongst the independent variables increases, effects are much less significant. Whatever the source of the multicollinearity, it is important to be aware of its existence so that its adverse effect can be minimized.

The major effects of multicollinearity are as follows:

1. The variances in the regression of coefficients are excessively inflated.

2. The magnitude of the regression of coefficients is different from what is expected.

3. The signs of the regression coefficients may be the opposite of what is expected.

4. The F ratio is significant, but the t-ratios are not.

5. The removal of a data point causes large changes in the coefficient or in the sign of the coefficients.

6. Adding or removing variables produces large changes in the coefficients or in the sign of the coefficients.

7.17.1   Correcting the Problems of Multicollinearity
Trial & Error

A trial and error process is often used to deal with the problem of multicollinearity. In this process, the effects of the inclusion of different independent variables on the modeling process are reviewed. The modeling process includes various independent variables and transformations that are independent of variables. The regression model is thoroughly scrutinized, and the significance of various combinations is used to test the independence of the variables. The process is designed to come up with the most parsimonious model, with the highest degree of predictive power.

Other Variable Selection Procedures

1. All Possible Regressions

   This method consists of running all possible regressions when k independent variables are considered and choosing the best model. For example, when there are four independent variables, then there would be 16 combinations of models to run. These models would be compared according to modeling criteria such as the model with the highest adjustments.

2. Stepwise Regression

   Stepwise is a combination of forward and backward elimination that reevaluates the significance of every independent variable at every stage. This procedure minimizes the probability of leaving out the important independent variables, while keeping in the non-important or independent variables. In this procedure, the most significant single variable regression model is identified. Next, the variables not included in the model are checked by using a partial F-test and the most significant variable, assuming it meets the entry significance requirement, is added to the regression model. Then the original independent variable is again evaluated to see if it still meets the significance standards for staging in the regression model, after the new variable has been added to the model. If this does not happen, then the independent variable is removed from consideration.

Next the independent variables not included in the model are evaluated to meet the entry requirement, and the most significant one, if found, is put into the regression model. All variables in the regression model are tested again for staying in the model. The stepwise procedure continues until there are no variables outside the model that should be added to the variable that is included in the model.

7.18 Multiple Regression Examples

In this section, two multiple regression analysis examples are given. The first example presents a forecasting problem with two independent (predictor) variables. The second example requires the use of categorical variables. Each example is first solved using the tools of Excel to develop the regression models.

Excel's regression analysis tool was used in Chapter 6 to develop a simple (single predictor variable) linear regression model. Excel's regression analysis tool can be used to develop multiple regression models and uses the least square method described at the beginning of the chapter to fit a line through a set of observations.

The forward stepwise regression procedure adds one independent variable at a time to the regression equation, starting with the independent variable with the most significant probability of the correlation (partial F statistic). The formula then recalculates the partial F statistic for the remaining independent variables, taking the existing regression equation into consideration. Independent variables are added until either independent variables are exhausted, a pre-selected stopping criteria, is reached, or the number of included independent variables reaches one-third of the number of data points in the observation set. The two stopping criteria are based on either the R-square value (or adjusted R-square) or the F statistic.

The iterative stepwise regression adds or removes one independent variable at a time to or from the regression equation. This add or remove procedure is repeated (iteratively) until no insignificant variables remain in the regression equation, or until the model runs out of independent variables, the regression model reaches one of the two stopping criteria (as described above), or the same independent variable is added and then removed. Both the forward and iterative stepwise regression procedures are intended to allow the analyst to determine the best subset of independent variables for the model.

7.18.1 Multiple Regression—Example 1

The marketing analyst for a leading electronics company that produces, in addition to other consumer devices, digital video disk players (DVD's), needs to be able to predict the sales of this item. One potential forecasting mechanism is multiple regression analysis. Based on related experience, it is hypothesized that DVD sales may be correlated to disposable income as well as to television sales. The logic here being that DVD's are more of a luxury item (they are certainly not a necessity), so disposable income, the amount households have available to either save or spend, might be a reasonable predictor variable. Also, DVD's and TV's would be considered complementary, i.e. goods that are used together. It would be expected then that as television sales increase or decrease, DVD sales would also increase or decrease. Data on sales of DVD's and televisions along with disposable income is shown in Figure 7.1.

Problem—Excel's Regression Analysis Tool

Using the data in Figure 7.1:

1. Prepare a multiple regression analysis using Excel's regression analysis tool;

2. Interpret the analysis; and

3. Forecast DVD sales for a disposable income of $178 billion and $1,425 million in television sales, first using 1, the multiple regression equation determined and then 2, the TREND function.

Solution—Excel's Regression Analysis Tool

1. Multiple Regression Analysis

A. First, arrange the data in columns with the two independent (explanatory) variables in columns on the left and the dependent variable on the right, immediately adjacent to each other. The data (with column headings) is placed in cells B4:D17.

B. It is helpful to view the scatter plots of the independent variables versus the dependent variable, as well as those of the independent variables against each other. The scatter plots help to confirm that a relationship exists and indicate what form that relationship takes (e.g. linear, logarithmic, exponential, power, or polynomial). Scatter plots also assist with diagnosing heteroscedasticrty and multicollinearity. In this particular problem, it is anticipated that the predictor variables will exhibit some level of multicollinearity, i.e. disposable income will be correlated with TV sales.

C. To generate a scatter plot, use the Chart Wizard (a four step process), which can be invoked from the "Insert menu" by choosing "Chart…", or clicking on the chart icon.

   i. At step one, Chart Type, choose the "XY (Scatter)" option, then "Next." See Figure 7.2.

   ii. Step two is Data Range, which should be "B5:BI7,D5:D17" for plotting disposable income

DVD Sales ($000,000)	Disposable Income ($000,000)	TV Sales ($000,000)
Y	X_1	X_2
272	151,000	1,389
275	161,000	1,471
275	174,000	1,504
290	175,000	1,530
290	181,000	1,602
290	183,000	1,641
293	184,000	1,703
301	187,000	1,721
310	191,000	1,724
315	194,000	1,791
320	201,000	1,826
340	207,000	1,841

Figure 7.1 Example 1 data.

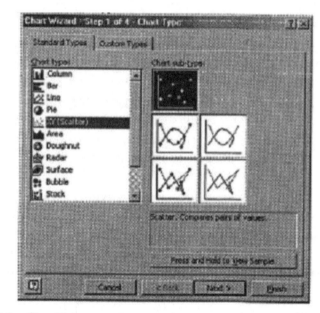

Figure 7.2 Chart type.

against DVD sales. Be certain to specify that the data is in columns (not rows). Select "Next" to go to step three. See Figure 7.3.

iii. Step three, Chart Options, allows entry of a chart title and the units for the X and Y-axes. Select "Next" to go to step four. See Figure 7.4.

iv. Step four allows the chart's location to be specified. Opt to have the chart as an object in sheet 1. Click on "Finish" to have the chart wizard generate the scatter plot. See Figure 7.5.

D. Repeat step 3 (Chart Wizard) and generate scatter plots for TV sales versus DVD sales (C5:Dl7) as well as disposable income against sales TV (B5:Cl7). The three scatter plots are shown in Figures 7.6–7.8.

E. Enter the information into the dialogue box as shown in Figure 7.9. The Y input range is D5:D17 and should include the label. Similarly, the X input range is B5: C17, including the labels. Be certain "Labels" is checked. Other options that should be checked are "Residuals," "Standardized Residuals," "Residual Plots", and "Line Fit Plots."

Note

From the scatter plots there appears to be a strong relationship between the two predictor variables (disposable income and TV sales) and the dependent variable (DVD sales). In addition, the shape of the scatter plot in Figure 7.6 suggests that the relationship between DVD sales and disposable income might be exponential. The shape of the scatter plot in Figure 7.7 appears linear. Finally (as anticipated), a multicollinear relationship appears to exist between the two predictor variables, evidenced in Figure 7.8. From the "Tools" menu, choose "Data Analysis" then "Regression" and then "OK." This sequence brings up the "Regression" dialogue box.

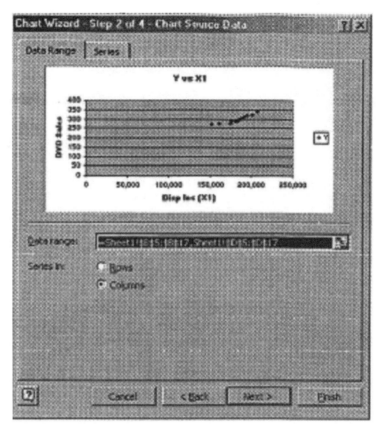

Figure 7.3 Data range.

Do not select "Normal Probability Plots" because this option is not implemented properly in Excel.

F. The column widths can be adjusted so that all the summary output labels and information is visible by using the "AutoFit" function. This adjustment is most easily accomplished by selecting the columns containing the regression output, columns F through L. Then click on "Format," "Column," and then "AutoFit Selection." The results are shown in Figure 7.10.

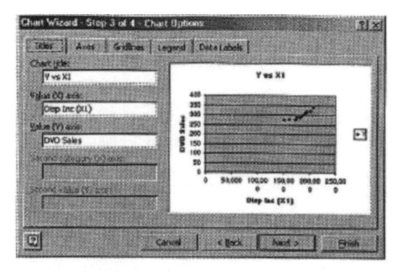

Figure 7.4 Chart options.

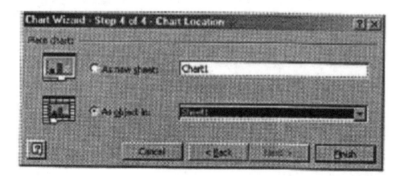

Figure 7.5 Chart locations.

2. Interpretation of the Regression Output

Refer to Figure 7.10 (previous page). The regression equation for the first order model, is given by the following equation (with rounding of the regression coefficients):

$$Y = 78.0551 + 0.000664X_1 + 0.059800X_2$$

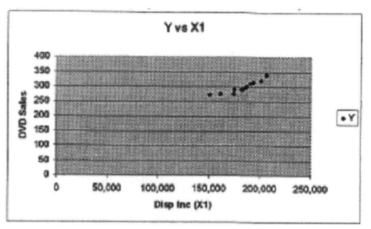

Figure 7.6 Scatter plot (Disposable Income vs. DVD Sales).

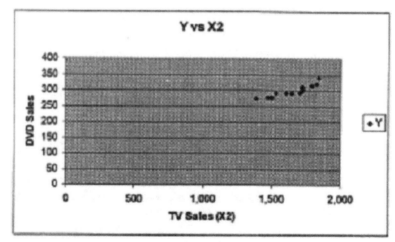

Figure 7.7 Scatter plot (TV Sales vs. DVD Sales).

or

DVD Sales = 78.0551 + 0.000664 * Disposable Income + 0.059800 * *TV* Sales

In a multiple regression formulation, the regression coefficients are typically referred to as *partial regression coefficients*. Here,

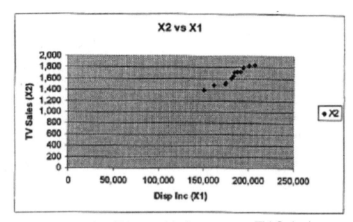

Figure 7.8 Scatter plot (Disposable Income vs. TV Sales).

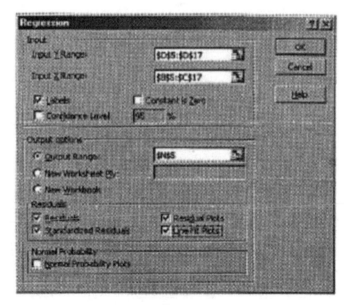

Figure 7.9 Regression Dialogue Box.

Summary Output

Regression Statistics	
Multiple R	0.933546489
R Square	0.871509047
Adjusted R Square	0.842955501
Standard Error	8.138105331
Observations	12

ANOVA

	Df	SS	MS	F	Significance F
Regression	2	4042.857841	2021.428921	30.52192084	9.77072E-05
Residual	9	596.0588253	66.22875837		
Total	11	4638.916667			

	Coefficients	Standard Error	t Stat	P-value	Lower 95%
Intercept	78.05514218	28.38097587	2.7502628	0.022467152	13.85286539
X1	0.000664096	0.000632409	1.05010511	0.321048245	-0.000766513
X2	0.05980009	0.067946269	0.88010851	0.401689963	-0.093905167

RESIDUAL OUTPUT

Observation	Predicted Y	Residuals	Standard Residuals
1	261.3958923	10.60410766	1.44054195
2	272.940455	2.059544974	0.27978412
3	283.5470999	-8.547099927	-1.161102507
4	285.7659978	4.234002208	0.575178788
5	294.0561774	-4.05617745	-0.551021732
6	297.716572	-7.716572014	-1.048277332
7	302.0882731	-9.088273105	-1.234619552
8	305.1569613	-4.156961321	-0.564712973
9	307.9927437	2.007256274	0.272680829
10	313.9916363	1.008363666	0.136983724
11	320.7333082	-0.73330821	-0.099618117
12	325.6148828	14.38511724	1.954182803

Figure 7.10 Regression outputs.

the interpretation of the two partial regression coefficients is that if TV sales could be held constant, then for every unit change in disposable income, DVD sales would change by 0.000664 units. Similarly, if disposable income were held constant, then for every unit change in TV sales, DVD sales would change by 0.059800 units. In both situations, if the change to the independent variables is positive, then the change to the dependent variable is positive. However, with the presence of multicollinearity, this interpretation is not fully applicable.

The p-values for the partial regression coefficients are quite high and correspondingly the t statistics are both low (less than 2). If these statistics were taken at face value, the null hypothesis that there is no relationship between disposable income or TV sales to DVD sales would be accepted. However, the scatter plots initially performed (or the line fit plots) indicate clearly that there is a statistical relationship. This result is again due to the presence of multicollinearity, which may result in the estimated individual regression coefficients being statistically insignificant even though a definite statistical relationship exists between the response variable and the set of predictor variables. Therefore, the null hypothesis will be rejected and the conclusion is that there is a statistical relationship. Finally, note that the t statistic and p-value for the intercept term is typically ignored.

Listed under the Regression Statistics, the R-square value of 0.8715 indicates that approximately 87 percent of the variation in DVD sales can be explained using this model. Note that the adjusted R-square value, 0.8429, should be used as one of the two criteria for evaluating different models (containing different or varying numbers of explanatory variables). The other criterion typically used is the mean square error (MSE), which is 66.2 for this model and is shown under the analysis of variance (ANOVA) section.

From the ANOVA output in Figure 7.10, the sum of squares (SS) column provides the values to determine the R-square value. This value is simply the sum of squares regression (SSR) divided by the sum of squares total (SST). This section also discusses the result of testing the null hypothesis that all regression coefficients are simultaneously equal to zero. The result is contained in the significance F value, which is actually a p-value. Here, the value is $9.77*10^{-5}$, which is slightly less than 0.0001. Therefore, for this model, the null hypothesis can be rejected and it can be concluded that both regression coefficients are not zero, i.e. that at least one significant relationship exists between a predictor and response variable. This statistic also helps to reinforce the explanation

(multicollinearity) of the high p-values for the individual regression coefficients presented earlier.

Residual analysis using plots of the residuals for the independent variables are valuable in assessing the validity of assumptions of linear relationships and constant variance. Excel provides these plots to the right of the regression summary output, as shown in Figures 7.11 and 7.12.

Prototypically, residual plots can exhibit four basic patterns (or a combination of them):

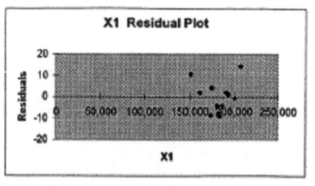

Figure 7.11   Residual Plot–Disposable Income.

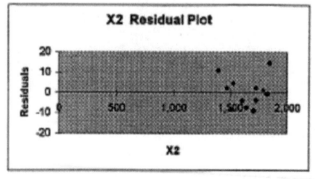

Figure 7.12   Residual Plot–TV Sales.

A. The residuals fall within a horizontal band centered around zero, displaying no systematic tendencies to be positive and negative (i.e. random). This type of pattern indicates that the regression model used is appropriate.

B. The residuals tend to vary in a systematic fashion between being positive and negative, i.e. curvilinear. This type of pattern indicates the need for a curvilinear function to be introduced into the regression model.

C. The residuals can also exhibit a non-constancy error, either increasing or decreasing. The residual pattern would take the form of a megaphone shape.

D. Finally, the residual plot can exhibit non-independence or time-related dependence, indicated by the residuals increasing or decreasing with time.

Both residual plots appear to be random. However, the small sample size (12) makes it difficult to detect nonlinear patterns.

3. Forecasting DVD Sales

A. Using the Regression Equation

Assuming that the model is satisfactory, the first means of making predictions is by substitution into the regression equation. To predict DVD sales (in millions of dollars) for a disposable income of $178 billion and $1,425 million in television sales, the substitution is simply:

DVD Sales = 78.0551+0.000664*Disp. Income+0.059800* TV Sales

= 78.0551+0.000664*178,000+0.059800*1,425

= 281.479 (with rounding)

B. Using the Trend Function

Again, assuming that the model is satisfactory, predictions of DVD sales dollars can be made by using the Trend function rather than by substitution into the equation. The syntax for this function is:

TREND (known_y's, known_x's, new_x's const).

Here, the *known_y's* and *known_x's* correspond to the cells containing the dependent and independent variables, respectively. *Const* is a logical value specifying whether to force the constant b (the intercept term) to equal 0. If const is TRUE or omitted, b is calculated normally. If const FALSE, b is set equal to zero.

The steps for using this function are as follows:

i. Enter the values for the explanatory variables for which the prediction is to be based on the worksheet. That is, enter 178,000 for disposable income in cell B18 and 1,425 for TV sales in cell C18. This procedure keeps the forecast figures in line with the original data.

ii. Select a cell that will contain the predicted value. Use cell D 18 for consistency. In cell Dl8 type the following, with the Trend function in lower case:

= trend (d6:d17, b6:c17, b18:c18)

and press enter. Here, the *const* term is omitted (left blank) because there is no need to force the regression line through the origin.

iii. Note that if several predictions were to be made simultaneously, the explanatory variables could have been entered as an array in the formula. For example, if it was necessary to predict three values, the new independent variables could have been entered into cells B 18: C 20. The cells that contain the predictions, D18:20, would be selected , and the appropriately modified function, = trend (d6:d17, b6:cl7, bl8:c20), would be entered but the ENTER key would not be pressed. Instead, for this array, the Control and Shift keys should be held down simultaneously and then ENTER should be pressed. The formula bar would display TREND in uppercase with curly brackets around the function, indicating that the array function was recognized and entered properly.

iv. The Trend function can also be accessed through the Paste Function dialogue box by clicking on the icon, f_x

Figure 7.13 shows the results which correspond exactly to those obtained by substitution into the regression equation.

Disposable Income ($000,000)	TV Sales ($000,000)	DVD Sales ($000,000)
X_1	X_2	Y
151,000	1,389	272
161,000	1,471	275
174,000	1,504	275
175,000	1,530	290
181,000	1,602	290
183,000	1,641	290
184,000	1,703	293
187,000	1,721	301
191,000	1,724	310
194,000	1,791	315
201,000	1,826	320
207,000	1,841	340
178,000	1,425	281.479

Figure 7.13   Trend function results.

To summarize, for a disposable income of $178 billion and $1,425 million in television sales, the model predicts DVD sales to be $281 million. Possibly a better indication would be the prediction interval. An approximate 95-percent prediction interval would be the estimate plus or minus two standard errors of the estimate, i.e. $281.479 \pm 1.96 * 8.138 \approx 281 + 16$. Stated another way, the analyst is 95-percent confident that DVD sales ($000,000) will be in the range of 265 to 297 million dollars. Unfortunately, the Trend function only provides a point estimate and an interval cannot be calculated.

There are, however, two comments that should be made concerning this prediction interval:

First, the standard error of prediction should be used instead of the standard error of the estimate. The standard error of prediction takes into account the uncertainty in the regression coefficients and not just the variability of the actual values around the regression line.

Secondly, with only 12 observations, the t statistic should be used (with 9 degrees of freedom), rather than the normal distribution, for calculating the confidence interval. The normal distribution would be appropriate for larger sample sizes (perhaps ≥ 30). Using the t statistic (2.262) would yield a larger interval (± 18).

7.18.2   For Further Insight

As a means for extending understanding of developing regression models, it is recommended that the reader construct simple linear regression models for each of the two independent variables. It is also suggested that a transformed model be evaluated, e.g. use an exponential transformation with disposable income. Using the adjusted R-square and mean square error (MSE) values as the criteria, determine if the first order multiple regression model developed in this example is the best model for predicting DVD sales.

7.18.3 Multiple Regression Example 2: Using Categorical Variables

A recruiter for a headhunting firm, specializing in technical professions, who works primarily with engineers, would like to be able to accurately predict the appropriate starting salary of a client based on years of experience and field of expertise. The recruiter believes that it would be possible to build a regression model and wishes to utilize data for the last ten clients as a representative sample for this purpose. The data is shown in Figure 7.15.

    EE : electrical engineer
    CE : civil engineer
    ChemE: chemical engineer

Problem—Excel's Regression Analysis Tool

Using the data in Figure 7.15.

1. Prepare a multiple regression analysis;

2. Interpret the analysis; and

3. Predict the starting salaries for 1, an electrical engineer with 1 year of experience, 2, a chemical engineer with 3 years of experience, and 3, a civil engineer with 7 years of experience.

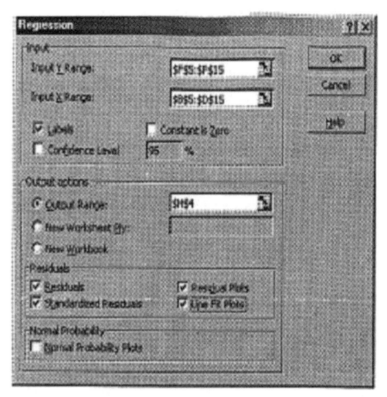

Figure 7.14   Regression Dialogue Box.

Starting Salary ($)	Engineer's Experience (years)	Major
65,000	2	EE
62,000	3	EE
65,500	4	EE
59,000	1	CE
71,000	3	CE
58,000	2	CE
73,000	5	ChemE
68,000	2	ChemE
60,000	1	ChemE
54,000	0	ChemE

Figure 7.15   Data for Example 2.

Solution—Excel's Regression Analysis Tool

1. Multiple Regression Analysis

The regression models previously constructed used only numerical variables. However, a non-numerical variable is now encountered, the engineer's major. This is a categorical variable, often referred to as an indicator, binary, or dummy variable (for somewhat obvious reasons). The number of indicator variables necessary is one less than the number of categories to be used. Here, there are three categories (EE, CE, and ChemE), therefore two indicator variables are necessary. The two indicator variables are binary, taking the values of 0 or 1. Enter the data with the two binary variables in cells B4:F15 of the Excel worksheet, as shown in Figure 7.17. The independent variables, including the indicator variables, should all be to the left of the dependent variable (starting salary). In addition, make sure that experience and the two indicator columns are to the left of "major" because Excel requires the independent variables' range to be contiguous.

Here, the interpretation of the EE variable is EE equals 1 if the engineer is an electrical engineer, 0 otherwise. Similarly, for the CE variable, CE equals 1 if the engineer is a civil engineer, 0 otherwise. When both EE and CE indicator variables equal 0, the engineer is implied to be a chemical engineer. This interpretation is the reason why one less indicator variable is needed relative to the number of categories to be represented. Because ChemE does not have an indicator variable, the value for all other indicator variables is 0, ChemE is frequently termed the *default category* or *base-case category*.

Note that if a large data set were being employed, an IF statement (along with the copy/paste commands) could be used in the worksheet to automatically generate the values of the indicator variables. To accomplish this, the formula =IF (E6="EE", 1, 0) would be entered in cell C6 and subsequently copied down

Summary Output

Regression Statistics

Multiple R	0.832824127
R Square	0.693596026
Adjusted R Square	0.540394039
Standard Error	4094.09014
Observations	10

ANOVA

	Df	SS	MS	F	Significance F
Regression	3	227655555.6	75885185.19	4.527330479	0.055184722
Residual	6	100569444.4	16761574.07		
Total	9	328225000			

	Coefficients	Standard Error	t Stat	P-value	Lower 95%	Upper 9
Intercept	56694.44444	2813.394348	20.15161667	9.69886E-07	49810.31144	63578.5
X1	3527.777778	964.9863003	3.655780167	0.010632786	1166.539637	5889.01
EE	-3111.111111	3272.427759	-0.950704291	0.378462189	-11118.45923	4896.2
CE	-1083.333333	3126.912995	-0.346454582	0.74082763	-8734.619393	6567.95

RESIDUAL OUTPUT

Observation	Predicted Y	Residuals	Standard Residuals
1	60638.88889	4361.111111	1.304624052
2	64166.66667	-2166.666667	-0.648157172
3	67694.44444	-2194.444444	-0.65646688
4	59138.88889	-138.8888889	-0.041548537
5	66194.44444	4805.555556	1.437579369
6	62666.66667	-4666.666667	-1.396030833
7	74333.33333	-1333.333333	-0.398865952
8	63750	4250	1.271385222
9	60222.22222	-222.2222222	-0.066477659
10	56694.44444	-2694.444444	-0.806041612

Figure 7.16 Regression output.

through cell C15. Similarly, the formula =IF (E6="CE", 1, 0) would be entered in cell D6 and copied down through cell D15.

The steps for generating the regression analysis are:

Select cell H4. From the "Tools" menu, choose "Data Analysis", "Regression" and then "OK." This brings up the "Regression" dialogue box.

A. Enter the information into the dialogue box as shown in Figure 7.14.

The Y input range is F5:Fl5 and should include the label. Similarly, the X input range is B5:D15, including the labels. Be certain the "Labels" is checked. Other options that should be checked are "Residuals," "Standardized Residuals," "Residual plots," and "Line Fit Plots." Do not select "Normal Probability plots" because this option is not implemented properly in Excel.

B. The column widths can be adjusted so that all the summary output labels and information is visible using the "AutoFit" function. This adjustment is accomplished most easily by selecting the columns containing the regression output, columns F through L. Click on "Format" "Column," and then "AutoFit Selection." The results are shown in Figure 7.16.

2. Interpretation of the Regression Output

Refer to Figure 7.16. The regression equation for the first order model, is given by the following equation (with rounding of the regression coefficients):

This equation can be stated as:

Starting Salary = 56,694.4 + 3,527.8 * Yrs of Exp – 3,111.1 for EEs;

Starting Salary = 56,694.4 + 3,527.8 * Yrs of Exp – 1,083.3 for CEs; or

Starting Salary = 56,694.4 + 3,527.8 * Yrs of Exp for ChemEs.

The p-value for the partial regression coefficient corresponding to the first predictor variable, years of experience, is very small

Experience (years)	Indicator	Indicator	Major	Starting Salary ($)
X₁	EE	CE		Y
2	1	0	EE	65,000
3	1	0	EE	62,000
4	1	0	EE	65,500
1	0	1	CE	59,000
3	0	1	CE	71,000
2	0	1	CE	58,000
5	0	0	ChemE	73,000
2	0	0	ChemE	68,000
1	0	0	ChemE	60,000
0	0	0	ChemE	54,000

Figure 7.17   Data with binary variables.

(and the corresponding t statistic is quite large). The null hypothesis should therefore be rejected because it implies that there is no statistical relationship between experience and salary, whereas it is concluded that there is, in fact, a relationship between these two variables.

However, the p-values for the partial regression coefficients for both categorical variables are high and correspondingly the t statistics are both low. Here, the null hypothesis would be accepted, and the conclusion is that there is no relationship between salary and the type of engineer. The t statistic and p-value for the intercept term is typically ignored. It would, therefore, behoove the analyst to rerun this regression analysis using only years of experience as the predictor variable, or to increase the sample size. In either event, a larger sample size would be preferable.

Listed under the Regression Statistics, the R-square value of 0.6936 indicates that approximately 69 percent of the variation in starting salary can be explained using this model. The model may be satisfactory (or not), depending partly on the application. The adjusted R-square value, 0.5404, should be used as one of the criteria for evaluating this model against the first order simple linear regression model. The other criteria would be the MSE.

Also, the ANOVA output provides the result of testing the null hypothesis that all regression coefficients are simultaneously equal to zero. The result is contained in the Significance F value, which is actually a p-value. Here, the value is 0.0552. Therefore, for this model, the null hypothesis would be rejected and the conclusion would be that not all partial regression coefficients are zero, i.e. at least one significant relationship exists between a predictor and a response variable.

3. Predicting Starting Salaries

To make predictions of starting salaries using this model, the independent variables' values must be substituted into the regression equation. The Trend function previously described cannot be used with binary variables. The three predictions would thus be:

A. An electrical engineer with 1 year of experience:

Starting Salary = 56,694.4 + 3,527.8* Years of Experience – 3,111.1

= 56,694.4 + 3,527.8 * 1 – 3,111.1

= 57,111.1

B. A chemical engineer with 3 years of experience:

Starting Salary = 56,694.4 + 3,527.8 * Years of Experience

= 56,694.4 + 3.527.8 * 3

= 67,277.8

C. A civil engineer with 7 years of experience:

No prediction can be made because there are no observations (data) regarding salaries of engineers with seven years of experience. The range for years of experience is from 0 to 5 years. Therefore, any prediction for experience outside this range, using this model, would be quite suspect.

A 95-percent confidence interval could be calculated for these salaries. First an approximate confidence interval could quickly be calculated based on the assumption that the data followed a normal distribution. This approximate interval would be plus/minus 1.96 times the standard error or:

$$\pm 1.96 * 4094 = \pm 8.024$$

However, with only ten observations, when at least thirty would be desirable, the more appropriate confidence interval would employ the *t* distribution with seven degrees of freedom:

$$\pm 2.365 * 4094 = \pm 9,682$$

Therefore, the electrical engineer with 1-year of experience could expect a salary, using the more appropriate distribution, ranging from \$47,429 to \$66,793 and the chemical engineer with 3 years of experience a salary from \$57,596 to \$76,960.

References

Abraham, B. and J. Ledolter. *Introduction to Regression Modeling.* Brooks/Cole, Belmont, CA: 2005.

Barreto, H. and F.M. Howland. *Introductory Econometrics.* Cambridge University Press, New York: 2006.

Bowerman, B.L., R.T. O'Connell, and A.B. Koehler. *Forecasting Time Series and Regression.* 4th ed. Brooks/Cole, Belmont, CA: 2005.

Weisberg, S. *Applied Linear Regression.* 3rd ed. Wiley, New York: 2005.

Chapter 8

Markovian Forecasting Models

8.1 Introduction

Markovian modeling has been used to predict or forecast individual choice and to forecast consumer buyer behavior. Markovian modeling attempts to determine customer brand choice, as well as to make predictions of customer response. Markovian modeling specifically deals with the probability of buying given brands, based upon what was previously purchased by the customer. The prediction of brand choice is influenced by ways of dealing with

1. *external market factors,*

2. *the effect of present purchase behavior on future purchase behaviors,*

3. *population heterogeneity.*

In the Markovian model of purchase behavior, only the last brand chosen affects the purchase decision. All the information needed to characterize brand choice in the Markovian model is found in the transition probability matrix $P=P_{ij}$.
Where P_{ij} is the probability of purchasing item i next, given that item j was purchased last time. Purchase-incidence forecasting models detail the occurrence of purchases, as well as the number of purchases that will happen in a given time interval. In a Markovian purchase incidence forecasting model, the transition probabilities are related to the decision variable. The transition probabilities are: P_{ijt}, $(i=j=1,..., n, t=1,...,T)$

8.2 A Markovian Model

The random sequence $(X_1, X_2, ..., X_n)$ is said to be a Markov process if the conditional probability

$$p(i_n | i_1, ..., i_{n-1}) = \Pr[X_n = i_n | X_1 = i_1, ..., X_{n-1} = i_{n-1}]$$

depends only on the values of i_n and i_{n-1}.

Thus $p(i_n | i_1, ..., i_{n-1}) = p(i_n | i_{n-1})$. If a system is known to have reached state (n–1) at the (n–1)st stage, it is immaterial what chain of sales is passed through on the way to this stage, as far as predicting the state it will enter at the next stage is concerned. Thus, the system has no memory that would allow it to use information about its behavior before a known state was reached, to modify the probabilities for the next stage. Basically, in a Markov-dependent sequence, knowledge of the present makes the future independent of the past.

In such a sequence,

$$p(i_1, i_2, ..., i_n) = p_{i_1}^{(1)} p(i_2 | i_1) p(i_3 | i_2) ... p(i_n | i_{n-1})$$

These probabilities $p(i_n \, i_{n-1})$ are referred to as the transition probabilities.

In a stationary Markov-dependent sequence, these transition probabilities were not assumed to depend on n. Thus, the quantity P_{ij} can be defined as follows:

$$p_{ij} = \Pr[X_n = j | X_{n-1} = i]$$

are the one step transition probabilities of the Markov process. Thus, the conditional probabilities satisfy the condition:

$$\sum_j p_{ij} = 1 \text{ for each } i,$$

where the sum is extended over the entire state space of the Markov process.

The matrix P whose entries are one-step transition probabilities P_{ij}:

$$P = (p_{ij}) = \begin{bmatrix} p_{00} & p_{01} & \cdots & p_{0n} \\ p_{10} & p_{11} & \cdots & p_{1n} \\ \cdots & \cdots & \cdots & \cdots \\ p_{n0} & p_{n1} & \cdots & p_{nn} \end{bmatrix}$$

is referred to as the transition matrix of the process, and states that the sum of the entries in each row of p is 1.

The n-step transition probabilities $p_{ij}^n = \Pr[X_n = j | X_{n-1} = j]$ for $i, j = 0, 1, 2, ..., n$, and for each $n \geq 0$. $p_{ij}^{(n)}$ is the probability of the system's ending up in state j after n transitions, starting from state i. That is, $p_{ij}^{(n)}$ is the probability that the process goes from state i to state j in n steps. Thus $p_{ij}^{(1)} = p_{ij}$ and $p_{ij}^{(1)} = \Pr[X_n = i]$ is the unconditional probability that the process is in state i after n steps.

8.3 The First-Order Markovian Model

To begin, a system in which events can be realized in a finite number of states $i = 1, 2, ..., n$. At each time period t, there is a distribution of events among the n-states, expressed in the form of vector(s). When expressed as relative frequencies, each vector(s) can be thought of as a probability vector, giving for each s_i the probability that the events of the system will be realized in state i at time t.

It can be assumed that this system is driven by a stochastic process such that the condition of the system at time $(t+1)$ depends only on its condition in the previous period and the set of stable transition conditional probabilities. These transitional probabilities p_{ij}, give the probability when the system is in state j and time t, and it will be realized in state i at time $(t+1)$. The movement of the system from period to period is given by:

$$s_{t+1} = P_{s_t}$$

where P is the matrix of transitional probability p_{ij}, where (i) is the row index, and (j) is the column index. Also, the elements of (s) and (p) are nonnegative

$$\sum_{i=1}^{1} s_t = 1 \text{ and } \sum_{i=1}^{1} p_{ij} = 1 \text{ for each j}$$

Furthermore, the elements of the vector(s) and each column of (p) sum to one.

For initial period t_0, $s_n = p^n s_0$, where s_0 is the initial condition. The transition matrix is positive, so the vector(s) converges and its limiting value is independent of its initial condition.

8.4 Computation of the Steady State

To calculate the steady state behavior of the transition matrix, p, algebraic methods using eigenvalues and eigenvectors will be applied. Given a transition matrix, the characteristic equation is used:

$$|p - \lambda I| = 0$$

From this equation, the eigenvalues λ_{ij} are found (if all N roots are district, the process fails.) Then solve equation $s_i A = \lambda_{ij}$, s_i where $A = S^{-1}ps$ for the nonzero eigenvector s_i, corresponding to each λ_{ij} for i = 0, 1,...,N–1. Then form S from the s_i; then find S^{-1} and then $p^n = S^{-1} p^n s$.

8.4.1 An Example Problem for Steady State Calculations

$$P = \begin{bmatrix} 0.75 & 0.25 \\ 0.50 & 0.50 \end{bmatrix}$$

$$|p - \lambda I| = 0$$

$$\begin{vmatrix} 0.75 - \lambda & 0.25 \\ 0.50 & 0.50 - \lambda \end{vmatrix} = 0$$

The characteristic equation is

$$(0.50 - \lambda)(0.75 - \lambda) - 0.125 = 0$$

$$\lambda_{00} = 1 \text{ and } \lambda_{11} = .25$$

$$s_{10} = 1 \; s_{11} = -1$$

$$S^{-1} = \begin{bmatrix} 0.667 & 0.333 \\ 0.667 & -0.667 \end{bmatrix}$$

$$P = S^{-1} \Lambda S$$

$$P^n = \begin{bmatrix} 0.667 & 0.333 \\ 0.667 & -0.667 \end{bmatrix} \begin{bmatrix} 1 & 0 \\ 0 & (0.25)_n \end{bmatrix} \begin{bmatrix} 1 & 0.5 \\ 1 & -1 \end{bmatrix}$$

8.4.2 Problem 1—Brand Calculations Steady State

In a northeastern city, the brands of soda bought by the city's population are given by the following matrix P_{ij}, shown in Table 8.1.

The number of people purchasing Brand 1 in the past year is 80,000, Brand 2 is 40,000, and Brand 3 is 30,000. Forecasts required:

1. Forecast the number of people using Brand 1, Brand 2, and Brand 3 in the current year.

2. Forecast the number of people purchasing Brand 1, Brand 2, and Brand 3 in the following year.

3. Determine the steady-state probabilities.

4. Forecast the number of people purchasing each Brand in the long run, defined as

"Note—Perform calculations in Excel Absorbing States for Use Brand Numbers; please list all formulae."

Solution

A (1x3)   P$^{(1)}$ (3x3)   Output (1x3)

$$[80,000 \quad 40,000 \quad 30,000] \cdot \begin{bmatrix} 0.75 & 0.10 & 0.15 \\ 0.15 & 0.65 & 0.20 \\ 0.05 & 0.10 & 0.85 \end{bmatrix} = [67,500 \quad 37,000 \quad 45,500]$$

Table 8.1   Matrix for Brand Comparison

Units = Bottles		To:		
		Brand 1	Brand 2	Brand 3
From:	Brand 1	0.75	0.10	0.15
	Brand 2	0.15	0.65	0.20
	Brand 3	0.05	0.10	0.85

Table 8.2   Transition Probability Matrix

		To Brand		
	From Brand	1	2	3
	1	0.75	0.10	0.15
$P^{(1)} =$	2	0.15	0.65	0.20
	3	0.05	0.10	0.85

1. Given that last year 80,000 people purchased Brand 1, 40,000 people purchased Brand 2, and 30,000 people purchased Brand 3, the prediction of the number of customers using each brand in the current year at the left:

Calculating in Matrix Multiplication in Microsoft Excel:

A. Insert the matrices A and $P^{(1)}$ to be multiplied, in the work sheet as shown in Figure 8.1.

B. Select a group of cells for output, with dimension 1x3.

C. Type =MMULT (range of cells for matrix A, range of cells for matrix B). The range of cells can be typed in manually, identifying the cell at the top left and the bottom right. Alternatively, the mouse can be used to highlight the matrix.

D. Then type Ctrl-Shift-Return (If this is not done, only a single value, not the entire matrix will appear). Refer to Figure 8.1.

Thus, the numbers of people using Brand 1, Brand 2, and Brand 3 in the current year are seen in Table 8.3:

2. Here, the first need is to calculate the two-step transition probabilities as follows:

Given that last year 80,000 people purchased Brand 1, 40,000 people purchased Brand 2, and 30,000 people purchased Brand 3, the prediction of the number of customers using each brand in the year following the current year is as follows:

$$[80,000 \quad 40,000 \quad 30,000] \cdot \begin{bmatrix} 0.585 & 0.155 & 0.260 \\ 0.220 & 0.458 & 0.323 \\ 0.095 & 0.155 & 0.750 \end{bmatrix} = [58,450 \quad 35,350 \quad 56,200]$$

Thus, the numbers of people using Brand 1, Brand 2, and Brand 3 in the year following the current year are seen in Table 8.4.

3. The state values, at steady state, will be represented by the symbol π. Multiplication of a state condition by the transition matrix yields the same condition at steady state, so it is possible to write

$$\pi = \pi.P$$

or

$$[\pi_1 \quad \pi_2 \quad \pi_3] = [\pi_1 \quad \pi_2 \quad \pi_3] \cdot \begin{bmatrix} p_{11} & p_{12} & p_{13} \\ p_{21} & p_{22} & p_{23} \\ p_{31} & p_{32} & p_{33} \end{bmatrix}$$

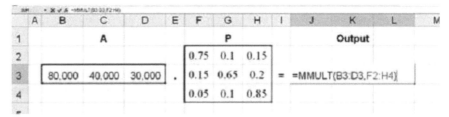

Figure 8.1 Formula view.

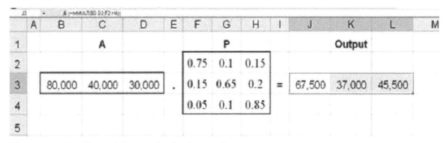

Figure 8.2 Resulting calculations view.

Table 8.3 Users in Current Year

Brand	Number of People
1	67,500
2	37,000
3	45,500
Total	150,000

Table 8.4 Users in Year Following Current Year

Brand	Number of People
1	58,450
2	35,350
3	56,200
Total	150,000

where

π = vector of state probabilities (relative proportions)

$P = P^{(1)}$ = one-step transition probabilities matrix.

The sum of the state probabilities must be 1.0.

$$\pi_1 + \pi_2 + \pi_3 = 1.0$$

$$\begin{bmatrix} \pi_1 & \pi_2 & \pi_3 \end{bmatrix} = \begin{bmatrix} \pi_1 & \pi_2 & \pi_3 \end{bmatrix} \cdot \begin{bmatrix} p_{11} & p_{12} & p_{13} \\ p_{21} & p_{22} & p_{23} \\ p_{31} & p_{32} & p_{33} \end{bmatrix}$$

$$\begin{bmatrix} \pi_1 & \pi_2 & \pi_3 \end{bmatrix} = \begin{bmatrix} \pi_1 & \pi_2 & \pi_3 \end{bmatrix} \cdot \begin{bmatrix} 0.75 & 0.10 & 0.15 \\ 0.15 & 0.65 & 0.20 \\ 0.05 & 0.10 & 0.85 \end{bmatrix}$$

which yields

$$\pi_1 = 0.75\pi_1 + 0.15\pi_2 + 0.05\pi_3$$

$$\pi_2 = 0.10\pi_1 + 0.65\pi_2 + 0.10\pi_3$$

$$\pi_3 = 0.15\pi_1 + 0.20\pi_2 + 0.85\pi_3$$

$$\pi_1 + \pi_2 + \pi_3 = 1.0$$

Solving these equations simultaneously yields

$$\pi_1 = 0.240 \quad \pi_2 = 0.222 \quad \pi_3 = 0.537$$

The simultaneous solution of the equations to obtain π_1, π_2 and π_3, actually solves for the steady-state proportions of the market share, or the probabilities of one customer being in any one of the states (i.e. a customer purchasing any one of the brands).

4. If it is desired to get the numbers of customers for each brand, simply multiply each of the probabilities, π_1, π_2 and π_3 by 150,000, which yields:

$$\pi_1 = 36,111$$

$$\pi_2 = 33,333$$

$$\pi_3 = 80,556$$

8.5 Absorbing States in the Markov Process

In a Markov process it is possible to go from one state to any other state between two periods. However, it is possible that if you are in a state of a Markov process, you cannot go to another state of the Markov process in future states. Thus, once you are in an absorbing state, you will always remain in it.

To deal with the Markov transition probabilities matrix, which includes absorbing states, it is necessary to partition the transition probability matrix

$$P = \begin{bmatrix} I & 0 \\ \hline R & Q \end{bmatrix}$$

Q matrix = the non-absorbing states of the overall Markov transition matrix

I = the identify matrix (ones on the main diagonal; zeroes elsewhere)

O = a matrix of all zeroes

The fundamental matrix N is computed in the following fashion:

$$F = (I = Q)^{-1}$$

8.5.1 Problem 2—Absorbing States Calculations for Credit

A department store has a 30-day billing cycle. At the start of each 30-day cycle, outstanding bills are classified into one of the four categories:

1. New

2. Less than 30 days old

3. Less than 60 days old

4. Less than 90 days old

5. Paid

6. Bad debt

Forecasts required:

1. Forecast the probability that the less than 30 days account will be paid.

2. Forecast the probability that the less than 60 days account will be written off.

Table 8.5   Bill Classification Categories

	New	Less than 30 days	Less than 60 days	Less than 90 days	Paid	Bad Debt
New	0	0.4	0	0	0.6	0
Less than 30 Days	0	0	0.6	0	0.4	0
Less than 60 Days	0	0	0	0.4	0.6	0
Less than 90 days	0	0	0	0	0.5	0.5
Paid	0	0	0	0	1	0
Bad Debt	0	0	0	0	0	1

3. If the store's average sales are $200,000 per month, how much money per year will go uncollected?

$$F = (I - Q)^{-1} \quad \text{Absorbing States in the Markov Process}$$

Label each state; List the formulae used, etc.

Solution

The transition probability matrix is as below:

1 2 3 4 5 6

$$P = \begin{array}{c} 1 \\ 2 \\ 3 \\ 4 \\ 5 \\ 6 \end{array} \left[\begin{array}{cccc|cc} 0 & 0.4 & 0 & 0 & 0.6 & 0 \\ 0 & 0 & 0.6 & 0 & 0.4 & 0 \\ 0 & 0 & 0 & 0.4 & 0.6 & 0 \\ 0 & 0 & 0 & 0 & 0.5 & 0.5 \\ \hline 0 & 0 & 0 & 0 & 1 & 0 \\ 0 & 0 & 0 & 0 & 0 & 1 \end{array} \right]$$

Now four submatrices exist that are in the following general form:

$$P = \left[\begin{array}{c|c} Q & R \\ \hline 0 & I \end{array} \right]$$

The first matrix operation determines the fundamental matrix, F, which gives the expected number of times the system would be in any of the non-absorbing states before absorption occurs (i.e. before the account is paid off or becomes a bad debt). The fundamental matrix is computed by taking the inverse of the difference between an identity matrix and Q.

$$F = (I - Q)^{-1}$$

$$F = \left(\begin{bmatrix} 1 & 0 & 0 & 0 \\ 0 & 1 & 0 & 0 \\ 0 & 0 & 1 & 0 \\ 0 & 0 & 0 & 1 \end{bmatrix} - \begin{bmatrix} 0 & 0.4 & 0 & 0 \\ 0 & 0 & 0.6 & 0 \\ 0 & 0 & 0 & 0.4 \\ 0 & 0 & 0 & 0 \end{bmatrix} \right)^{-1}$$

$$F = \left(\begin{bmatrix} 1 & -0.4 & 0 & 0 \\ 0 & 1 & -0.6 & 0 \\ 0 & 0 & 1 & -0.4 \\ 0 & 0 & 0 & 1 \end{bmatrix} \right)^{-1}$$

$$F = \begin{array}{c} \\ s_1 \\ s_2 \\ s_3 \\ s_4 \end{array} \begin{array}{c} s_1 \, s_2 \, s_3 \, s_4 \\ \begin{bmatrix} 1 & 0.40 & 0.24 & 0.10 \\ 0 & 1 & 0.60 & 0.24 \\ 0 & 0 & 1 & 0.40 \\ 0 & 0 & 0 & 1 \end{bmatrix} \end{array}$$

Calculating the Matrix Inverse in Microsoft Excel:

1. Insert the matrix F in the work sheet as shown in Figure 8.3.

2. Select a group of cells for output, with dimensions the same as matrix F (i.e. 2×2 in this example).

3. Type =MINVERSE (range of cells for matrix F). The range of cells can be typed in manually, identifying the cell at the top left and the bottom right. Alternatively, the mouse can be used to highlight the matrix.

4. Then type Ctrl-Shift-Return (If this is not done, only a single value, not the entire matrix will be processed). See Figure 8.4.

$$F.R = \begin{bmatrix} 1 & 0.40 & 0.24 & 0.10 \\ 0 & 1 & 0.60 & 0.24 \\ 0 & 0 & 1 & 0.40 \\ 0 & 0 & 0 & 1 \end{bmatrix} \cdot \begin{array}{c} p \quad\;\; d \\ \begin{bmatrix} 0.6 & 0 \\ 0.4 & 0 \\ 0.6 & 0 \\ 0.5 & 0.5 \end{bmatrix} \end{array} = \begin{array}{c} s_1 \\ s_2 \\ s_3 \\ s_4 \end{array} \begin{bmatrix} 0.95 & 0.05 \\ 0.88 & 0.12 \\ 0.8 & 0.2 \\ 0.5 & 0.5 \end{bmatrix}$$

This procedure yields the following information:

A. The probability that the less than 30 days account will be paid:

Refer to the F.R matrix above. S_1 = New, a_1 = Paid. Thus, the probability that a new account will be paid is = 0.95

B. The probability that the less than 60 days account will be written off:

Refer to the F.R matrix above. S_3 = Less than 60 days, a_2 = Bad debt. Thus, the probability that a 'Less than 60 days account' will be written off is = 0.20.

C. The yearly accounts receivables are $24,000. The F.R matrix above, shows that 5 percent of all debts are eventually written off. Hence, (0.05) ($24,000) = $1200 per year will be written off or uncollected.

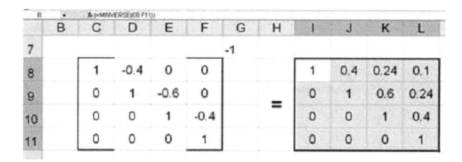

Figure 8.3 Matrix inverse calculation.

8.5.2 Problem 3—Inventory Questions

An owner of a nursery has 10,000 shrubs in inventory. Each spring he selects shrubs for sale. In viewing his previous spring's operation, he noted the following four states:

State a: shrubs sold

State b: shrubs lost to disease

State c: shrubs too small for sale

State d: shrubs available for sale but not sold

The following transition matrix is produced:

$$P = \begin{bmatrix} 1.00 & 0.00 & 0.00 & 0.00 \\ 0.00 & 1.00 & 0.00 & 0.00 \\ 0.105 & 0.15 & 0.50 & 0.20 \\ 0.30 & 0.20 & 0.00 & 0.50 \end{bmatrix}$$

Question: How many of the nursery's shrubs available for sale will

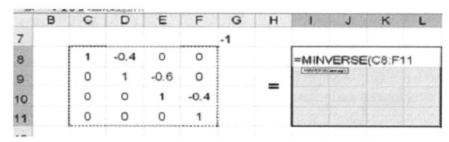

Figure 8.4 Final matrix inversion calculation.

$$F = (I - Q)^{-1} \quad \text{Absorbing States in the Markov Process}$$

Solution

The transition probability matrix is shown below:

$$P = \begin{bmatrix} 1 & 0 & 0 & 0 \\ 0 & 1 & 0 & 0 \\ 0.15 & 0.15 & 0.5 & 0.2 \\ 0.3 & 0.2 & 0 & 0.5 \end{bmatrix}$$

Four submatrices exist that are in the following general form:

$$P = \left[\begin{array}{c|c} I & 0 \\ \hline R & Q \end{array}\right]$$

$$P = \left[\begin{array}{cc|cc} 1 & 0 & 0 & 0 \\ 0 & 1 & 0 & 0 \\ \hline 0.15 & 0.15 & 0.5 & 0.2 \\ 0.3 & 0.2 & 0 & 0.5 \end{array}\right]$$

The first matrix operation determines the fundamental matrix, F, which gives the expected number of times the system will be in any of the non-absorbing states before absorption occurs (i.e. before the shrubs are sold off or lost). The fundamental matrix is computed by taking the inverse of the difference between an identity matrix and Q.

$$F = (I–Q)^{-1}$$

$$F = \left(\begin{bmatrix} 1 & 0 \\ 0 & 1 \end{bmatrix} - \begin{bmatrix} 0.5 & 0.2 \\ 0 & 0.5 \end{bmatrix}\right)^{-1}$$

$$F = \left(\begin{bmatrix} 0.5 & -0.2 \\ 0 & 0.5 \end{bmatrix}\right)^{-1}$$

$$F = \begin{bmatrix} 2 & 0.8 \\ 0 & 2 \end{bmatrix}$$

$$F.R = \begin{bmatrix} 2 & 0.8 \\ 0 & 2 \end{bmatrix} \cdot \begin{bmatrix} 0.15 & 0.15 \\ 0.3 & 0.2 \end{bmatrix} = \begin{bmatrix} 0.54 & 0.46 \\ 0.6 & 0.4 \end{bmatrix}$$

From the F.R matrix it is seen that 60 percent of the shrubs will be sold, and 40 percent of the shrubs will be lost to disease. Hence, (0.6) (10,000) = 6,000 shrubs will be sold and (0.4) (10,000) = 4,000 shrubs will be lost to disease.

References

Bhat, U.N. and G.K. Miller. *Elements of Applied Stochastic Processes*. 3rd ed. Wiley, New Jersey: 2002.

Hoel, P.G., S.C. Port, and C.J. Stone. *Introduction to Stochastic Processes*. Waveland Press, Illinois: 1986.

Searle, S.R. *Matrix Algebra Useful for Statistics*. 1st ed. Wiley-Interscience, New Jersey: 2006.

Isaacson, D.L. and R.W. Madsen. *Markov Chains*. John Wiley & Sons, , New Jersey: 1976.

Chapter 9

Diffusion Modeling and Forecasting

9.1 Introduction

To forecast sales of raw products, prior to their introduction, the concept of the product life cycle will be used here. The first part of this process is to apply a simple analytic forecasting model, which allows one to generate an entire product life cycle from very few interpretable parameters, such as market size. With such a model, the problem of forecasting the entire life cycle is reduced to that of predicting two or three model parameters. The second component deals with estimating the key model parameters and their changes with time, prior to the existence of sales data.

The process of diffusion mimics the growth pattern of an S-shaped curve (typical of a product life cycle). An innovation is an idea, product, or service, that the firm or the individual believes is new. The process that a firm or individual goes through in gaining exposure and eventually adopting, consists of five basic steps:

1. Awareness: the potential buyer becomes aware of the innovation.

2. Interest: the potential buyer seeks or receives additional information about the innovation.

3. Evaluation: after enough information is acquired to allow the individual or firm to evaluate (worth of actual use).

4. Trial: the potential adopter secures some of the innovation and tries it out.

5. Adoption: the buyer is sufficiently satisfied with the trial to go ahead with further usage.

An important concept in the launch of a new product or service involves the adoption of an innovation by individuals and firms, and then its diffusion through a group or an industry.

An innovation is a product or service that the individual or firm perceives as being new. Buyer behavior will reflect the perception, not the reality.

Awareness: the potential buyer must become aware of the existence of the innovation, whether it takes the form of awareness of the brand name or of some specific or unique product feature.

Interest: the potential buyer seeks or receives additional information about the innovation. The interest may be active or passive.

Evaluation: as soon as enough information is acquired to allow judgments, the individual or firm attempts to evaluate the product. This step is used to trigger the trial decision as to whether the new product is worthy of a test.

Trial: the potential adoption agency secures some of the innovation and tries it out.

Adaption: graphically, the adoption process across the total population takes the form of an S-curve.

Figures 9-1 and 9-2 capture an important generalized pattern related to the life cycle of a new durable product.

The process of adoption is executed at varying rates depending on the innovation and on the person and firm. Some innovations get almost instant adoption, and others are adopted very slowly.

Innovators: are the group of adopters who are in the first wave of adoption.

Early Adopters: are sometimes referred to as an early minority who are less venturesome than the innovators; they are clearly not waiting for others to adopt.

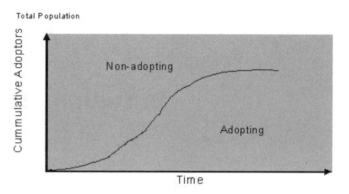

Figure 9.1   S-shaped diffusion curve.

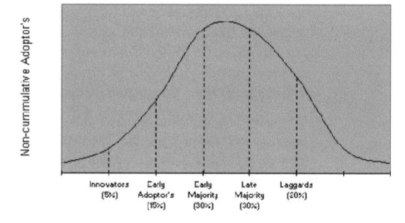

Figure 9.2   The Bass adopter categories.

Early Majority: is a group that is more deliberate than the innovators and early adopters, and desire to benefit from the experience of those who adopted earlier.

Late Majority: is a group that consists of skeptical latecomers who require considerable persuasion to adopt.

Laggards: are the last group to adopt.

Marketers are very interested in two categories, the early adopters and the innovators, because they provide the initial sales volume. Also, these two categories influence the remaining groups as the innovation is diffused throughout the firms or industries.

9.2 Diffusion Model

A good starting point to begin the discussion of the diffusion model is the forecasting of a new technology and new durable products. The cumulative probability that someone in the vulnerable market segment will adopt the new technological innovation by a certain time will be represented by a continuous function $F(t)$ (cumulative distribution function that approaches one as time gets large). The derivative of $F(t)$ is the probability density function $f(t)$ (the rate at which the probability of adoption of the new technology is changing at time t).

To estimate the cumulative distribution function $F(t)$, an estimate of the conditional likelihood that a customer will adopt a technological innovation at time t is given by $A(t)$.

$A(t)$ is defined as:

$$A(t) = F(t)/1 - F(t) \qquad (9.1)$$

In 1969, Bass proposed the following diffusion model

$$A(t) = p(1 - F(t)) + qF(t)(1 - F(t)) \qquad (9.2)$$

where

$F(t)$ = Cumulative proportion of adopters
$f(t)$ = Non-cumulative proportion of adopters

$N(t) = mF(t)$ = Cumulative number of adopters at time t
$n(t) = mf(t)$ = Non-cumulative number of adopters at time t
m = Total market potential for the new product
p = Coefficient of innovation
q = Coefficient of imitation

The coefficients p and q capture the proportional adoptions in $f(t)$ due to mass media $p(1 - F(t))$ and interpersonal communications $qF(t)(1 - F(t))$. These coefficients have also been termed the coefficients of external influence and internal influence respectively.

$$\frac{dN(t)}{dt} = p(m - N(t)) + q\frac{N(t)}{m}(m - N(t)) \qquad (9.3)$$

$$N(t) = pN + (q - p)N(t)[N(t)]^2 \qquad (9.4)$$

where N = Total number of customers comprising the target market.

Table 9.1 involves telecommunications services (cable TV, cellular phone, and home phone) and references the forecasting of these services by the use of the Bass diffusion model.

Table 9.1   Telecommunication Services Example

Cable TV	1981–1996	p = 0.100	q = 0.060	N = 68
Cellular Phone	1986–1996	p = 0.008	q = 0.421	N = 45.1
Home	1982–1988	p = 0.121	q = 0.281	N = 75.8

9.3 Another Model for Estimators: The Product Life Cycle Using Excel Computation

This second model (Lawrence and Lawton) has been applied to many classes of products. The model takes the following form:

$$\frac{dS(t)}{dt} = p * \frac{N_0 + S(t)}{N + N_0}[N - S(t)]$$ (9.5)

or

$$S(t) = \frac{N + N_0}{(1 + (N/N_0)e^{-p*t})} - N_0$$ (9.6)

where

$S(t)$ = Cumulative unit of sales of product up to time t

N_0 = Cumulative number of adopters at time t_0

N = Market size

$p*$ = A diffusion rate parameter

To forecast factors for a new product introduction, three key parameters N, $p*$ and N_0 need to be estimated. Once this estimation has been done, a plot of product sales as a function for the entire product life cycle is given.

Using this model over 30 new product life cycles, estimates of the rate parameter points are found in Figure 9-3 which shows a plot of the various values for products.

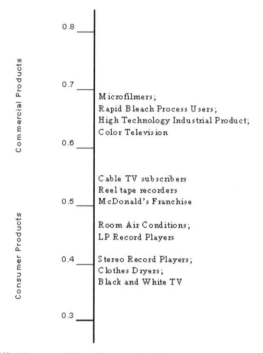

Figure 9.3 Diffusion model rate constants.

9.4 Excel Computations—Forecasting

Using the model

$$S(t) = \frac{N + N_0}{(1 + (N/N_0)e^{-p*t})} - N_0$$ (9.7)

$$N_0 = \frac{NS_1 e^{-p*}}{[N(1 - e^{-p*}) - S_1]}$$ (9.8)

where $S_1 = S(1)$, the sales in year 1.

The values of S_1 and N are estimated by traditional market research methods and are assumed to be as below.

$$p^* = 0.5$$

$$N = 500,000$$

$$S_1 = 40,000$$

Substituting these values in Equation 9.8, gives

$$N_0 = 77,396.$$

Plot results for $S(t)$, where t = 1, 2,...., 15 are shown in Table 9.2, which contains the data used in Figure 9.4. Figure 9.5 shows the Excel calculations for N_0.

An updated example will now be given using a slight modification of the original example at the beginning of Section 9.4.

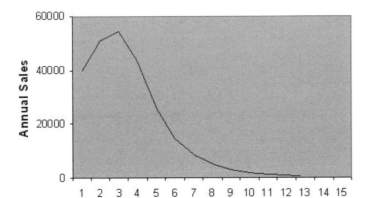

Figure 9.4   Sales forecast for t = 1, 2,..., 15.

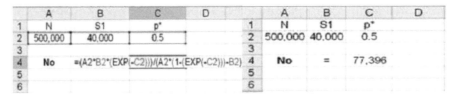

Figure 9.5   Excel formulae (left) and calculation (right).

Table 9.2   *S*(*t*) by year & cumulative by year

t	Cumulative Sales	Annual Sals
1	40,000	40,000
2	91,253	51,253
3	145,769	54,516
4	189,137	43,368
5	214,595	25,458
6	229,129	14,534
7	237,582	8,453
8	242,549	4,967
9	245,518	2,969
10	247,289	1,771
11	248,364	1,075
12	249,005	641
13	249,402	397
14	249,632	239
15	249,783	151

Changes made to parameter example are showin in Table 9.3: For the years 2000 – 2006, N = 600,000 and $p^* = 0.5$, calculate N_0:

$$N_0 = \frac{NS_1 e^{-p^*}}{[N(1-e^{-p^*}) - S_1]}$$

$$N_0 = 92,875$$

Restart the $p^* = 0.5$. Table 9.3 produces the result show in Figure 9.5. Subtract out $\Sigma S(t)$ from N = 500,000. Now, from the data matrix in Table 9.3

$$\Sigma S(t) = 285,099$$

The new $N_{0new} = N_{0original} + \Sigma S(t)$ and is recalculated. Therefore,

$$N_{0new} = 92,875 + 285,099$$

$$= 377,974$$

9.5   A Markovian Customer Demand Level Model and the Diffusion Model

A problem that is often faced is the forecasting of sales prior to the introduction of the product. The Markovian model of demand will be used here to estimate the overall market vulnerability of various customer segments with regard to their long-run spending on similar products, as a first step in estimating sales,

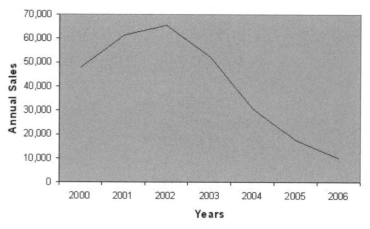

Figure 9.6   Sales forecast for 2000–2006.

Table 9.3   Cumulative and Annual Sales by Year

Year	Cumulative Sales	Annual Sales
2000	48,000	48,000
2001	109,503	61,503
2002	174,922	65,419
2003	226,965	52,043
2004	257,513	30,548
2005	274,955	17,442
2006	285,099	10,144

N = vulnerable market derived from the long-term expected value of the Markovian customer demand

$$N_0 = \frac{NS_1 e^{-p^*}}{[N(1-e^{-p^*})-S_1]}$$

where S_1 = First year sales (market research).

If, for example, the vulnerable market size is estimated to be 400,000 potential customers and is derived from the sum of the long-term steady X_t of the Markovian customer demand model segments 3 and 4, then the diffusion ratio $p^* = 0.5$ and N_0 is 106,460. A ten-period-ahead forecast of cumulative sales would be 198,573.

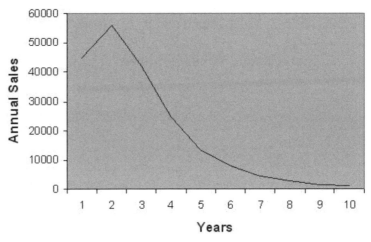

Figure 9.7 Sales forecast for t = 1, 2, 3,..., 10.

References

Bass, Frank (1969), "A New Product Growth Model for Consumer Durables," *Management Science*, 15 (January), 215–227.

Bass, Frank (1993), "The Future of Research in Marketing: Marketing Science," *Journal of Marketing Research*, 30 (February), 1–6.

Bass, Frank (1995), "Empirical Generalizations and Marketing Science: A Personal View," *Marketing Science*, 14(3), G6–G19.

Blackman, A. Wade, Jr. (1974), "The Market Dynamics of Technological Substitutions," *Technological Forecasting and Social Change*, 6(1), 41–63.

Lawrence, Kenneth and Michael Geurts. "Converging conflicting forecasting parameters in forecasting durable new product sales." *European Journal of Operational Research* 16 (1984): 42–47.

Lawrence, Kenneth and William H. Lawton. "Applications of Diffusion Models: Some Empirical Results." In *New Product Forecasting*, edited by Y. Wind, V. Mahajan, and R. Cardozo. Lexington Books, 1981: 525–541.

Mahajan, Vijay and Yoram Wind. *Innovation Diffusion Models of New Product Acceptance*. Ballinger Publishing Company, Cambridge, MA: 1986.

Rogers, Everett. *Diffusion of Innovations*. 3rd ed. 5th ed. Free Press, New York: 1983, 2003.

Chapter 10

Miscellaneous Forecasting Methods

10.1 Gravity Modeling
10.1.1   Introduction

This section will deal with forecasting the flows of goods or people. In these spatial interaction models, the flows are the dependent variables, and the independent variables measure a structural property in a flows environment. The type of spatial interactions model that will be used is the gravity model.

The gravity referred to here is based upon the laws used in physics. The inverse square of distance derived from the gravitational attraction F_{12} between bodies 1 and 2 is as follows:

$$F_{12} = g * m_1 m_2 / d^2_{12}$$

where mass of 1 is m_1, mass of 2 is m_2, distance between 1 and 2 is d^2_{12} , and g is the constant of gravity. Thus, as the mass of either body increases, the attraction between them grows. The gravity model interaction between 1 and 2 is directly proportional to the masses of m_1 and m_2, and inversely proportional to the distance between them. Also, reductions in the distances between 1 and 2 increase the attraction between 1 and 2.

The gravity concept was initially used in statistics in predicting migration. In this application, the origins of migrants in area 1 and area 2 are regarded as being inversely proportional to the distance between area 1 and area 2. Other early applications of the gravity model included the forecasting of retail trade between two areas by assuming that trade is in direct proportion to the population in the two areas, and that the retail trade between the two areas is inversely proportional to the square of the distance between the two areas.

10.1.2 Journey-to-Work Model and the Need for Gravity Model Constraints

In the journey-to-work model, the masses are the total numbers of journeys to work in origins, O_i, in a zone and the total number of destinations in D_j (time). The modified gravity model becomes

$$r_{ij} = k \, O_i D_j / d_{ij}^{\,b} \qquad (10.1)$$

where r_{ij} is the total number of trips from i to j. In this model structure, the level of dependence between the interactions of the masses is defined from the data set.

It is assumed that the model has been calibrated and $k = 1/1000$ and $b = 2$. The city is divided into zones A and B, one mile apart. If zone A has (100) jobs and zone B has (100) workers… and if this city is a very prosperous one with no unemployment, then the population is attracted to zone A. Thus, the flows are

$$T_{AB} = (0.01) * (100*100/1^2) = 100$$

If during an expansion, both the number of workers and the number of jobs double, then the expectation of the number of trips also doubles to 200. However, the model inaccurately forecasts 400 units of flow:

$$T_{AB} = (.01) * (200*200/1^2) = 400$$

What is needed to prevent this inaccuracy (there are not enough jobs or workers) is information to produce restrictions on the gravity model during the calibration process.

In the gravity model, the following constraint is needed to ensure that the number of flows is forecast:

$$\sum_{i=1}^{n}\sum_{j=1}^{n} r_{ij} = \sum_{i=1}^{n} O_i = \sum_{j=1}^{n} D_i \qquad (10.2)$$

in n zones.

The constraint equation provides the condition that the number of trips should be the same as the total number of origins and the same as the total number of destinations.

To incorporate this constraint requires the formulation of k as a scaling factor. Thus,

$$k = \frac{\sum_{i=1}^{n} O_i}{\sum_{i=1}^{n}\sum_{j=1}^{n} r_{ij}} = \frac{\sum_{i=1}^{n} D_i}{\sum_{i=1}^{n}\sum_{j=1}^{n} r_{ij}} \qquad (10.3)$$

In the previously given T_{AB}, let $k = 0.01$. Given the addition of workers and jobs, a new value of k is needed. The flows predicted without k are

$$\frac{(200)(200)}{1^2} = 40,000$$

given O_i and D_j are 200. Thus,

$$K = 200/40{,}000 = 0.005$$

such that

$$T_{AB} = (1/200) * (200*200)/ 1^2 = 200 = O_i = D_j$$

Next, the gravity model structure referred to as the totally-constrained gravity model will be given as

$$r_{ij} = \frac{kO_iD_j}{d_{ij}^b} \qquad (10.4)$$

where

$$k = \frac{\sum\limits_{i=1}^{n} O_i}{\sum\limits_{i=1}^{n}\sum\limits_{j=1}^{n} r_{ij}} = \frac{\sum\limits_{i=1}^{n} D_i}{\sum\limits_{i=1}^{n}\sum\limits_{j=1}^{n} r_{ij}} \qquad (10.5)$$

There must be a constraint for the production of trips. This gravity model is given by

$$r_{ij} = \frac{S_iO_iD_j}{d_{ij}^b} \qquad (10.6)$$

where S_i is the scaling factors for all O_j. Thus, there is a special constant for every origin zone.

Thus,

$$S_i = \frac{1}{\sum\limits_{i=1}^{n} D_i/d_{ij}^b} \qquad (10.7)$$

To satisfy the constraint,

$$\sum_{i=1}^{n} r_{ij} = O_i \qquad (10.8)$$

Thus, the number of trips leaving zone i that equals the number of origins is i.

To develop a gravity model that is attraction-constrained, the following model form is specified:

$$r_{ij} = T_j O_i D_j/d_{ij}^b \qquad (10.9)$$

where T_j are the scaling factors for all Dj, where

$$T_j = \frac{1}{\sum\limits_{i-1}^{n} O_i/d_{ij}^b} \qquad (10.10)$$

and satisfy the

$$\sum_{i=1}^{n} r_{ij} = D_i \qquad (10.11)$$

which states that the number of flows into zone j is equal to the number of destinations in zone j.

The three constraint production-attraction constraint gravity model takes the following form:

$$r_{ij} = \frac{S_iT_jO_jD_j}{d_{ij}^b} \qquad (10.12)$$

where

$$S_i = \frac{1}{\sum_{i=1}^{n}(T_j O_i D_i / d_{ij}^b)} \qquad (10.13)$$

$$T_i = \frac{-1}{\sum_{i=1}^{n}(S_i O_i / d_{ij}^b)} \qquad (10.14)$$

and

$$\sum_{i=1}^{n} r_{ij} = D_i \text{ for each } D_j \qquad (10.15)$$

$$\sum_{i=1}^{n} r_{ij} = O_i \text{ for each } O_j \qquad (10.16)$$

which ensure that

$$\sum_{i=1}^{n}\sum_{j=1}^{n} r_{ij} = \sum_{i=1}^{n} D_i = \sum_{i=1}^{n} O_i \qquad (10.17)$$

10.1.3   Estimation of the Model Parameters

This model structure provides scaling factors for both origins and destinations. To estimate the model parameters fitting an empirical process, it is necessary to determine the parameters that minimize the differences between observed values and predicted values.

Table 10.1   Data for Origin and Destination Flow Between Locations

Location	Origin Flow	Destination	Destination Flow
1	24,000	1	20,000
2	30,000	2	25,000
3	5,000	3	4,000

Distance in Miles (d_{ij})			
	1	2	3
1	2	4	8
2	5	1	7
3	7	6	3

Given the set of data shown in Table 10.1:

$$\sum_{i=1}^{n}\sum_{j=1}^{n} r_{ij} = \frac{k_i l_j D_i O_j}{d_{ij}^2 e^{-0.5 d_{ij}}} \qquad (10.18)$$

if $O_1 = 24,000$ and $D_1 = 20,000$, then

$$O_2 = 30,000 \quad D_2 = 25,000$$

$$O_3 = 5,000 \quad D_3 = 4,000$$

and

$$\sum_{i=1}^{3}\sum_{j=1}^{3} r_{ij} = 59,000$$

A sample calculation in Excel for l_1 is shown in Figures 10.1 and 10.2.

$$l_1 = \frac{1}{k_1 D_1 d_{11} + k_2 D_2 d_{21} + k_3 D_3 d_{31}} = 0.0009$$

$$l_2 = \frac{1}{k_1 D_1 d_{12} + k_2 D_2 d_{22} + k_3 D_3 d_{32}} = 0.00014$$

$$l_3 = \frac{1}{k_1 D_1 d_{13} + k_2 D_2 d_{23} + k_3 D_3 d_{33}} = 0.0005$$

Figure 10.1 shows the Excel calculation methodology for l_1, and Figure 10.2 shows the value of l_1. Figure 10.1 includes the formulae indicating various cells used for calculating l_1. The cells used in the formulae are highlighted in Figure 10.1.

Sample calculations in Excel for k_1 are shown in Figures 10.3 and 10.4.

$$k_1 = \frac{1}{l_1 O_1 d_{11} + l_2 O_2 d_{21} + l_3 O_3 d_{13}} = 0.0041$$

$$k_2 = \frac{1}{l_1 O_1 d_{21} + l_2 O_2 d_{22} + l_3 O_3 d_{23}} = 0.0055$$

$$k_3 = \frac{1}{l_1 O_1 d_{31} + l_2 O_2 d_{32} + l_3 O_3 d_{33}} = 0.0023$$

Figure 10.3 shows the Excel calculation methodology for k_1, and Figure 10.4 shows the value of k_1. Figure 10.3 includes the formulae indicating various cells used for calculating k_1. The cells used in the formulae are highlighted in Figures 10.3 and 10.4.

Figure 10.1 Calculations for l_1.

Figure 10.2 Further Calculations for l_1.

Figure 10.3 Calculations for k_1.

There now are six equations with six unknowns, which are needed to compute the flows once the values k_1, k_2, k_3, l_1, l_2, and l_3 are found. Using Excel, the values of the flows are found as follows:

$$r_{11} = l_1 k_1 O_1 S_1 / d_{11} = 2016$$

$$r_{12} = l_1 k_2 O_1 S_2 / d_{12} = 2490$$

$$r_{13} = l_1 k_3 O_1 S_3 / d_{13} = 266$$

$$r_{21} = l_2 k_1 O_2 S_1 / d_{21} = 1613$$

$$r_{22} = l_2 k_2 O_2 S_2 / d_{22} = 9916$$

$$r_{23} = l_2 k_3 O_2 S_3 / d_{23} = 235$$

$$r_{31} = l_3 k_1 O_3 S_1 / d_{31} = 148$$

$$r_{32} = l_3 k_2 O_3 S_2 / d_{32} = 223$$

$$r_{33} = l_3 k_3 O_3 S_3 / d_{33} = 12$$

Sample calculations for r_{11} are shown in Figures 10.5 and 10.6. Figure 10.5 shows the Excel calculation methodology for r_{11}, and Figure 10.6 shows the value of r_{11}. Figure 10.5 includes the formulae indicating various cells used for calculating r_{11}. The cells used in the formulae are highlighted in Figure 10.5.

10.2 Input-Output Modeling

10.2.1   Introduction

Input-output analysis recognizes the existence of many goods, and the consideration that some goods are used to produce others. Input-output is designed for the quantitative study of inter-industry relationships.

Figure 10.4   Further Calculations for k_1.

Figure 10.5   Calculations for r_{11}.

Figure 10.6   Further Calculations for r_{11}.

The information that underlies the study of inter-industry relationships can be given in the form of the transactions matrix shown in Table 10.2.

Where

$$Z_i = \sum_{i=1}^{4} X_{ij} \text{ (elements of the row)}$$

$$X_i = Z_i + Y_i \tag{10.19}$$

$$S_i = T_i + F_i \tag{10.20}$$

$$V = Y \tag{10.21}$$

Z_i is the total value of the output of the ith industry used up in the production process, not available for final demand. And Y is the total final demand, or the value of output that goes to the consumer, to expand productive capacity, and to the government:

$$Y = C + I + G \tag{10.22}$$

Also, $X_i = Z_i + Y_i$ is the total value of the output of the ith industry (balance equations).

Each column of the matrix contains the value added in each industry group. The value added is reflective of the ways S_i and the return of capital F_i. When the sum of the S_i is taken, the national income is formed.

When the elements of the column are summed, then

$$\sum_{i=1}^{n} X_{ij} + S_i = X_1 \tag{10.23}$$

Table 10.2 Transactions Matrix for Inter-Industry Relations

Sector	1	2	3	4			
1	x_{11}	x_{12}	x_{13}	x_{14}	Z_1	Y_1	X_1
2	X_{21}	X_{22}	X_{23}	X_{24}	Z_2	Y_2	X_2
3	X_{31}	X_{32}	X_{33}	X_{34}	Z_3	Y_3	X_3
4	X_{41}	X_{42}	X_{43}	x_{44}	Z_4	Y_4	X_4
	S	S	S	S			

and the value added, the total value of the output of the jth industry is equal to the value of its intermediate inputs, its wages, and what is left over, F_i.

The value of the ith industry's output X_{ij} required by the jth industry is a function of X_j, the output of the jth industry. Thus, it can be assumed that

$$X_{ij} = a_{ij} = X_i \tag{10.24}$$

Thus, a constant technology is assumed, described by fixed coefficients, and the coefficients a_{ij} can be computed:

$$a_{ij} = x_{ij} / x_j \tag{10.25}$$

If all requirements are strictly proportional to outputs, the total output of each good must be equal to the total amount of it that is used up in the production of other goods, plus the total amount going to final demand. In matrix notation,

$$X = AX + Y \tag{10.26}$$

Subtracting AX from both sides gives X = AX = Y and factoring out X gives (I-A)X = Y. (I-A) is the Leontief matrix.

If given the components of Y, the final demand is known. Thus, if the problem is: given the coefficient matrix A and the final bill of goods Y, find the outputs required of each industry X, then the problem can be stated as

$$X = (I - A)^{-1}Y \qquad (10.27)$$

Forecasting company sales based on other sales is typically used when the products are of a complementary nature. A sales forecast in baseball may be made by using the forecasting of sales of baseball bats or gloves. This projection, from another forecast, provides for an analysis in terms of a "what if" scenario. For example, what will happen if the sales of a customer segment increase by 30 percent? A method for dealing with such a scenario is to use an input-output modeling technique.

The input-output modeling structure allows for detailed analysis of the interdependence of business from a structured-dependent system. The systematic relationship in the input-output model defines the flow of services among and between goods and services. Input-output modeling directly allows for what happens to outputs if the inputs change. The matrix multipliers associated with the input-output model provide for such analysis.

10.2.2   Regional Input-Output Models

The information provided about the macro U. S. economy by the input-output model often is not sufficiently detailed to provide a breakdown of industries by geographic region (i.e., by state). Some regions trade with one another to a significant degree. To examine these regional economics, a breakdown of each industry is made by region. Data can be found in a construction of an inter-industry input-model table.

The regional technical coefficients are defined as

$$a^s_{ij} = T^s_{ij} / x^s_{ij}$$

where

T^s_{ij} = the dollar value of input from section 1 used by sector j in Region T

x^s_j = the gross output of the jth sector in Region T

Regionalized coefficients are not always available. However, this data can be generated from a product-mix approach. Underlying such an approach is the fact that the input requirement per unit output is tabled from region to region.

Such an approach creates an interconnection among the regions by means of trade coefficients. These trade-flows of the regional input-output model are estimated by industrial sectors. Thus, T_{12} represents the dollar flow from product j from region 1 to region 2. These flows include shipments of the product sectors in region 2, as well as the demand in region 2.

The total shipments are of good i into all regions from all other regions. For two regions for goods,

$$P_i^2 = T_i^{12} + T_i^{22} + \ldots + T_i^{N2}$$

When each element in a given shipment-matrix column is divided by the column total, then the coefficient ties the proportion of all goods i used in column B that comes from each other region. Therefore, the inter-regional trade coefficients $D_i^{12} = T_i^{12} / P_i^2$.

For each possible origin/destination grouping in the n region of the input-output model, a C_i^{12} vector with elements C_i^1 (where i = 1, 2, …, n) can be developed. Each element of the vector gives the proportion of the total number of goods used in region 2 that come from region 1.

In a similar fashion, an intra-regional trade analysis can be developed. The elements of the vector will give the proportion of goods in region 2 that come from within the region.

The overall regional input-output model takes the following form:

$$(I - DA)X = D^Y$$

where

$$D^{11} \dots D^{1n}$$

$$D^{21} \dots D^{2n}$$

$$D = \dots\dots\dots$$

$$D^{n1} \dots D^{nn}$$

A = technical coefficients matrix for the nth region system
X = total output vector for the nth region system
Y = final demand vector for the nth region system

Input-output modeling allows the forecaster to capture the full array of inter-relationships among all industries and the potential impacts they have on each other in the forecasting process. Such modeling allows for the direct translation of macroeconomic forecasts into industry-specific forecasts.

10.2.3   An Example Problem

The following data sets define the example problem.

In the following example, the forecasting of product (H) sales in industry (T) over the (D) year period is to be developed. Table 10.3 shows data for a four-year period of economic activity for industrial sector (T).

Table 10.3   Total Output in Millions of Dollars for Industrial Sector (T) by Quarter by Region for a Four-Year Period

Year	Quarter	Region 1	Region 2	Region 3
1	1	14,367	12,548	13,475
1	2	14,403	12,556	13,501
1	3	14,412	12,563	13,511
1	4	14,418	12,575	13,525
2	1	14,432	12,588	13,538
2	2	14,454	12,591	13,545
2	3	14,474	12,598	13,557
2	4	14,498	12,604	13,565
3	1	14,515	12,631	13,576
3	2	14,527	12,639	13,581
3	3	14,550	12,651	13,592
3	4	14,577	12,668	13,601
4	1	14,560	12,676	13,612
4	2	14,565	12,681	13,626
4	3	14,597	12,694	13,635
4	4	14,608	12,704	13,641

A set of three simple linear time series regression models was run to forecast the total output of industrial sector T by quarter by region. Table 10.4 shows the forecast total output of industry (T).

The time series regression analysis output for each of the three regions is shown below.

Table 10.5 contains data for the sales of product (H) in industry (T) over a three-year period.

Table 10.4   Forecast of Total Output ($M) Industrial Sector (T) by Quarter by Region

Year	Quarter	Region 1	Region 2	Region 3
5	1	14,632	12,715	13,656
5	2	14,648	12,726	13,666
5	3	14,664	12,736	13,677
5	4	14,680	12,747	13,687
6	1	14,696	12,758	13,697
6	2	14,712	12,769	13,708
6	3	14,727	12,779	13,718
6	4	14,743	12,790	13,728

Region 1
SUMMARY OUTPUT

Regression Statistics	
Multiple R	0.989087304
R Square	0.978293696
Adjusted R Square	0.976743245
Standard Error	11.64408572
Observations	16

ANOVA

	df	SS	MS	F	Significance F
Regression	1	85550.42812	85550.42812	630.9739067	4.80168E-13
Residual	14	1898.18625	135.5847321		
Total	15	87448.61437			

	Coefficients	Standard Error	t Stat	P-value	Lower 95%	Upper 95%
Intercept	14362.5	6.106210063	2352.113643	1.39187E-40	14349.40347	14375.59653
Var	15.8625	0.631489211	25.11919399	4.80168E-13	14.50808914	17.21691086

Figure 10.7   Regression output for Years vs. Region 1.

Region 2
SUMMARY OUTPUT

Regression Statistics	
Multiple R	0.994819225
R Square	0.98966529
Adjusted R Square	0.988927097
Standard Error	5.430593097
Observations	16

ANOVA

	df	SS	MS	F	Significance F
Regression	1	39537.8106	39537.8106	1340.658266	2.64965E-15
Residual	14	412.8787794	29.49134139		
Total	15	39950.68938			

	Coefficients	Standard Error	t Stat	P-value	Lower 95%	Upper 95%
Intercept	12531.345	2.847827046	4400.318137	2.16394E-44	12525.23701	12537.45299
Var	10.78367647	0.294515262	36.61500056	2.64965E-15	10.1520035	11.41534945

Figure 10.8   Regression output for Years vs. Region 2.

Region 3
SUMMARY OUTPUT

Regression Statistics	
Multiple R	0.994915789
R Square	0.989857427
Adjusted R Square	0.989132957
Standard Error	5.174827667
Observations	16

ANOVA

	df	SS	MS	F	Significance F
Regression	1	36588.4756	36588.4756	1366.320337	2.32327E-15
Residual	14	374.9037794	26.77884139		
Total	15	36963.37937			

	Coefficients	Standard Error	t Stat	P-value	Lower 95%	Upper 95%
Intercept	13479.3675	2.713702523	4967.150005	3.96753E-45	13473.54718	13485.18782
Var	10.37367647	0.280644434	36.9637706	2.32327E-15	9.77175349	10.97559945

Figure 10.9   Regression output for Years vs. Region 3.

Region 1
SUMMARY OUTPUT

Regression Statistics	
Multiple R	0.037300588
R Square	0.001391334
Adjusted R Square	-0.098469533
Standard Error	9.14724E-07
Observations	12

ANOVA

	df	SS	MS	F	Significance F
Regression	1	1.16578E-14	1.16578E-14	0.013932724	0.90837566
Residual	10	8.3672E-12	8.3672E-13		
Total	11	8.37886E-12			

	Coefficients	Standard Error	t Stat	P-value	Lower 95%	Upper 95%
Intercept	3.08939E-05	5.62974E-07	54.87626544	9.78714E-14	2.96395E-05	3.21483E-05
Var	-9.02901E-09	7.64931E-08	-0.118036959	0.90837566	-1.79466E-07	1.61408E-07

Figure 10.10   Regression output.

Intensity-of-use data for products from an industry is equal to the total number of products used by an industry divided by the total number of products of the industry. Next, by dividing the sales of product (H) to industry (T), the intensity-of-use of product (H), the intensity of use of product (H) industry (T) is shown in Table 10.6.

The regression output for the intensity of use for region 1 is shown in Figure 10.10.

The intensity-of-use can be forecast by a regression. The forecast intensity-of-use of product (H) in industry (T) is shown in Table 10.7.

By simply multiplying the total forecast output for industry (T) by the forecast intensity-of-use of product (H) in industry (T), the forecast sales of product (H) in industry (T) is as shown in Table 10.8.

10.3 Combination of Forecasts

10.3.1 Introduction

In recent years, not only have methods of forecasting changed and improved, but the concept of combining forecasts to improve the accuracy of results has been developed. This strategy of combining forecasts seeks to minimize the effects of bias.

The advantages of combining forecasts are:

1. Providing more accurate forecasts.

2. Removing the need to fund the best model. The combination of forecasts outperforms individual forecasting methods because:

    A. Error variance is reduced in the combining process.

    B. The accuracy is improved.

    C. The time series pattern is changeable.

Table 10.5   Product (H) History in Industry (T) for Region

Region	Year	Quarter	Output ($)
1	1	1	460,081,671
1	1	2	475,348,974
1	1	3	458,891,008
1	1	4	441,943,322
1	2	1	481,081,397
1	2	2	478,911,707
1	2	3	491,031,202
1	2	4	475,835,127
1	3	1	468,321,581
1	3	2	475,941,394
1	3	3	455,801,696
1	3	4	471,706,705

Table 10.6   Intensity-of-Use of Industrial Sector (T) for Region 1

Region	Year	Quarter	Intensity of Use
1	1	1	0.000031
1	1	2	0.000030
1	1	3	0.000031
1	1	4	0.000033
1	2	1	0.000030
1	2	2	0.000030
1	2	3	0.000029
1	2	4	0.000030
1	3	1	0.000031
1	3	2	0.000031
1	3	3	0.000032
1	3	4	0.000031

10.3.2 Methods of Combining

One of the easiest methods of combining forecasts is simply by averaging the individual forecasts produced by various forecasting methods. If one has three forecasts such as (F_1, F_2, and F_3), then the combined forecast C is equal to

$$C = (F_1 + F_2 + F_3)/3 \qquad (10.28)$$

Using combined forecasts with a simple average can sometimes be unsatisfactory when it results in combining forecasting variances that are greater than the individual variances.

Another very viable method of combining forecasts is to use weighted averages. The combined forecast would take the following form:

$$C = w_1F_1 + w_2F_2 + w_3F_3 \qquad (10.29)$$

Weights are w_1, w_2, and w_3 where $w_1 + w_2 + w_3 = 1.0$. Those forecasts that have the lower error variance should get the greatest weight. A likely extension of the weighted methods would be to use weights that are derived inversely to the square of errors (Σe^2_i):

$$W_1 = \frac{1/(\text{sum of squared errors } F_1)}{\dfrac{1}{\text{Sum of squared errors } F_1} + \dfrac{1}{\text{Sum of squared errors } F_2} + \dfrac{1}{\text{Sum of squared errors } F_3}}$$

$$W_2 = \frac{1/(\text{sum of squared errors } F_2)}{\dfrac{1}{\text{Sum of squared errors } F_1} + \dfrac{1}{\text{Sum of squared errors } F_2} + \dfrac{1}{\text{Sum of squared errors } F_3}}$$

$$W_3 = \frac{1/(\text{sum of squared errors } F_3)}{\dfrac{1}{\text{Sum of squared errors } F_1} + \dfrac{1}{\text{Sum of squared errors } F_2} + \dfrac{1}{\text{Sum of squared errors } F_3}}$$

Table 10.7   Intensity-of-Use Forecast for Industrial Sector (T) for Region 1

Region	Year	Quarter	Intensity of Use
1	4	1	0.0000307765
1	4	2	0.0000307675
1	4	3	0.0000307585
1	4	4	0.0000307494
1	5	1	0.0000307404
1	5	2	0.0000307314
1	5	3	0.0000307223
1	5	4	0.0000307133

Table 10.8   Forecast for Product H for Industry Sector (H) for Region 1

Year	Quarter	Output ($)
5	1	450,328
5	2	450,682
5	3	451,039
5	4	451,396
6	1	451,749
6	2	452,105
6	3	452,457
6	4	452,813

Regression analysis is another method used to derive weights for combining forecasts. The combining weighting forecast F_c is given by

$$F_c = b_1F_1 + b_2F_2 + b_3F_3 \qquad (10.30)$$

where

b_1 = regression coefficients (i = 1, 2, 3)

F_1 = individual forecasts (i = 1, 2, 3)

The predicted value F_c is estimated by dependent variables given by forecast models 1, 2, and 3. A weighted example is $y = b_0 + b_1t$.

Excel calculations of the three forecasting methods are shown in Table 10.9.

10.4 Combined Forecasting Method

Figure 10.11 shows an example of a weighted forecast. In this method, weights w_1, w_2, and w_3 are found, using the forecast methods F_1, F_2, and F_3. A combined forecast is developed using the following equation:

$$C = w_1F_1 + w_2F_2 + w_3F_3$$

where, $w_1 + w_2 + w_3 = 1$

which gives

$$w_1 = 0.3551$$

$$w_2 = 0.3207$$

$$w_3 = 0.3242$$

Table 10.10 shows the combined forecast results.

The next method used to derive weights for combining forecasts is regression analysis. However, a drawback of the combined regression forecasting method is that the regression coefficients, or the weights, are statistically insignificant when incorporated in the model.

SUMMARY OUTPUT

Regression Statistics	
Multiple R	0.23060446
R Square	0.053178417
Adjusted R Square	0.010141072
Standard Error	27.08518792
Observations	24

ANOVA

	df	SS	MS	F	Significance F
Regression	1	906.4704348	906.4704348	1.23563425	0.278314776
Residual	22	16139.3629	733.6074045		
Total	23	17045.83333			

	Coefficients	Standard Error	t Stat	P-value	Lower 95%	Upper 95%
Intercept	350.9855072	11.41235709	30.7548655	1.42256E-19	327.3177018	374.6533127
Time Period	0.887826087	0.798698618	1.111590864	0.278314776	-0.768575244	2.544227418

Figure 10.11   Regression output.

	A	B	C	D	E	F
1			F_1	F_2	F_3	
2	Time Period	Units Sold	Time Series Regression	2-Month Weighted Moving Average	Exponential Smoothing	forecast
3	1	336	352			336
4	2	380	353		336	336
5	3	310	354	=(B3+B4)/2	349	349
6	4	350	355	345	337	337
7	5	300	355	330	341	341
8	6	361	356	325	329	329
9	7	341	357	331	338	338
10	8	390	358	351	339	339

Figure 10.12   Calculation of two-month moving average forecast.

	A	B	C	D	E	F
1			F_1	F_2	F_3	
2	Time Period	Units Sold	Time Series Regression	2-Month Weighted Moving Average	Exponential Smoothing	forecast
3	1	336	352			336
4	2	380	353		=F3+0.3*(	336
5	3	310	354	358	B3-F3)	349
6	4	350	355	345	337	337
7	5	300	355	330	341	341
8	6	361	356	325	329	329
9	7	341	357	331	338	338
10	8	390	358	351	339	339
11	9	390	359	366	354	354
12	10	360	360	390	365	365
13	11	400	361	375	364	364
14	12	381	362	380	375	375
15	13	373	363	391	376	376

Figure 10.13　Calculation of exponential smoothing forecast.

Table 10.9　Excel Calculated Values for Three Forecasting Methods

Time Period	Units Sold	F_1 Time Series Regression	F_2 2-Month Weighted Moving Average	F_3 Exponential Smoothing
1	336	352		
2	380	353		336
3	310	354	358	349
4	350	355	345	337
5	300	355	330	341
6	361	356	325	329
7	341	357	331	338

Table 10.9　Excel Calculated Values for Three Forecasting Methods (Continued)

Time Period	Units Sold	F_1 Time Series Regression	F_2 2-Month Weighted Moving Average	F_3 Exponential Smoothing
8	390	358	351	339
9	390	359	366	354
10	360	360	390	365
11	400	361	375	364
12	381	362	380	375
13	373	363	391	376
14	395	363	377	375
15	321	364	384	381
16	387	365	358	363
17	371	366	354	370
18	393	367	379	371
19	374	368	382	377
20	350	369	384	376
21	374	370	362	368
22	341	371	362	370
23	352	371	358	361
24	360	372	347	359
25	375	373	356	359
26	381	374	368	364
27	349	375	378	369

Table 10.10   Data Generated by the Combined Forecast Method

Time Period	Units Sold	F_c Combined Forecast
1	336	352
2	380	380
3	310	354
4	350	346
5	300	343
6	361	337
7	341	343
8	390	350
9	390	360
10	360	371
11	400	366
12	381	372
13	373	376
14	395	372
15	321	376
16	387	362
17	371	364
18	393	372
19	374	375
20	350	376
21	374	367

Table 10.10   Data Generated by the Combined Forecast Method (Continued)

Time Period	Units Sold	F_c Combined Forecast
22	341	368
23	352	364
24	360	360
25	375	363
26	381	369
27	349	374

References for the Gravity Model

Anderson, James E. "A Theoretical Foundation for the Gravity Equation." *American Economic Review* 69, no. 1 (1979): 106–116. A first attempt to provide theoretical foundations to the gravity model.

Bergstrand, Jeffrey H. "The Gravity Equation in International Trade: Some Microeconomic Foundations and Empirical Evidence." *Review of Economics and Statistics* 67, no. 3 (1985): 474–481. A second attempt to provide theoretical foundations to the gravity model.

Deardorff, Alan V. "Determinants of Bilateral Trade: Does Gravity Work in a Neoclassical World?" In *The Regionalization of the World Economy*, edited by Jeffrey A. Frankel. University of Chicago Press, Chicago: 1998. A helpful review and assessment of the gravity model.

Feenstra, Robert C., James R. Markusen, and Andrew K. Rose. "Using the Gravity Equation to Differentiate among Alternative Theories of Trade." *Canadian Journal of Economics* 34, no. 2 (2001): 430–447. Tests of the gravity model over differentiated and homogenous goods, focusing on differences in estimated parameter values.

References for Input-Output Modeling

Baumol, William J. and E.N.Wolff. "A Key Role for Input-Output Analysis in Policy Design," *Regional Science and Urban Economics* 24 (1994): 93–113.

Hartwick, J.M. "Notes on the Isard and Cheneg-Moses Interregional Input-Output Models." *Journal of Regional Science* 1 (April 1971): 73–80.

Leontief, Wassily W. *Input-Output Economics*. 2nd ed. Oxford University Press, New York: 1986.

Maddon, M. and P.W.J. Batey. "Achieving Consistency in Demographic-Economic Forecasting." *Papers of the Regional Science Association* 44 (1980): 91–106.

Miller, R.E., Karen R. Polenske, and Adam Z. Rose, eds. *Frontiers of Input-Output Analysis*. Oxford University Press, New York: 1989.

Richardson, H.W. *Input-Output and Regional Economics*. Wiley, New York: 1972.

Sastry, M. Lakshminarayan. "Estimating the Economic Impacts of Elderly Migration: An Input-Output Analysis." *Growth and Change* Winter (1992): 54.

References for Combination of Forecasts

Clemen, R.T. "Combining Forecasts: A Review and Annotated Bibliography." *International Journal of Forecasting* 5, no. 4 (1989): 559–583.

Makound, E. "Combining Forecasts: Some Managerial Issues." *International Journal of Forecasting* 5, no. 4 (1989): 599–600.

Makridakis, S. and Winkler, R.L. "Averaged Forecasts: Some Empirical Results." *Management Science* 29 (1984): 987–996.

Popp, A.E. "On Combining Forecasts: Some Extension and Results." *Management Science* 31, no. 12 (December 1986):1492–1497.

Index

FUN & FUNKY
Fingers and Toes